BROKEN SILENCE

Dialogues from the Edge

André Stein

LESTER
&ORPEN
DENNYS
PUBLISHERS

The Publisher wishes to thank the Multicultural Program, Government of Canada, for its support in the publication of this book.

CANADIAN CATALOGUING IN PUBLICATION DATA

Stein, André
    Broken silence: dialogues from the edge

ISBN 0-88619-082-7

1. Stein, André.   2. Holocaust survivors — Canada —
Biography.   3. Jews — Hungary — Persecutions.
3. Holocaust, Jewish (1939-1945) — Psychological aspects.   I. Title.

D810.J4S86 1984   940.53'15'03924   C84-099292-0

Design by Jack Steiner Graphic Design

Printed in Canada by John Deyell Company for

LESTER & ORPEN DENNYS LIMITED
78 Sullivan Street
Toronto, Ontario M5T 1C1

Dedication

To the memory of my mother, Piroska Csengery Stein, whose life was absurdly ravished from her, from us, at the age of forty-two, in the desert of Bergen Belsen;

To Raoul Wallenberg, one of the noblest men in history. His totally altruistic heroism resulted in the survival of thousands of Jews in Budapest, including myself, and in his loss of freedom and possibly his life to another version of darkness;

To the memory of all the victims of the engineers, technicians, and active and passive supporters of the Nazi regime. I offer my tale to the six million martyrs. May it speak for those whose voices were gagged by the breathless void.

For the sake of their cherished memory, I break the silence of forty years.

Contents

Acknowledgements

Elie Wiesel: when out of the amorphous fog, I stepped into the light of your awareness, you extended to me your wisdom, your experience, your warmth. A few words here, a few comments there, and I always knew how to continue. Such is the magic of your discreet guidance. A self-effaced Virgil, you led me through the many levels of my private hell—always from a distance, yet always available for a moment of support, just enough to go on with the task. You have taught me the value and the mystery of searching for questions, instead of chasing the mirage of assertions. For all these proofs of spiritual and intellectual generosity, I thank you, Elie.

Harry James Cargas: you embraced me without ever having laid eyes on me. You showed genuine Christian respect for another man's struggle—mine. You extended to me the caring hand one hopes for from an older and wiser brother. You offered valuable suggestions without offending the integrity of the tale. I am grateful to you, Harry, for all these gifts and for your enthusiastic faith in my work.

Louise Alcan: you have been my guide on several tentative, fearful incursions into the abyss of Auschwitz, your second cradle. For the quiet camaraderie and for the sad dialogues—both indispensable ingredients of the essence of my tale—I thank you, Louise.

Janet Hamilton: you have given me so much more than just erudite editorial assistance and advice. You welcomed my awesome dialogues into your heart and you helped me articulate more clearly not only the pain and the rage but also the urgency of the telling of the tale. You were there for me, a total stranger, when my morale threatened to cave in under the burden of harsh realities governing the publishing world. For these acts of genteel and elegant humanity, Janet, I thank you.

Sarah Shadowitz, my friend, Sarah: without your editorial wizardry and integrity, without your commitment to the fate of these dialogues, this book would not exist as it does today. You have worked your way through this awkward labyrinth with the mastery of a virtuoso and the experience of a veteran of many battles with bewildering manuscripts. You lent my work your expertise and you gave it your heart. For all this and much more, I thank you and I love you, my friend, Sarah.

Ted Grosberg: thank you for sharing with me your wife, Sarah, during our travails on the rough waters of my rather choppy opus. I appreciate your patience, your kind friendship, your numerous insights.

Ted Todd, my cousin, my friend, my brother: you and I have been gathering the same dust on our backs since the beginning of it all. We shared the molasses and the carrots, the dark dampness of the cellar, and the tears of mourning and fear. Wherever you and I might have been, we have never been too far from each other. I just had to fine-tune my awareness onto your weather-beaten face and I immediately felt your presence. You courageously volunteered to accompany me on my pilgrimage to the pit where evil used to blossom. And we bled together. Again. Ted, this is our tale, lived by the two of us, told for the two of us. Your spiritual and substantial share is on every page of this volume. Thank you, Ted.

Hilda Rosner: for the unconditional faith in the outcome of this project, for sustaining me when body and spirit were faltering, for welcoming me into your mothering heart, I thank you with all my love.

Cybèle, my first-born: of all my children you alone were old enough not only to give me your sturdy love but to hold my hand when the solitude of gazing into the night became blinding. In spite of your tender years—or perhaps because of them—you truly understood and felt the necessity and the impossibility of my task. Thank you, my child.

Tristana, Adrian, and Eliana—my children: without the sunshine of your innocence I would have continued to live the story in silence. I engaged in these lightless dialogues for the sake of the brilliance in your eyes, so that they could sparkle unimpeded by evil deeds of evil men. My children, I thank you for being near me when I could have been swallowed by the quicksand of my memories.

Vicki, my wife: the journey was rough for you, too, I know. Often it made little sense; often you felt that you lost me to the unburied. And yet, you sustained me. You trusted this seemingly absurd project which, at times, undermined the sanity of our home. But because your trust was inspired by love and respect, you stood by me. Thus, this book belongs to you, as well.

And, finally: I thank the Social Science and Humanities Research Council and Principal Paul Fox of Erindale College of the University of Toronto. Their generous grants helped to defray the financial costs of the journey that took me from Toronto to California, to various locations in Europe, and, finally, to Israel. And into the invisible realms of the living past....

Every writer today attempts to achieve the same thing. We live in a generation of darkness, so much darkness that we want to bring some light to it, or, at least, to give an intensity to the darkness. There is so much suffering that we try, at least, to evaluate it and see where it comes from, if not to redeem it.

—Elie Wiesel

"With words you can create either angels or demons. Be careful. Do not create demons. Create only angels; create only the good and the humane."

—Elie Wiesel, quoting his teacher in
In Conversation with Harry James Cargas

To the Reader

I wasn't born to be a writer, nor am I a teller of tales by vocation. But this tale must be told and it falls on me to break the silence of forty years and tell it. Nothing predisposes me to abandon the anonymity to which most humans are predestined; no gift distinguishes me from my parents or their ancestors—small-time merchants and craftsmen. Nothing, except that I am a Jew born in Budapest in 1936. Is there a more ordinary statement than that? But this particular place of birth and this date thrust me, at the age of eight, into the Devil's limelight: for I was born into the desecrated skin of a Jew when and where that was the greatest crime of all.

I had a mother, a father, and a sister, Agi, five years older than I. We lived in a two-room flat in the centre of the cursed capital of Hungary. He was the meek youngest son of poultry mongers. She was the timid eldest daughter of a printer. Between them they had twelve brothers and sisters, all married, and twenty-one nieces and nephews. And Agi and me, of course. Our daily existence was so monotonously simple that hardly a shred of memory surfaces to prove that I was, indeed, alive for over eight years before the sky fell upon the Jews of Budapest. My family had only a marginal Jewish identity; we were essentially assimilated. I think my parents were too busy making ends meet, providing us with a thin cushion of comfort in the heart of a hostile city, to have energy or concern for religion. I don't even recall visits on High Holidays to the synagogue, which was only three blocks from our house. Like most Jews in Budapest we spoke Hungarian and only Hungarian. There were no candles lit on Friday nights, no prayer books, no Seder celebrations on Passover, no fasting on Yom Kippur.

And yet I knew I was Jewish. Of course, I was circumcised. That would have been sufficient proof. But then there were my classmates in Grade 2 who called me dirty Jew, which made no sense at all since I was meticulously clean and they sported, more often than not, black fingernails, soiled shoes, and other signs of neglected personal hygiene. And when I was six, there were the children in my hospital ward who beat me up and took the first orange I ever owned. And there were the gendarmes, in their foreboding rooster-feathered coifs, who interrupted my sister's eleventh and my sixth birthday party held the same day at an uncle's country home. They came to usher away my aunt, my uncle, and my eight-year-old cousin, Tomi, because my aunt's husband was a Jew from Poland. What a peculiar way to acquire an identity!

Only many years later, in the lap of sad adult wisdom, did I learn that nearly a thousand years of hatred and persecution of Jews in millennial Hungary preceded what seemed to the ignorant child an unfathomable curse upon my family. I didn't know that anti-Semitism was a part of the national character in Hungary from the early kings of the Arpad dynasty throughout the centuries. I certainly didn't have any notion of the assimilationist thrust of Hungarian Jewry throughout the previous century, a tendency that committed them to a fatal illusion. As a result of the illusion they failed to predict that the acquisition of the Magyar language, the total immersion in secular culture, the conscientious participation in most aspects of society, was not going to earn them the right to survive as Hungarians. They underestimated or failed to perceive at all the impenetrable exclusivism of Hungarian Christians. They were blinded by civil emancipation, superficial privileges, and some constitutional rights. Victims of a trap they unwittingly helped to erect, they chased the elusive mirage of real, palpable citizenship. The awakening for most of them came at the threshold of untimely death. Thus, when the barrage of anti-Jewish laws and communiqués saw the grey light of day, they were stunned. "Jews are Jews, not Jewish Magyars. Only Christians are Magyars!" proclaimed the Prime Minister even before the Germans marched into Budapest on 19 March 1944 to prepare to execute the already well-oiled deportation process. Thousands of converts learned in labour and concentration camps the inevitability of being Jewish: one didn't become a Magyar, one's ancestors had to be born into that state of grace.

After 19 March 1944 all other aspects of our lives receded into dark irrelevance. Whatever else we seemed to be or do was altogether negligible: being Jewish overshadowed everything. Soon after that harshly lit spring day, when I watched with silent fascination as the *Wehrmacht* settled into our lives without a sound, events followed each other in machine-gun succession. First, a law forced us to brand ourselves with a yellow star so that everyone could always recognize us as Jews. Until then, I knew only that to be Jewish was dangerous. On 3 April I learned that it was also shameful. Three weeks later, looking insignificant and defeated under his giant knapsack, my father disappeared from our lives, leaving our little family truncated and scared. My mother took us out of school. We spent all our time at home or at our grandmother's flat. What also vanished from our lives was the smile on the adults' faces. And little by little, we, the children, stopped playing—as if daily existence had become a continuous funeral, waiting for worse to come.

About six weeks after my father's departure for forced labour, the three of us moved into grandmother's flat. My Aunt Sari and her three-year-old son, Tibi, joined us. Grandmother's building was one of the some 2,600 buildings designated with a large Star of David on the front door as approved housing for Jews. Life at grandmother's was cramped, tense, and mostly devoid of any active hope. The children learned to whisper even without being told. The adults whispered feverishly uttered words at night. Every night. Except when the shrill sound of sirens forced us to take shelter against nightly bombing raids. Then, we were stunned to silence; none of us ever cried.

For reasons that were opaque to me, my mother decided to have us converted to Catholicism. The priest, a coarse, cruel old man, horrified me more than all the guns and all the bombs: he never failed to threaten me with eternal hell. He accused me of being the Devil's messenger because I made signs of the cross with my left hand. That daily panic "cured" me of being left-handed. What followed was a murky confusion in my young mind about Jesus and the God of Christians and a manual clumsiness that has been my unshakeable mate since I became a budding Catholic.

Then, on 15 October, a moment of euphoric illusion freed us of our captivity. The amateur ruler of the country, Admiral Horthy, Regent and Supreme War Lord, proclaimed on radio the cessation of hostilities. Magically having regained our voices, we ran into the streets screaming with free air in our lungs our liberation from the yoke of the yellow star and the arrow cross, symbols of the oppressed and the oppressor. For the first time in my life, I tasted the sweet nectar of real happiness.

But only hours, meagre little hours, later, our elation turned into bitter poison. No one took Horthy's proclamation seriously or literally, except the Jews. His own high-ranking officers disobeyed him. In the Parliament, Veterans of the Eastern Front colluded with the Hungarian fascist party, the dreaded Arrow Cross Party, to declare Horthy's proclamation unconstitutional. The Germans entrapped his younger son and exacted his abdication. And the infamous head of the Arrow Cross Party, Ferenc Szálasi, became Prime Minister. That date—15 October 1944—was to inaugurate the darkest period in the history of Budapest Jewry. While I had no awareness of the day's significance for the 200,000 Jewish inhabitants of the capital, at age eight I learned to recognize the ugly head of despair on the very same day that I discovered happiness.

Despair seemed to spread in our family and among our neighbours like an inevitable epidemic. I grew to live with it as I imagine one resigns oneself to the loss of one's sight.

Szálasi was at the helm of a cursed ship. Mad hatred never soared higher than during those interminable three months. The mobs ruled, but not without the not-so-tacit permission of the Germans, the real masters of Hungary. Whatever control Szálasi commanded, he concentrated on the most rapid massacre of the Jews. The day after he became Prime Minister, Jewish houses were sealed for ten days, leaving us without food or medical aid. The dead and the living were competing for space in their makeshift cages. Why? Because according to the Minister of the Interior we deserved it for our previous and present conduct. The enthusiasm, the dedication, and the obscene brutality of the Arrow Cross militia and of the unaffiliated mob of wild youths surpassed all expectations of their leaders. Thus, the same minister ordered restraint two days later, but to no avail. The rulers of the streets were no longer under anyone's control. What seemed to emerge, however, was an absurd contest between Eichmann's *Sondereinsatzkommando*, which feverishly endeavoured to keep the number of deportable Jewish bodies the highest possible, and the masters of the street, whose thirst for Jewish blood seemed unquenchable.

My mother and my aunt were running around a great deal, leaving us children with grandmother, our obese, very childish, always scared grandmother. I found out much later that they were trying to pull whatever strings they could to get us into one of the buildings protected by neutral countries. A young Swedish lover of humanity, Raoul Wallenberg, came to Budapest to make it his life's mandate to save as many Jews as he could. To this end, he devised the ersatz passport referred to as a *Schutzpass*, or safe-conduct letter, which, as evidence of Swedish citizenship, protected the bearer from Nazi persecution. Charles Lutz, the Swiss Consul, and some other diplomats representing neutral governments followed the example of the noble Swede. Alas, mother's and Sari's efforts were not crowned with success and our family lapsed into the dismal fate shared by most Jews of the capital.

When the war effort could no longer afford even the cattle wagons, over 20,000 Jews were marched off toward the Austrian border where the German SS were expecting them. On the nearly 200-kilometre trek, half of them succumbed to the endless marches, the almost complete lack of food, and the constant dread of the looming shadow of the gas chamber. The relentless savagery of their guards only added to their being reduced to what the Swedish Ambassador referred to in a protest note to the Arrow Cross government as people "who no longer possess human shape and lack all human dignity." Again, we learned later, tragically too much later, of the superhuman efforts of Wallenberg who, day after day, literally tore hundreds of victims from the diabolical snares of the murderers. He lied, manipulated, threatened, bluffed, and used whatever ruse he could think of; his only concern was to save lives. One man against the Reich! How many more were needed, my God! We were waiting for the arrival of the Soviet soldiers as if mounting a fanatic vigil for the Messiah. The Red Army advanced to thirteen kilometres from the capital in chaos. Alas, there they suffered a massive setback which exacted three more months before they could rid the city of its plague. For thousands of Jews those thirteen kilometres meant the difference between life and death, between raving insanity, famine, spiritual discomfiture, rape, and death.

Then mother was deported. Silent terror settled into my young body. Surrounded by the loneliness of an orphan, I was learning to cope with an increasingly pressing daily reality. Nothing was beyond the realm of the possible. I lived every day in the shell of a prematurely aged old man. I don't recall ever saying out loud, "I am going to die, we are all going to die." But certain truths need no words to be convictions governing every living moment. The air attacks became a more regular part of our routine than eating. We spent entire nights in the dark, damp cellar.

Until 26 November came, when the central ghetto was inaugurated: some 63,000 Jews were herded into 293 apartments. I'll never forget the march through the streets of Pest amid constant beatings and machine-gun bursts from avid Arrow Cross militia and just plain, "apolitical" Jew-hating citizens. With pitiful parcels on our backs, deadness in our hearts, and stony terror in our eyes, we marched into the evacuated, ghostly territory in the bowels of the city designed to be our grave or, at least, its antechamber. Food? Some molasses, a turnip, and a slice of sawdust bread. Medical aid? Nonexistent. Hope? Well....Corpses stacked like frozen logs began to clutter the ghetto landscape.

Budapest was in the hands of obsessed, rabid youths killing, raping, torturing Jews in the ghetto or on the banks of the Danube. The atrocities reached such proportions that even the German sensibilities were ruffled and they complained to the government about the horror flooding the streets. It was "upsetting" to their orderly plan of action. While the Germans quickly gave up on Szálasi and his "Asian savages", they decided to defend Budapest to the last man, in order to slow the advance of the Red Army toward the Reich. The defeated government slipped out of town leaving it in the hands of the SS and the Arrow Cross militia.

The ghetto was liberated in a house-to-house sweep by Soviet troops. While within shooting range of Soviet soldiers, the Arrow Cross men continued with their bloody massacre, maniacally committed to their goal that not one Jew should survive their rampage. In fact, they planned to blow up the ghetto; but, ironically, a German general foiled their evil project. So they had to do it the hard way, inspired by the infamous Arrow Cross priest, Father András Kun: "In the sacred name of Christ, fire!"

Freedom didn't greet all of my family. My father returned from the copper mines of Bor blinded, with the weight of torture etched forever into his extinguished eyes. Mother perished in the hell of Bergen Belsen. Most of my aunts, uncles, and cousins were killed in one camp or another. Survival took its toll in every Jewish household.

What followed was not a joyous reconstruction, a gleeful enactment of the rites of spring. The new year seemed dedicated to the dead and the pain and confusion of the survivors. Where to begin? What to do first? How to go about starting over? Father was possessed by a dark depression nurtured by his indelible memories of the pit and of the sweetness of our simple life before the deluge. My sister and I were wards of a Zionist-funded organization providing us with daily food and some gentle nurturing toward the art and craft of living. Tentatively an anemic growth of new childhood began to take hold. At times, I recall, we even sang and danced. But fear never left me. Neither did shame. Fear that it might happen again and shame for having had to live through it once and forever.

And life did begin to pick up a faster cadence. Father, as a result of surgical intervention, regained some of his sight; thus he was able to take a job. He was no longer totally dependent on us, children.

In fact, for our sake, he allowed a marriage to be arranged. He was to wed a survivor of Mauthausen. My stepmother was a physically and emotionally emptied woman who married into our morose family to escape the loneliness of her memories and to escape the stigma of spinsterhood. She quickly demonstrated to Agi and me the cool madness of torture she had learned at Mauthausen at the expense of her soul. She pushed my sister into marriage at the age of seventeen, when she was still a needy child. I hated being home, where I felt hunted by my stepmother and haunted by my father's lethargy and my ache for my mother. I hated school, where I was brutalized by my Christian classmates, all of them bigger and stronger than I. I escaped into solitude. I cut school for days, weeks, months, hiding out on the hills of Buda, in hospital waiting rooms, in movie theatres. Hungary's new masters, the Russians, beyond saving my pitiful skin, did not endow me with any optimism about life. It was still horrible to be a Jew. The fear and the shame received a new companion: rage. I refused to submit myself to the Bar Mitzvah, the Jewish rite of passage for boys. I refused to wear the shameful and dangerous cloak of a people that allowed its own massacre.

As for God, I had had to get along without His support for so long that it never occurred to me that it was even available to me at all. In that sense, the Marxist regime offered me a viable alternative—a society built on a godless principle. Only much later did I awaken to the grim reality that to live without God as a metaphor in one's conscience leaves a moral vacuum in the essence of man and society. But in a rudimentary, tentative manner, I soon articulated to myself that the new regime was only a variation on the old theme and that not even the might of the victorious Soviet Union could succeed in extinguishing the sacred fire of anti-Semitism in the heart of the Hungarian.

On the day of Stalin's funeral, my demented stepmother attacked me with a butcher's knife. The years of accumulated, merciless memories of torture finally found an expression of rightful rage. But why me? Because in her life I was the weakest, the most likely candidate for successful victimization. Her foaming explosion of violence found resonance in the turmoil of my viscera: with one arm I easily disarmed her, and with the other I hit her across her purple face at the bottom of which two bloodshot eyes seemed to scream: "I hate!" There was immeasurable hatred in the blow with which I demolished this wretched shadow of a woman. And I have never felt so good in my life, or so clear. And now, as I tell you this story, I feel shame as tears well up in my eyes: she, too, was a victim, just like me, and I became just another torturer in that tattered existence of hers. But back then, for the first time, the puny boy I was felt mighty. How

I cherished my brand-new power. She screamed out in horror as I struck her, and her indignant fear and shock only swelled my glory. "Shut up, or I'll give you another one!" I yelled at her with the cruelty of all victors. Six weeks later my father divorced her and married a friend and partner of my Aunt Sari.

Father's third marriage coincided with my entrance into gymnasium, the Hungarian version of high school. It was a kind of new birth for me. My classmates were mostly Jewish, our teachers were mostly anti-Communist and not anti-Semitic. It was from some of these marvellously human, hence vulnerable teachers that I put together a tentative concept of loving, and especially the love of children. For the first time, I had friends. I was doing what is natural for teenagers: playing soccer, swimming, studying as little as possible (except languages, which had a mysterious hold on me), day-dreaming, and running after girls. My rapport with my sister Agi and her husband was tender and *almost* successful in eradicating in me the endless thirst for real parents.

Upon graduation, I found myself defeated again by the dictatorial exigencies of the so-called Communist regime: I was obliquely declared ineducable. It was unlawful to be unemployed; thus, abandoning my dreams of becoming a physician, I went to work in the largest printing plant in the country. At least I could still nourish my hearty appetite for books. But again, I landed in an exclusively Christian domain. In addition to a "natural" distrust and spite for Jews, my colleagues resented my high school education. A constant flow of references lashed out at my alleged Jewish identity. I say alleged because, by 1955, I had given up the struggle for a Jewish survival: I had assumed a Protestant identity, inventing Austrian aristocratic ancestors for myself to account for my Germanic family name. My pathetic attempts led me into a dimly lit fool's paradise. No anti-Semite worthy of the name gave any credence to my feeble cover-up. I would have had to give some real tangible proof of a noble Gentile descent: derogatory comments, anti-Jewish jokes, observance of Christian holidays—other than Christmas and Easter—would have sufficed. While I didn't feel shame for my cover-up or for the counterfeit banishing into exile of my family's Jewish past, I wasn't free to cover my own head with the scum of slurs. It was more than enough to have to bite my tongue and feel the blood empty from my stomach every time I heard vicious comments uttered at the expense of the Jew. The familiar bitter taste of hatred was invading my mouth once again. And, this time, it seemed there was no hope for any escape: this was for life.

October 1956: the miracle occurred. The people of Hungary rebelled against the Soviet yoke. The road to freedom was open for a brief, intoxicating moment. When the "patriots" thought that they triumphed over the Red Devil, their old hatred of Jews, slithering in unlit corners for over ten years, came right into the November mist. Caught between two walls of hopelessness, I opted for the only worthwhile choice: to risk escape to the West. In spite of my father's adamant protests and threats of locking me in the cellar, I fled to Austria, and two days later I was flown to Paris. It was at the festive Le Bourget airport that nearly ten thousand French enthusiasts welcomed me, at the age of twenty-one, to my second birth.

Life in Paris exploded into a continuous spectacle of fireworks as day after day I discovered sparks of possibilities, marvellous bits of street life, enticing sounds of a language that I wished to devour. In this strange kaleidoscope of a city I felt at home—for the first time in my life. I knew I could hide in any of its myriad hospitable corners. Or should I choose to be visible, there was enough benevolent light for me to bask in. With a stubborn, religious fervour, I threw myself into the French language. I opened all my pores to soak up "Frenchness". Aiming to enhance the purity of my new identity, I wanted to exorcize the Hungarian in me. I wanted to be French. More French than the French. I tamed the language in six weeks. I finally lost myself in the endless depths of Françoise, a sunlit eighteen-year-old from heavy-footed Perpignan. She was bursting onto Paris ready to be thrust into real living. Our thrust was greedy and parallel. We created one another.

But she didn't know I was Jewish. Her virginity sheltered me from the shameful unmasking of my circumcised identity. I cursed this symbol of the covenant. Again, fear settled into my heart. It took her aunt—a stiff-spined *grande bourgeoise* with deeply seated spite for all Jews—to rip to shreds my pitiful fable about an aristocratic lineage. The old loneliness reappeared in my heart, but manifold grown, more grotesque than ever. I clung onto this dark-haired, desperate lover as if my life depended on her. And, in a melodramatic yet certain way, she held the key to my survival in the French capital that suddenly lost its indomitable lustre for me. I clung to her with childlike fanaticism: with her immeasurable love and lust for strong experiences she was my lifeboat to safety. Together, in our tiny mansard crowning the Ile St. Louis, we thought we were undefeatable.

And yet, the stubborn solitude of my secret defeated us. I needed more and more vigorously to be at peace with the inevitable: "I can't hide from being Jewish. I may be able to lull the past to sleep but it keeps waking up. I must find refuge," I kept repeating with increasing desperation.

In February 1959 I arrived in San Francisco to start yet another life in the land of unlimited freedom, in the world without horizons. I joined my sister and her husband in Berkeley, California. We reunited what was left of our family.

Seven months of depression followed. I never felt the need to pierce the secret of California. I relied exclusively on my French to make a contact here and there. I found work and shelter thanks to my fluency in French, and I enrolled in the mighty University of California as a senior in French. I saw California through layers of translucent veils all woven in France. I never saw naked California. I never really left Paris.

I married into a bizarre Sicilian family. Sandwiched between endless moments of nostalgia for what life could have been with Françoise and the crude reality of my wife's hostile clan, I escaped into my familiar loneliness. You see, even my wife didn't know that I was Jewish, and I was not about to reveal it to her since I knew that her family harboured the most primitive version of Jew-hatred. I married into a fascist family! Oh, they were harmless—the way the guard outside a prisoner's cell is harmless: he doesn't do the sentencing, he just makes sure that you remain captive and that you never forget your captivity. The triumvirate of fear–shame–rage gained a new partner: alienation. I lived the homeless existence of a stranger even in the privacy of my bedroom.

Out of that depth of solitude was born my first child, the one who was going to lead me out of the wilderness. I insisted that we name her after the mother of all Greek gods. She was baptized as a Catholic. I felt the emptiness and the ache of an amputated past. I buried my dead even deeper in the sky. But through this brand-new life I experienced a possibility of escape toward the future. When I finished my doctorate, our limping family left California. This time, Toronto was to be the shadow of the Promised Land. Canada seemed harmless, hospitable, silent like a cemetery. A suitable home for the final abode. I looked forward to shedding as much of the dead skin accumulated over the years of disillusionment as the frost would permit. Soon after my second daughter's birth, I shed the last inert layer: I divorced my children's mother. At the age of forty, after so many spurious births, I finally stepped out into a shower of genuine, unimpeded light: I linked my life to a Jew. Our wedding was celebrated in a temple! As with all newborns, my identity was tentative, my faith inarticulate and clumsy; I still proclaimed that it was the company of Jews that I was seeking, not that of their God. But the ancient vigour was already absent from my voice. I began to feel comfortable in the skin of the Jew. Now, the reconstruction could really begin.

My wife, Vicki, and our son, Adrian David (a first wobbly step toward my self-definition as a Jew, and a kind of indirect blessing to my son as the heir to an ashen history with a plausible happy ending), were vacationing in southern California four summers ago. One morning, I awakened from a dream that delighted me beyond the brilliance of the summer sun. I dreamt that Vicki and I gave birth to a baby girl whom we named Eliana Tovah. I held the infant in my hands a moment after she was separated from her mother's body. She looked at me with a penetrating glance that I knew to be a unique bond between her and me, and even beyond....I told my wife about the apparition. She was touched by the tale, but unmoved toward conceiving.

Back in Toronto, I was preparing to participate in a conference in Israel the following summer. And, as part of my research, I was getting ready to go to Auschwitz. I had decided that I didn't want to go to either place without having proclaimed to all my affinity with and commitment to my people: I went to see a rabbi to help me prepare for my Bar Mitzvah. In the rabbi's study, I learned that Eliana means in Hebrew "and God answered me" and that Tovah is the feminine form of the adjective "good". I wasn't aware of having posed a question to God for longer than I cared to remember. And, in my dream, I received the gift of an unsolicited answer, a kind of timid, tentative offer of divine friendship. Vicki and I agreed to give in to the mystic bargain and our new daughter was ceremonially named Eliana Tovah during my Bar Mitzvah, sharing with me the relief and the joy of affirming to be who I was born to be. The despair of alienation vanished on its own.

Prologue

As a child I used to love the darkness, that weightless, soothing blanket that gently wrapped my body every night when sleep's invitation became irresistible. As I closed my eyes, a host of friendly shadows would visit me, keeping me company until darkness saturated my whole being with its familiar lull. I would let my body sink into an all-dissolving reassurance that the next morning, when I opened my eyes, a nourishing light would welcome me back into my life. A new day would greet me with the exuberance of spontaneous pleasures which only a well-nurtured child knows. No, indeed, darkness held no surprises for me. It was there, as taken for granted as the air.

And then one morning, in the ninth year of my existence, I opened my eyes and the darkness was still there. It was not the familiar uterine night, but a frightening dampness, a thick, slimy substance like clotting black ink. The wider I opened my eyes, the less I could see. Thinking that maybe I had done something wrong, I closed them again to start the day all over. Anguished, sensing that something had broken in me forever, and very tentatively, I summoned light to chase away this worrisome intruder. Instead, it slapped me in the face. Moments of panic slowly slipped into guarded curiosity. I began to scan what appeared to be an impenetrable black horizon. At first I guessed, more than discerned, the bobbing silhouettes of others on this involuntary journey. Little by little furtive whispers and hasty prayers uttered practically without breathing reached my ears. An indescribable atmosphere of fear invaded the darkness of this foreign place.

I must have made a sound or a gesture of concern, for an unexpectedly warm breath brought within whispering distance my mother's muffled voice: "We're in the cellar, my little boy. There was an air alert but you didn't hear the wailing of the sirens so I carried you down in my arms. Everyone from the building is here, and we have strict orders for observing a total blackout. Go back to sleep; I'll wake you when it is over."

"Air alert" sounded so distant, so technical, so non-threatening. Yet I knew that under the deceitful cloak of this sterilized word lurked a monster; we could be killed, for no reason at all, by a bomb falling indiscriminately from a sky roaring with Allied planes. It made no sense to me as an eight-year-old, and it is still an absurdity of civilized life that our lives had to be in danger. What did we, the children, do to deserve such a cruel fate? A web of fear, anger, and confusion reduced me to an unresolved silence. And from that moment on, I never again trusted the night.

Seeing the face of night banished me forever from the realm of childlike concerns and ignorance. The age of innocence was ripped out of my life. Hunger, abandonment, defilement, and the ceaseless pounding of bombs swelled the net of terror into which my family was caught like so many nameless fish in unimportant waters.

Since then, when the night arrives, I stare at the black screen of the winter of my ninth year. And my gaze freezes to a pile of corpses, still and chilled, upon which I was thrown, pitched like a shovelful of coal to be covered with further layers of dead Jewish neighbours and friends. How to free my body from the crushing, cold weight of fear, disgust, and madness at having been shrouded in a blanket of cadavers? Oh, the desperate dilemma of continuing or not continuing to *play* dead! (The cruelty of speech forces me to use this word, for we don't have words for tales we don't dare to tell. I have never since been able to *really play* at anything else.)

Then darkness descends and it begins to speak to me. It uses voices that I often cannot distinguish from my own or from that of the cadaver on my belly. At other times it sounds as if there is no one out there; only the echo of my memory of the dead reverberates in my empty bones. Again, at other times, faces poke through the nocturnal silence with disapproving frowns on their foreheads, with well-nourished fingers wagging at me accusingly, as if to say: "Haven't you done enough harm by molesting us with your very presence? The ugliness of your tale is a malignant intrusion on *our* version of reality.

Go, crawl back into the cave of darkness where you and your sick imagination can be kept under control." Often, because of my mournful familiarity with the darkness, I recognize them: here a professor of humanities, there a famous film-maker, over there again a social scientist, a friend, a well-intentioned psychiatrist.

How can I talk to the night? How can I stay silent against the night?

So, year after year, day after day, I restlessly roam the streets, the houses, the shelters, the bomb craters, the bath houses, the synagogues, the improvised depots for the flood of dead in the ghetto. From that desolate depth, I speak to any voice, without knowing who is out there and what he will answer. I dialogue as if I were in the company of life, as if I were really alive as a whole person. I hear voices born in a living soul and die in the memory of the corpse. I hear friends that sound like judges and judges that chant apologies for the murderer. I hear the voices of malicious magicians who, with a murderous sleight of hand, turn the rape of my body, the death of my mother, the disappearance of our large family into "the hoax of the century". I hear silence that howls back, ushering darker and darker clouds above my head, as answers to my questions aimed at man and God.

Lately, I have also been hearing new voices, voices that thin the mist of solitude with words that seem to have warm hands instead of the chilly cadaverous grips to which I am accustomed. Voices that sound strange, for they sound as hollow as my own, yet I know that they belong to other dwellers of the darkness. They ask no questions, offer no answers. Tentatively, without modulation or trust, in stark words they begin to talk about life on the flip side of sanity. They speak not of mythical beasts or fantastic creatures. They use literal, guttural, minimal language to account for their lives beyond the smoke and ashes. They tell of brothers, sisters, mothers, fathers, sons, and daughters whose fallen bodies made the clay and the mud bleed and groan.

They just keep telling their stories. They don't always wait for one to finish before the next one begins.

Strangely, this new polyphony is soothing. More and more often I close my eyes, stretch my arms, dip my pen in the hope of touching another soul out there beyond the wall, another survivor whose pain is akin to mine. We can travel together without carrying the other's burden, being fully aware of the ones already rounding our respective backs. As we journey on, who knows in what direction and with what purpose our numbers may swell and the sound of our tales may drown out the night and the curse of its guardians.

And there are also other voices....

Dialogue
with a
Torturer

" *F*OR YEARS I have been rehearsing my part in this confrontation, always knowing what I wanted to do to you should you have the audacity to force your presence upon my life again. I have had more fantasies of revenge than a painter's palette has colours. But I had no words to whirl at you, should it be inevitable to look into your eye and speak to you as if you were really human. How am I to gather into a coherent discourse my inarticulate howls and whimpering memories? Fearing that a collapse of my inadequate vocabulary would drag with it my seemingly sophisticated manners of social intercourse, I have chosen to cower. Not, though, like a snake in the grass, for that reptile is in a constant state of readiness to lash out when its survival depends on it. Rather, I have been lying low so as to avoid a paralysing encounter with you in my superficially ordinary routine existence.

"Should you emerge in a bank, should I lay eyes on you in the blasé ambience of a suburban supermarket or in the bustling crowd in the foyer of a movie theatre, would I tremble and bleed? Would my tongue freeze? Would my lungs refuse to propel air to my rescue? Would you triumph over me once again? Or would I be able to take a moment's vacation from my normally peaceful nature? Would I be able to step back far enough from you so that I could still see who you were but no longer feel the human affinity needed to contain the disdain and rage I have been harbouring for forty years?

"So many breathless conditions crowd my awareness each and every time your imprint makes its appearance on the murky screen of my memory! Here is but another version of torture: you are still holding on to my life with your icy cruelty, relentlessly and tenaciously; I am the fulfillment of your desire to continue dominating your faceless victims. This victory is so unexpected, even by you, that to formulate it in your consciousness would have been a wasteful embodiment of the absurd. And yet the absurd is truth and other truths travel the elevated but imaginary paths of artful fiction. I have given you more power than you thought you could ever extract from me. You probably don't even know that I still breathe vigorously enough to remember you at all. That is where *you* have made your fatal miscalculation. From the multitude of shapeless lives you ripped apart, one managed to mend itself sufficiently to function without attracting too much attention from the curious and apathetic tumult of human traffic. Yes, I, too, have power over you, a power engendered in the meticulous drudgery of cohabiting with the schism in my soul year after year, moment after wounded moment.

"The amorphous wait is over. No more trepidation, no more hypothetical limping from one catastrophic fear to the next. For days you have been loitering around my bowels, my quivering veins and arteries. I have been seeing your unmistakable ugliness in the dulled reflection of my bathroom mirror morning and night. To be sure, your cavernous face defies the world of interplay between light and shadow. You dare not cross the threshold between the integrity of radiance and the malice of darkness, the boundary between life and its negation. Yet, I *know* with cursed clarity that you have returned to haunt me."

"I haunt no one. I live in a suspension without energy. You should look, rather, at the obsessive tenacity with which you hold onto a memory without merit, without future for either one of us." I heard these words resonate with an acoustic flatness. They failed to engage me deeply enough to honour them with a feeling, with an overt acknowledgement.

"Forty years ago you seared your portrait on my consciousness; only death will separate me from your parasitic image. Do you doubt my sanity? My madness is as real and as palpable as it was when you bestowed it upon me forty years ago. But I am also armed with a saneness that has allowed me to avoid succumbing to your murderous commerce. I look over my shoulder and you linger in the air, surrounding me like a protective aura. You invade my body again with an arrogant insistence that claims squatter's rights on my life. I am confused about the essence of you, you who are so close yet the opposite of me.

"I can't loosen your stronghold on me until I deal with you face to face, even if your face is more a stench than an apparition. I smell the breath of raw human flesh where I should see your mouth. Blood still oozes between your teeth because the cannibal in you bit off more than he needed to satisfy the requirements for his survival and thriving. Your curse is to live with a mouthful of my flesh until the grave and beyond. Mine is that I shall never hear your words filter through that evil barrier; I shall never hear you utter outbursts of remorse, guilt, shame; and, above all, I shall never hear your sincere oath: 'I'll never torture again!' That you are condemned to this bloody silence is your inescapable fate, and I have not an instant's worth of compassion for you. That I have to live with *your* silence is another version of torture I hold *you* responsible for. You will remain a mournful enigma to me even if I free myself of the heavy burden of confusion and mystery about your essence. But unloading it will allow me to stand straighter and stronger, with my anchor more deeply sunk into the present. You understand, of course, that my query is meant to relieve me and to hurt you by refreshing your memory, in case you plead for mercy on the grounds of fading memories."

"You can't hurt me, for I am not vulnerable to you. I'm separate and committed only to living beyond moments of my own creation. You are obsessed with causing me pain; you don't even notice that you are your sole victim." His words fell without life.

"I forgot nothing! Some clamour for forgiving. I won't! The pain in my body won't let me forget or forgive. Forgiving you would be an invitation to start it all over if you still fancy torture as your preferred mode of creativity. Suffer my questions, and if it helps you, I am not ashamed to share with you that I suffer not only in the process of posing them but also from the ensuing silence. Were you born for good and later suffered the corruption of the commerce of men? Or did you enter this world carrying in you the seeds of the curse: being and doing evil? If you were destined to be evil, so was I. If you were robbed of your moral innocence, so was I, or, at least, so could I be. The road from you, the doer of evil, to me, the target of your malefic acts, may be sinuous, but it is uninterrupted. Without a doubt, you and I were condemned to a brotherhood neither of us wished to embrace. Your version of humanity denies me the right to an inviolate body, to a destiny not designed by mortals. Your evil—innate or bestowed— denies me the reassuring luxury of a belief in my absolute goodness. If for nothing else, for this rape of my optimism alone, I wish you to suffer, I want you to die a painful death."

"You can't hurt me," he countered. "Your curses die without penetrating my skin."

"The impenetrable darkness of the horror you immersed me in fills my mouth with shame. You have exposed the flaw in me without my having committed even one single reprehensible deed. Your guilt has robbed me of my innocence. Your 'guilty' verdict implicates me in possible future foul acts against human beings who look as I used to before you lacerated my body and my name. Now I often stare at the screen of my opaque conscience attempting to tease out a tolerable answer to the ultimate question: am I also fatally infested with the potential for perversion? Could the same generous mind that presents the gift of lyric poetry to a humanity eager to be enhanced by the lull of a soothing metaphor also devise more ingenious, more refined, more expedient ways to torture and murder? One mournful night could I raise a gun, instead of the tender glass eye of my camera, to the unsuspecting face of a child?

"Do not make haste with the answer. Leave me my illusions— above all, the illusion that I have survived the defilement of my person. I don't have to pass on the curse, yet it's there in every story I tell. I am committed to tell our story, yours and mine, to all my children. Their birth attests not so much to the truimph of good over you, the evil, but to your demise, and thus to the liberation of life.

"There are so many marvellous things children can do, if only we tell them the right stories while they are still free and willing to listen. The tale I *must* tell about you robs them, too, of some of the wonders they could create. For the theft of some of the glitter in my children's hearts, I wish you to die in the agony of the full awareness of your villainy. You have planted cancer where healthy blood should flow. You have covered all the oceans, all the lands, all the spheres with graves for the millions who decomposed without burial. Where there should be vast gardens, nurturing wheat fields, dancing waters blistering with life, the weeds of destruction dominate the horizon. The new vegetation of granite monuments to the martyred multitudes punctuates the air saturated with the endless shriek of souls. The new poetry is a monotonous litany composed of the ceaseless procession of names of murdered women and their brothers, mates, and sons. Can you hear their doomed chant for which you composed the lyrics? 'Vera Rosenberg, young of ten summers spent in the silk slippers of the apprentice ballerina, beaten and shot to death at Kamenets-Podolsk....Piroska Schlesinger, lived forty-two simple years, mourned by two little orphans, tortured and killed at Bergen Belsen....Alexander Stein, saw forty-two undistinguished years with his myopic eyes, blinded in the copper mines of Bor, the fire of life extinguished in him by the loss of his family....Judit Weisz, six weeks old, starved to death in the ghetto of Budapest....' and the chant continues with only the names changing. But your name remains impassibly the same, guilty, evil, and soiled: murderer of dreams, assassin of six million futures. What you have left us with is the painful realization that human perfectibility includes, and perhaps dominates, the growth of the capabilities and talents for more evil."

"As long as there are humans, we'll do what our destiny orders us to do. Posterity makes sense of it to explain the urgency of a different moment. How incredibly corrupt!"

"Once upon a time our magic memories enabled us to profit from mistakes, to establish continuities in our lives, to master complex feats of learning. Now that same gift of memory has (per)/(con) verted our beautiful minds into depots filled with mass traumas, howling fears, nightmarish anxieties, unresolved conflicts, and, above all, the souvenir of a landscape of rape and untimely deaths. Yes, indeed, you have done away with our age-old human conception of expanses of time and space without which no hope can flourish. The anemic, scarcely whispered optimism that plaintively grows from beneath the panorama of rubble you have left us with allows less for the spurt of hope than for the tired sigh of relief and mourning.

"What do you shelter in the depth of your mind? What feelings make your entrails churn? Could I possibly hope for a glimmer of sorrow or an occasional flash of compassion? Does pain ever visit you when you are absolutely alone and no one is there to see your tears? Or are you *ever* alone? Do your victims ever leave you a moment's grace of solitude? And what about guilt? Does your memory ever lean back over your conscience to whisper with sincerity and humility: 'I am sorry for the evil I did, I am guilty, atrociously guilty'?"

"I'm not any more guilty than any other man ever born. We are compelled by our biographies to conduct ourselves in good faith toward our destinies."

I have come to pause for a breath of air. My heart is skipping beats from the burden of confronting the murderer not as a murderer but as a fellow traveller on this human journey, as a stepbrother. I am covered with cold sweat and my eyes are foggy with the steam of my hatred and the tears of my sorrow for him, for me. I am in a trance. My struggle to remain humane is at crucial odds with my urge to stay human: the surge toward a higher moral plane is duelling with the raw cruelty slowly building in my groin. Humane versus human, what absurd polarity!

What seems to rescue me from this stalemate is really a defeat of hope; it is a kind gesture from my memory serving up to me a morsel of wisdom forged by Nathaniel Hawthorne in *Twice-Told Tales*: "There is no such thing in man's nature as a settled and free resolve either for good or evil, except at the moment of execution." Not a total victory for a joyous rebirth, but at least a repossession from the darkness of that which survived Auschwitz. The murderer is at home only in the company of victims and other murderers. The rest of us have this limping but still vigorously breathing universe.

"Could it be that you torture and murder without *really being* evil? Could it be that evil and good exist out there as independent mercenaries waiting patiently to serve any interested master? How

does it happen that you choose to shelter a wounded puppy one
minute, to nurture him back to the life his biological destiny owes
him, and that the next minute you let your body fall prey to ripping
the flesh of an eight-year-old boy you never saw before as if he were a
sheet of toilet paper? What has he done to you? How is your destiny
enriched by the rape of his unsuspecting, uninvolved body? Does it
come easily, naturally to you to do evil, or do you have to ritualistically
condition yourself to afflict pain on the innocent? Is this how you pay
tribute to some mystical deity holding you captive with threats or
promises?

"Maybe you don't recognize in me any resemblance to you, maybe
my humanness is not at all visible to you. What is it about me that
exiles me to a region more distant from your heart than a dog? If I
can't arouse in you the same sympathy as an animal, what does that
make me? Certainly not a vegetable being, for you surround yourself
with luxuriant plants, you express your passion with richly scented
bouquets of flowers, and you sustain your being with nourishing
vegetables and fruit. Would this mean that you relegate me to the
realm of inanimate objects? But you amass objects of all origins to
embellish, shelter, and simplify your existence! What am I, then? You
have robbed me not only of a name but also of membership in the
natural order of creation. How strange it is that I recognize an
essential similarity between you and my father, my rabbi, my cousin,
me! And you treat me as a nightmare!"

"You are you, and I am I. Therein lies our commonality."

"How is it that *you* invade my body with your brutal thrust and *I*
end up feeling like an intruder? Could it be that I have given you more
power than you really have?

"Can you feel the awesomeness of the fear I want to inspire in
you? I want more than anything the certainty that in the privacy of
your bed you tremble with unshakeable terror that one day, sooner or
later, I will hurt you. I want the evil pain you inflicted upon my person
to imprison you for the rest of your living days because you can't
escape from settling our account. But you don't know when. Or how!
Or whom you will have to face. You won't know if it will come, as you
did, sneakily, with the fear of the coward, from behind. You don't

know whether I will be alone or surrounded by avenging judges looming as gigantic as you and your cohorts seemed to me on that distant December morning."

"You can't hurt me. Your threats are words that spin no wheels. I alone can hurt me. Just as you have been hurting yourself. Therein lies our separateness."

"But you see, I am free today. Desolate and free. Wounded and free. Having breathed beyond your assault liberates me from the nightmarish, catastrophic fantasies that ordinary people conjure up when they imagine the ultimate pain. To have seen the face of evil and to come back to spit into it and put it on public display endows me with a knowledge of freedom that only having been tortured affords a human being. A sorrowful wisdom, indeed; one that can be converted, however, into monumental power.

"You, on the other hand, have spent your last energy, there is nothing for you to hope for, nothing to discover. You have shrunken the space available to a human life. You reduced your plane to one gruesome act of extreme ugliness. You are henceforth neither man nor beast. You are a torturer of children. You may have long forgotten the taste of a child's blood, the smoothness of a child's skin; your ears may no longer be delighted with the scream of wounded flesh. But you are still going to be accountable—forever. To me, to the others, and to your own children. Especially to your children! They can't remain inviolate in your venomous shadow. You have robbed them, too, of their day in the sun. Their tragic lineage compels them to the damp darkness of a cavernous existence. 'What did you do in the war, daddy?' Shreds of my skin must be clouding your eyes when confronted with this question. Their suspicion, their disgust, their shame is one of the walls of your prison. I pity your children for no other reason than that they are *children*, just as I and my contemporaries were. I bleed for all the children who are born to suffer for the mere reason that they came to see the light of life in a corner of the earth belonging to the masters of darkness, be they offspring of tortured or torturer.

"I have but cruel fantasies when your image springs into my awareness. When it comes to you, I am not better than you, although my torturous deeds are limited to raging words and visceral upheaval tormenting only myself. I fear more than another visit from you that my fantasies of your endless suffering are just that: idle, self-afflicting fantasies. But for your children, I am filled with anguish and concern: will they have a chance to retain even a thread of their gentle innocence or does just the mere fact of being *your* children force them into an existence in the disquieting regions of penumbra? Torn between the natural bequest to thrive and an almost inescapable destiny of filial loyalty, what version of childhood is available under the roof of the torturer? Can you keep the reflection of my blood from your eyes when you smile at your son, whose tender face is not unlike mine used to be? Can you not see me in your son's open face or do you not have the courage to risk looking him in the face, for fear of betraying your perverted identity?"

"I see in your face only the familiar traits of strangers. In my life I've encountered only strangers. And I've never violated the boundary beyond which I cease to be a stranger for you, or anyone else. My son is not less a member of this endless fraternity than you or anyone else."

"I also fear your children, I recoil in cold anguish when I hear their powerful voices. Perhaps you instilled in them the love of evil before they had a chance to learn of another life energy. I fear that they have not been able to escape the curse of being your children. And if they have emerged as apprentices of that in which you are the uncontested master, then I must be vigilant that they don't perpetuate the world you handed down to them. In that case, I must rush to prepare my children for a relentless readiness for your assault on their peaceful and joyous existence. Before the fine arts, dramatic arts, and poetic arts I must strengthen their untempered bodies with the martial arts. Before teaching them the resplendent tranquillity of a blazing sunset, I must educate them in the wisdom that springs from the ashen past of their ancestors—a version of wisdom that blossoms into the even mood of peacefulness in a minor key. There is an ocean of strength in this version of tranquillity, but the fire of the setting sun over the rhythmic waves is absent. For absconding with the passion that is the birthright of all children, I curse you again and command God's and man's revenge to fall upon all the moments of your life!"

"You can't hurt me. Your curse dies without penetrating my skin."

"For setting the trap of hatred and violence for future generations I have devised a just consequence for you: day after day, I see you in a glass cage, naked, so that no artifice can hide your genuine evil essence. In this revealing captivity I would exhibit you in the heart of all human communities in which your face may be unknown—especially in human centres in which people doubt whether you ever existed. I would certainly want you to be exposed to the young sabra who denies that your foul deeds have any relevance to his sun-drenched existence—an existence nearly overwhelmed by the struggle with evil-doers clad in a bile of different tint, spitting murderous words of a different melody than yours. But the essence is the same: kill, torture, shut off the air supply to the Jews who managed to defeat you, you, who seem to be of a negligible import to those whose hearts and minds have been blinded and, at the same time, fascinated by the new face of evil. I want all of them to see you, I want all of them to know that you are the prototype for all the evil intentions this century has lavished on the house of Israel."

"I am who I am. You are who you are. Therein lies our commonality."

"On top of your ambulant glass prison I would place a sign informing all spectators not about who you are but about what you have done. Let them conclude as to your identity: 'At the time when the master race gave free reign to all who felt they had anything to contribute to its natural superiority, I, as a proud specimen of high-flying *Übermenschen*, showed my privileged superiority by raping, torturing, and murdering Jewish children.' And I would want to take all precautions that no physical harm be inflicted upon your body. Because, you see, in this way you would be useful to me and my comrades. Time will do the clement justice no creature born of human mother was either able or willing to bring upon your head. You have a very short time left in the company of men. I want to make sure that before you escape the wrath of your victims, you are properly exposed to those who are prone to forget, to those who claim you never existed, to those who lull themselves in the spurious reality that your face has nothing in common with those of decent men, to those who blindly beat their ignorant chests that the like of you can never see the light again. There are millions living in one kind of darkness or another. You must serve my purpose: to dissipate as much of the night as you and I—a grotesque, symbiotic pair—can. I want to flood the night with the clarity of the truth that only you and I know in its full disgrace.

"Watching you, I know that words don't leave you indifferent. You seem inclined to respond, to justify, to trim to ordinary dimensions the enormity of your evil deeds. No, not just yet. I want you to savour the chill of my hatred for you. I want to purify my body of the scum you forced upon it many, many years ago. You may think that in conducting myself as an avenger-judge, I am mirroring your cruelty. Far be it from the truth. The pain you may feel oppressed by, the horror that slowly seeps into your body pore by pore, is of your own production. I have sheltered it for all these years. Now, finally, I am able to return to you what is yours."

"I feel no pain. I don't know the meaning of horror. My life is uninterrupted by words of pathos."

"Keep in mind also that you are not a scapegoat upon whom I arbitrarily dump the trash of which I must rid myself. I have been searching for you, waiting for you. My soul has been torn for more years than I would like to remember about what to do with you if and when I ever came face to face with you again.

"I have even considered letting you off the hook by admitting you into the pitiful society of victims. But, damn you, I won't do that! It would be the ultimate madness to place you in the same grave next to my mother, my cousins, my own destiny. You chose us to be your victims. You chose to be a torturer, a murderer. However understanding, however benevolent I may be inclined to feel toward you in the name of generosity, you should never forget, because I certainly don't, that you chose to act as the most depraved cannibal on this planet. The seduction of your parasitic greed helped you to succumb to the promises of artificial mirages. Remember that many of your friends, neighbours, co-parishioners, resisted the pull of evil. The righteous in heart remained righteous in deed. 'Situational forces', 'social conditions', and 'peer pressure' are instances of mystical language which you invented to help you fall asleep with an anesthetized conscience.

Good-intentioned but blind guardians of academic, abstract wisdom became your unwitting buttresses. But remember that, at the moment of dragging a child under a dark doorway with the intention of gratifying the basest human urge there is, you acted out of *your choice*, out of *your own body*, with *your own purpose*. You did what you did with the awareness that only shame and disgrace would have covered your bestial head had you perpetrated the reduction of flesh into meat in the light of day. You knew that by raping a child you paid tribute to your own dehumanization."

"Whatever I did or do, I was born human and remain human, and I'll die human. You need to broaden your definition of humanity: you'll discover a multitude of strangers you chose to banish from your sight, endowing them with the mystique of evil, whatever that is."

"So you hid with your prey until your appetite was satiated. You are not a beast—for beasts of prey only kill, they do not intentionally torture. They must feed themselves; such is the order of nature. But they are neither wasteful nor capricious. You have wasted my innocence. The hunger you sought to assuage was a depravation of your mind, not an existential need of your body. I won't therefore disgrace even the most repulsive of animals by likening you to them.

"You, I am sad to say, are a man. You have not only deflowered my innocence, you have also shed light on a corner of the human potential that no one wants to know about, let alone see. I am here to remind you and the world of that last horizon where it is still accurate to state that this, too, is the work of man."

I grow silent. The torrent of uncontrolled words has parched my mouth, imposing restraint. My head is spinning. In a moment's clear presence of mind, I realize that not once in the course of my lengthy cathartic confrontation did I raise my glance. Was I avoiding my interlocutor? I sense where he is. His presence, once more, deprives me of the air needed to sustain my body. A vacuum indicates that he is standing in front of me, as still as a mausoleum. Yes, I am afraid to lock my gaze into his, dreading the possible loss of self-control I have been building doggedly and almost fanatically for years. Yet I know I have to make it clear to him that I no longer am his slave. This, however, can't be accomplished without piercing the mask on his face with my eyes. He mustn't believe for a moment that I am still living the shredded drudgery of my victimization. A victim can be a winner if he converts his wounds into fortifications. This doesn't mean, of course, that he will no longer feel the pain. Nor can it lead to losing the memory of whence the pain originated. What it amounts to, under optimal conditions, is a decreased vulnerability clearly communicated to anyone who sets himself up as a potential torturer in search of a victim. Never again can I walk around looking like a person available for victimization. At the risk of emanating an air of excessive self-assurance easily mistaken for arrogance, I must appear no more vulnerable to be hurt than the rock of Masada.

This is all so clear to me, I have been over it a thousand times and more. So what is the source of my reluctance to look him in the eyes? I will count to three—then I'll engage his gaze. No, I have to do more than that: I'll look him squarely in the eye so that he can see as deeply into the source of my strength as his guilt or shame permits him. At the same time, I will take a methodical inventory of each of his features so that I can discover even the minutest detail in his face that attests to a radical difference between him, the skin and bone manifestation of evil, and the rest of humanity. It would be so comforting, so elevating to unearth some primeval distinctive feature which would prove that his physical resemblance to human beings collapses under close scrutiny. What a relief it would be to be in a tenable position to disqualify him from the entire human species, to disown him!

One: my heart is pounding, the wound is opening, the details of memories protrude in contours forgotten for so many years....*Two:* I can't survive looking at him, he is still stronger than I am, he will always have an indomitable power over me, I feel tiny, very insignificant again. Though it's early autumn, my skin is rubberized by a December frost I haven't allowed myself to suffer for forty years. I must revolt, I must free myself from this shadow existence, even if it costs me my sanity, my life. I must affirm unequivocally that, regardless of the consequences, I am not a thing, I am a man. *Three:* I look at him with all the pores of my face. Our gazes lock each other to a visual standstill.

It takes me I don't know how long, owing to my complete loss of temporal awareness, to realize that there is no vigour, there is no aggression or even self-defence in his eyes. His are eyes without energy, without *élan vital*, without commitment. Need I fear this stone-like face? Is this a mask beyond which lurks the calculating evil waiting for a propitious moment to pounce on me and reaffirm his domination over my life? Or am I looking at a burnt-out shell of what used to be a formidable might?

He doesn't seem too different from those enormous dispensers of fire and death that littered the post-war European landscape for quite a while as accusing reminders of the rape of a continent. Where tiny children used to laugh and play, these over-scale emissaries of death —tanks, armoured trucks, cannon—dominated the horizon, silencing the child forever. After the triumph of good over evil the world around us did not bounce back onto its feet, since the child was never again able to laugh and play. The grooves were filled with decomposed, frozen families: there was no room left for returning the earth to what it had been. In the dismembered silence these man-made monsters littered the high road and the low. Their mass was still foreboding but their lifelessness invited one to take a chance on rebirth.

Facing my torturer ushers the similarity more clearly into my awareness. His body is imposing but there seems to be no one in it to guide it to a show of strength. He seems vacant, abandoned, uninvolved. The most impressive factor about him is that *he was there* and now *he is here.* One of us was not supposed to live beyond, one of us was supposed to perish in the flames or frost. I feel his presence mostly by the weight he imposes, in his motionless mass between me and the sun. I am no longer frightened of him. First of all, he is much smaller than I remembered; in fact, he is shorter and slighter than I am. And yet, how enormous he was, how invincibly, unquestionably mighty he was! I guess I grew up, and the years have taken their toll and repossessed some of his bulk. Physical aggression adds awesome inches and pounds to the most insignificant perpetrator's stature. The violence sapped from his muscles, he probably seems smaller than he really is.

I scrutinize his face without shame, as if he were a wax figure, a mannequin on exhibit. I meticulously search for a sign that will allow me to disclaim membership from the same species.

But I find nothing of the sort. His placid, emotionless, distant visage could be substituted for that of the farmer in the now clichéed painting, *American Gothic*. His eyes communicate only fatigue. The rigourless muscle tone in his face, the unblemished skin, the lack of eagerness in his jaws, all suggest a man at peace with his destiny much more than the torments of an anti-man ravaged by guilt or shame, or the well-controlled eagerness of a vanquished sadist ready to take bloody revenge. This man is neither smaller nor larger than life; he seems to be an ordinary mortal, nothing to distinguish him from any septuagenarian fatigued by the number of his years, the weight of his memories, the sclerosis of his horizons.

He seems impassible. Not because he planned his mask to be inpenetrable, but because he is hardly breathing. A modest man, I think, he takes less than his fair share of air and light. I can't see in him any of the stereotypical features of the retired conqueror. Nor do I perceive any sign of lost battle with his conscience. The longer I stare at him, the better I am acquainted with his insignificance, the more clear it becomes to me that I have never seen this man before face to face. Our first encounter was hastily executed and completed without introductory formalities. Back then, I only felt him, I only suffered him, I heard his inarticulate grunting and meaningless, obscene outbursts.

And now he stands here speechless. If there were just a tiny indication of tension in his stance, I'd be inclined to guess at his well-contained arrogance. His posture, however, doesn't reveal any effort greater than that needed for standing more or less erect. His clothing betrays the fact that life has not been generous to him on the material front. He obviously wasn't able to convert his short-lived might into creature comforts. His suit, his wrinkled, off-colour shirt point to a man whose existence does not include a concern for self-presentation or a sense of pride or interest in vestimentary aesthetics. He must be poor. Probably just making ends meet. My father, in his obsessive preoccupation with a bursting shine on his shoes, repeated endlessly: "Show me the shine on your shoes, and I'll tell you what kind of a man you are." This man definitely would have been labelled by my dad as asocial, a loner, for no sociable person can afford to appear in public with shoes "displaying the length of the road he has travelled". My torturer has forty years of dust on his feet; I couldn't even guess at the tint of his footware. There is nothing in this aged torturer of children to reveal the object of the nefarious practices of yesteryear. Nothing in his appearance gives any reason to indict him as the opposite of man. He could be my father, just on the image he presents. When you go far enough down the road and you look carefully, very carefully, at the traits, the gait, the eyes of the travellers, *all* the travellers, it is very difficult, if not impossible, to tell which one took the road of the perpetrator and which one journeyed with the victim's burden on his back. In the end, they both display only the evidence of having covered a great distance, at great cost.

The more I look at him, the harder it is for me to chase the haunting verdict: he looks exactly like my father at the end of his life, except for the shine on his shoes. Maybe this man is just unluckier than my dad. Could it be that if father had lived a few more years, he, too, would have stopped caring for the depth of the shine on his shoes?

I begin to resent him for his resemblance to my father and to all the other victims. How dare he assimilate to this extent the victim's portrait, to exploit the equalizing work of passing time? The victims deserve to be distinguished as martyrs of these assassins. The victims on one side, the murderers on the other; posterity must be able to tell them apart at a glance. I am about to open my mouth to attack this silent old torturer. Yes, he is a torturer, an assassin, just as I am still the tortured and my mother is the victim of assassination. Time doesn't have any effect on what has been once done and completed. Once raped, always raped. I feel the daggers in my bowels again, the burning nails in my groin, my sky is inundated with a red blanket of pain. I am now clear, I have found the unerasable difference between him and me. Not drastic enough to disclaim any commonality, but damning enough to insist forever on remembering: the victim remains the victim, even if later he joins the rank of another group of perpetrators, and the torturer will always remain the torturer even if later he falls victim to his former prey. I must tell him my discovery so that we can be clear on what to expect from one another. The war is over, but the barbed wires still run through our living rooms. What a sad new meaning for the Eternal Flame! Yes, I must speak my mind at least on that; he must learn the depth of the schism between us, he must learn the flavour of my bitterness for looking like a beaten old man and not like some kind of side-show freak. I resent his silent intrusion into my gallery of ancestors. I resent him for somehow sneaking into my family, into the family crypt that he will occupy alone, for the others were murdered in the four corners of the thousand-year Reich.

You have ripped my body apart, now you violate the boundaries of my lineage. You despicable, cruel old man, you keep on torturing me one way or another, you keep on insinuating yourself under my skin. I don't even care if you live or die. Because dead or alive, I can't disown the kinship between you and all the other old men in my life who passed away clutching onto a tragic memory of a loved one murdered by your brethren. I must tell you all this, so you can be aware of the curse you have been in my life, so that you know what to expect from me. Now you will know from my mouth that you can't escape the consequences of your crime, even in the distance of forty years. Just as I have been carrying in me the living wound for forty years, and now, your very presence has inflicted a new gap in my restless life. You must know all that.

If I only had the right words!

"You look as if you are fighting a violent battle with yourself. I imagine it's on my account. Don't bother. I know about all the things you want to spit in my eyes. I have heard them so many times I can quote you verbatim. No, it isn't just from other victims of my violent past. I have looked at that past with the powerful torchlight of a cooled-off heart and a regained sanity. Your words may ventilate your burning entrails, so if you are so inclined, you need not spare me. I won't take it personally anyway.

"But first, let me clarify some matters about which you are completely in the dark, judging from the impassioned flow of your questions about how I can go on living with the memory of my foul deeds.

"I am an ordinary man. Not *the* prototype for all men, but one of the most common ones. When the time came with its blatant invitation to feel powerful, mightier than all the might known to common folks, when the invitation changed into pressing demands to act or the moment would be wasted, I seized the gift before it was too late. Who doesn't dream of absurd gestures, of violent passions, of extravagant pleasures? Most of the time we let the dreams evaporate and disappear into emptiness, leaving behind nothing more than a bitter taste of insignificance. Then history takes a turn in a direction that favours the fulfillment of our fantasies. Better yet, it encourages us to take advantage of unique opportunities for the most creative and most selfish movement of the heart and body. Better yet, it exempts us from any accountability, of any moral compromising. So what is there to keep us, for once in our stinking lives, from being fulfilled as desired?

"You had nothing to do with what I did to you. And I am not saying that I am sorry that I did what I did. I wanted to do it. It was as much your fault for being where you were, as mine, for being where I was, at the time our destinies were linked to one another. I meant no harm to *you* as a person. I wanted to attend to my own needs for which, finally, I had all the permission I morally required. Don't misunderstand me. I don't have and I never did have an overwhelming need, for my survival, to violate children. As hard as this may be for you to accept with your victim's pain and your victim's rage, rape for me was nothing more than an adequate metaphor to rise above the confinements of a mediocre, lacklustre horizon. Being devoid of outstanding talents, appearance, or skill urged me to ascend to the other pole even more. From the ordinary respect for one's fellow human being, for the sanctity of the innocent child, it is only a matter of flipping a coin to discover the easiest, the shortest road to transcending triviality, especially the triviality of being. I stress again, I rose to the occasion only with the invitation, blessing, and moral protection of my place in history.

"As a man, I am free of guilt or remorse. I am not troubled by shame. Once a new momentum in history wiped out the old, I no longer needed to continue to taste forbidden fruits. I had learned the flavour of the extraordinary, I was able, easily, to lapse into the grey existence offered to the mediocre. You see, I am not a sexual pervert. I am a little man in search of a moment of greatness. I could have died any time after that height of self-fulfillment; mediocrity has little attraction to keep me alive. Why don't I kill myself? What's more banal for a little man than to choose the back door out of life?

"I can understand your endless curses, your limitless wishes for me to suffer until the moment I die and after. I don't resent you for it. If we were to change places, I imagine I wouldn't act in a significantly different manner. I am almost sad to disabuse you, however. Think what you may, but having committed acts of violence, having behaved in what therapists and sociologists would label antisocial manners, doesn't disqualify me from the rank of morally committed members of my community. On the contrary, I showed evidence of the ultimate commitment to a moral stance: I kept my integrity to the extent that I remained faithful to my ideal being, fully aware of the greatest consequences.

"You will find me arrogant and absurd to set myself up as an instance of integrity and I will propose it anyway: I have no illusion about the pain I have caused, nor do I try to whitewash myself of what I have done. And I have been prepared to pay the consequences on *your* terms, since the victims and the winners always have the right to define the limits of tolerable acts, especially those executed by the vanquished: such is the demand of natural law. For forty years I have been waiting for you folks who interpret my acts as bestial, heinous, and depraved to come to 'make sure that justice is done'. No one has come to take me away, no one has disturbed my peaceful, routine existence.

"It is also true that no one has tried to break my door down in his eagerness to befriend me. Instead of including me in your world as the inevitable 'bad' that enhances the value of your version of 'good', you have chosen to let me be. And that's just what I have done in the past forty years. I took stock, I put myself through a rigorous cross-examination (the logical stringency of which would stagger any court official in your systems of retribution), and I emerged as a morally clean man. My verdict to the charges of being a war criminal is 'not guilty', for the notion of a war criminal is an absurd one. The very essence of war dictates that physically harsh acts must be perpetrated. Before and after all, the process and the goal of war is to annihilate the enemy in the most efficient, the most expedient, and the most total fashion. Those who serve their country in this endeavour are law-abiding citizens and not war criminals. Have you noticed that, upon the conclusion of wars, it is extremely rare to find the triumphant nations endeavouring to produce before the courts of justice 'war criminals' from their own ranks? To be a 'war criminal' is usually the privilege and the logical lot of the loser. I was a 'war hero' while my side was winning, I was even decorated for military and patriotic valour. Need I say that I find this just as absurd as being labelled a war criminal? At war just as in peace time, we all do what our knowledge of the moment dictates us to do.

"No, I don't agree that I *chose* my acts. My acts were the inevitable fruit of a biography that yielded only some rules that you and I could agree on as beacons of conduct. But then again you didn't have my personal history, social or physiological. I was not deserving of praise, but neither did I earn the erroneous definition of evil. In the same way, you have no choice but to demand that the wrath of heaven and earth crush my body and soul for what became your unfortunate biography. I merit no less, no more than this same recognition. We are products of our heredity, and we curse our forefathers for the mediocre or poor genes they handed down to us when we find ourselves in the ranks of the disenfranchised. We are also offspring of a cultural and historical lineage that further pigeon-holes us, and we rant and rave when we slip into the midst of the underprivileged.

"The choices you keep throwing in my face as evidence of my free will in doing 'evil' are all predetermined. I don't have free choice, nor does anyone else. If I did, I would not have been a mediocre little man all my life except for one brief, glorious moment. I didn't *choose* to have power, to excel, to rise above my biography—rather, I was permitted to enrich, to cajole, to embellish my depressingly grey existence. You support your accusation with instances of moral and practical decisions opposite from mine which were made by my neighbours, friends, co-parishioners. You miss the nature of how decisions and interpretations come to see the light. Had I been one of them, I would have collapsed into their stances. Had they been me, they would have encountered you and others like you in the same manner in which you and I got acquainted.

"You may think that this is a sleek way to shirk responsibility for one's acts. No, I am not saying that I am not responsible for what I have done to you. I am only saying that it is not my job to determine the consequences of my acts to satisfy your thirst for 'justice' (which is, more honestly, for revenge). I have already embraced my responsibility according to my own code of justice: I have not sought the commerce of your world. But responsibility has nothing to do with guilt. I am not guilty of anything. No, I can't be held guilty by your tribunals, only responsible for specific acts. You alone can judge me for the pain I have perpetrated on your body. If it soothes your suffering, I am prepared to die at your hand. That would be justice. But how would your act of violence in terminating my life be different from mine? Do you want to live with the knowledge of having performed an *evil* act? For there is the difference. In the context of my violent self-gratification, what I did was within the rights of the privileged. Within the context of your violent gesture, robbing me of my right to a natural death, you would contravene moral and legal edicts. While I have never had to live with the torment of bad conscience, since my act was anchored in the rule of might, you would suffer the anguish of having sunk to the depth, having fallen into the well of that same darkness in which you imagine to locate my habitat. Think about that.

"Shame and fear have never kept me company, either. Since I am a product of history, I am contented with what I am. I am what has been made possible for me to be. Shame is also the product of comparative assessment. I find no grounds on which to compare my deeds with those committed by others, for I am not them. To tell you the truth the only shame I have ever suffered from is my reprehensible mediocrity, my inability to shine and soar. Don't misunderstand me, please. I am not comparing myself to the accomplishments of others,

I define my mediocrity based on what I would have liked to achieve and what was given to me as my meagre lot. I was poor but honest. You must have heard the cliché before. I would propose to you that the key word in it is 'poor'. It seems to be an exclusive virtue of the little man to be honest. Have you ever heard of someone who is 'wealthy but honest'? The moment that sealed our destinies in the same envelope didn't make me less honest, but it made me richer in my heart. Material wealth was not the bounty I was seeking. I needed the complex flavour of limitless power to elevate me above the subterranean life of a rodent, an insect. How banal, you may agree with me, to soar to gigantesque heights by means of redefining you as the embodiment of all that was pest-like in a human being.

"When I was in public school, there was a Jewish boy in my class. He was tall, strong, well fed, well clad, his hair was golden like a king's crown. And I was puny, pasty-faced, clothed in hand-me-downs from another Jewish kid for whose family my mom used to be a maid. I was more often hungry than not. He was the captain of the soccer team, we played with his ball, but no matter how many times I made pitiful attempts to gain acceptance to the team, this boy would look down at me with disgust and mockery in his face. 'Get lost, bedbug,' he'd say. So I got lost in places typical for bedbugs and other parasites. That is the only time I remember having felt shame. Not because he called me a bedbug. After all I could have retaliated by calling him a 'pig' or better yet a 'Jewish pig'. But I didn't. I did what he ordered me to do for lack of any other knowledge. I felt ashamed of having obeyed him, in assuming the posture and the identity of a bedbug. With the hindsight of a life span of reflexion I feel only sadness for the little boy I was but I feel no shame—for shame turns no wheels for me.

"As to fear, what do you want me to be scared of? You can't hurt me, no one can! So what else is there to fear but pain? Death? I am not actively seeking it but I am not consciously doing anything to avoid it, either. I have seen it face to face many times. It holds no mystery for me, I am not fascinated or obsessed by it. It will come when it is inevitable. Pain? I have experienced it before, I know that it never stays for longer than what I can cope with. And if I am vanquished by a hitherto unknown intensity of suffering it will give me another chance to rise above mediocrity by overcoming it. And if I succumb to it, there is certainly no more to be said about it.

"The rejection of people? I have lived in the shadow of human traffic for so long that a sudden change would be intolerable. I didn't choose this solitary mode of existence, it seemed to be naturally emerging around me. It wrapped me in a blanket of isolation which felt quite tolerable, especially given my disdain for the universal hypocrisy dominating and guiding social intercourse. I never needed warmth, or even physical gratification, to prove that I was just as human as my next-door neighbour.

"I don't find pleasure in sexual encounters. Remember, I warned you that ours had nothing to do with venereal satisfaction. In fact, the practice of immersing parts of one's body in the wastes of another evokes upheavals of disgust in my stomach. Yes, I did procreate, don't ask me how, and above all don't ask me why. I never was possessed by the demon of parental instincts. Like Rousseau, I have abandoned my progeny to the care of those possessed by the annoying spectre of the joys of seeing one's childhood reduplicated. I was even less tempted by the vicarious folly of raising little ones as a version of revenge, or one-upmanship: 'my kids will have it better than I.' They'll have what they'll have. The women whose wombs bore the burden of my seed were faceless entities whose caresses and sweet words had nothing to do with my consenting to the embrace. I entered their bodies strictly from obedience to nature's plans for man and woman. We have been made with a sexual component, and it was my inevitable duty to obey the order of creation. It is of no consequence to our encounter. I bring it up since you seemed to have some predilection concerning my children. I have no idea whether or not they even know who their biological father is. They probably live with or in the shadow of their natural father. (After all, the natural father is the man who defines himself as the 'father' and acts on this definition in manners typical of fathers. This is certainly not my case.) You must feel relieved that they didn't imbibe, along with the maternal milk, the paternal 'curse', the penchant for 'evil'.

"I am getting tired. I am not accustomed to speaking. I have put together more words on this occasion than during the past year. I am not even used to subvocal discourse. Words seem to amount to more bother than anything else. Silence, total silence, is the only way to pay tribute to this inevitability. But I wanted to tell you one more thing before I return to my tacit existence.

"Since the trial of Adolf Eichmann, a man not without similarities to yours truly in philosophy of living, so much has been wasted on the cleverly turned phrase 'the banality of evil'. It is well put, but it turns no wheels. Men such as Eichmann, and myself, and millions of others—some of them likely to be pillars of your community—are banal only in the sense that there is nothing in our portraits to distinguish us from the select few who travel through life on higher planes. Our deeds are no more evil than yours, who are now in the privileged position of churning out definitions and assigning moral values to your own definitions. This can't amount to anything else but the arrogant statement that 'what I do is good, and those who act otherwise are evil'.

"For your information, I have never killed an animal, any animal. What makes me more evil than you is that I have inflicted self-serving pain on humans, and you do it to other animals. There is also the difference that I no longer need to enhance the quality of my life at the expense of another's suffering. Whereas you have personally killed a mouse, under the most atrocious circumstances, leaving the miserable wretch to agonize for more than two days, at the end of which you and a friend terminated his life by throwing him, *live*, into an incinerator. I have been a vegetarian all my life, for the idea of sustaining my existence at the expense of another creature of nature repulses me. You who live within smelling distance of the slaughter-house, you who see the convoys of gloomy tell-tale truckloads of pigs and cattle drive by your home, you who drive by the arrogant abattoirs every week, how can you thrive on the flesh of those defenceless, massacred lives?

"You have asked time and again: 'How could the people of Oświęcim live in the shadow of the chimney stacks endlessly exhaling smoke, black with human mourning? How could they sit down to a family meal only walking distance from the death factory where thousands are dying of starvation?' Don't you feel just a bit ashamed at this version of the banality of evil? Don't answer me just yet: think about it, let my words invade your one-track conscience. Go ahead, grope for a rationalization which will allow you to regain your composure and continue perpetrating evil on creatures I consider my equals, if not my superiors. For they are not losing the struggle for a consistently moral existence, they just live with the natural morality of self-preservation without waste. We—you and I—cannot claim such purity of conscience.

"Just to round out the picture, let me answer one more question that seems to singe your flaming rage. How can I have more concern for the well-being of a puppy than for a human child? The puppy is much less likely to turn on man than is the human child. This would be the easy, facile reply. The fact of the matter is that I have more respect, more love, for any creature other than the human one because the latter is dishonest, full of noxious flaws, and, most of all, resembles me. No other animal has this curse as his burden in life. And when I say me, I could just as well have said you. Like it or not, we are of the same species, we just have different historical moments of effervescence. By disowning me as your stepbrother, by excommunicating me from the rank of human beings, you would do me a favour. Unfortunately, you do not have the power to do so. And if you seized it and acted on it, you'd have to join me at the very moment of leaving the company of humans forever.

"There is more, but what's the use? You can't benefit from my words any more than I can benefit from yours or mine. Now you understand why I have been living under the protective cloak of the wisdom of silence."

Having uttered his favourite word, he turned his back on me, and without concern for a reply or any other reaction from me, he left. Without hurry, without energy, without commitment. I remained alone with a mountain of confusion erected by the landslide of what I had expected to be his self-defence and what turned out to be, instead, a universal indictment of man, and, more specifically, the immediate "guilty" verdict for me.

His reasoning was not without seduction or truth. I had mistaken him all these years for an insanely cruel, perverted degenerate. Instead I had just encountered a man in the fullest sense of the word. No longer demented, but still with a very dangerous ideology. His lack of warmth, his refusal to belong, his inability to love another human being, make him into a very dangerous man even if he is no longer driven by the need to assert himself through acts of violence. What a sad man, an obvious victim of an emotionally very deprived childhood. No, I change my mind: he isn't harmless any more, he is still a psychopath if he is as yet unwilling or unable to step into the shoes of a tortured child and feel the child's pain. No matter how justified and how clever his indictment of man for abusing animals, I still condemn him for the atrocities he inflicted upon my life. A man's arrogance toward the rest of creation cannot exempt him from the responsibility for debasing a human destiny.

My God, how cold I feel and how empty and unconvincing my words ring to my ears! Could it be that I am *not* as strongly convinced of the morality of my condemnation of this man for the pain he caused me and others like me? I no longer know with the fire of absolute certainty. My words are the distant, clinical parlance of therapists too concerned with contamination. Am I turning mad, did he infect me with his strain of anti-human virus? No, this can't be. I can never lose my love of man, I may even die for improving conditions of existence for the next generations. These words, though, just don't feel authentic. They are justificatory attempts. The truth is that my torturer has touched me with his affectless low-key disengagement from my power. I wanted him to suffer and to die a horrible death. And he informs me that I have no control whatsoever over him. I feel unvindicated, unfinished, I want to shout: "But what about my pain? What about justice for the torture he committed in full possession of his wits, what about the consequences of his crime?" To no avail. The man has accepted himself as a righteous man. But he must suffer because he made others suffer. If he gets away with it, tomorrow a new generation of torturers will be encouraged to continue where he left off. But what about his counter-accusations of universal guilt for the continuous slaughter of animals? It changes nothing about the facts of his atrocious treatment of children: he is a twisted, depraved man full of hate, full of danger, full of guilt. He almost succeeded in turning the tables on me. How diabolical! How human! I want to hurt him, yet I know I can't, which further deepens the wound in my soul. The torturer gets off free, and there is not one free man who is willing to prosecute him, not one judge who wants to see him in his court, not one mother who wants to see his tired blood shed.

I do.

But why do I feel so timid? Where has my rage gone?

I feel tentative, unsure. Alone.

My torturer has done it to me again. He violated the certainty of my anger, the passion of my urgently pressing need for public justice. Forty years ago he deflated my innocence with a single stab. Forty years later he has made a malefic attempt to convert the shreds of my innocence into a numb mass of silent guilt.

He has partially won. But how? In my heart I feel he is one hundred per cent guilty as charged, he is a vicious, cold-headed, calculating assassin. So what is my hesitancy about?

I am disgusted by the futility of seeking justice, of mending what was ripped forever. I am exhausted from the battle against the absurd. Time is not my ally, it is his. And so is the pain that will never be soothed.

I shall never dialogue with my torturer again.

Dialogue
with a
Victim

O F THE FEW OF US living today, no one possesses a family
album. The family perished in the flames of Kamenets-
Podolsk, Bergen Belsen, Auschwitz, and countless unnamed
corners of Eastern Europe, wherever Jews burned. The albums went
up in flames in Budapest as if to wipe out the faces that vanished from
our midst, the certainty that we ever existed as a family. With the
faces and their photographic imprints gone, a whole history has gone
up in smoke, leaving behind hallucinatory bits and pieces tossed
randomly across the globe. One in Melbourne, one in Rishon-le-Zion,
one in Budapest, one in Los Angeles, and one in Toronto—a macabre
balance sheet for a family that numbered three scores of living souls,
half of them life-worthy children endowed with all that is the
birthright of any generation. Truncated souls, strewn around the
globe, we carry within our centre-core of life the faces we can now
only feel, having lost the photo album.

We have grown so tightly to these shadow people that most of us
are riddled with doubt about our own sanity. We are suspicious of
each other's memories. Contradicting details undermine the credibility
we so desperately need to prove to ourselves that, if we hallucinate, it
is about our own survival and not about whether or not they ever
existed. We tear our insides into duelling phantoms: those who
avoided the flames and continue to burn as survivors, and those
whose portraits throb within us. We are the few pages from the
album that a benevolent wind rescued from the inferno erected
without help from the Devil. Our souls have been agonizing for forty

years, yet they sizzle so intensely that, if we moved any closer to each other, the proximity of those hot ashen faces would ignite and incinerate us at once.

Our family album used to bulge with sixty lives: dressed in holiday best, proud parents boasted with self-satisfaction as they presented their thriving progeny on festive occasions like so many living milestones on the road of a family's history. The gauchely posed photographs that perished in the destruction, as if we had perished with them, could not suffer living beyond the men, women, and children for whose existence they were the inert proofs. Even the pictures vanished. Only half a dozen of us keep asking ourselves between two nightmares: which one of them *really* exists and which came to see the light in my hysterical fever? Was she tall, slender, and pretty as I'm used to seeing her in my dreams? Or does the dream mould her looks into an image that never existed in flesh and blood? Will I ever know the truth? What would she look like now? What would she do now that I need her to speak to me? Questions, only questions; dreams are never answers.

There is one dream that I remember more vividly than any other. In this dream an incinerated reality rises out of its own ashes to warm for a spurious moment a deadly, cold existence. I am lying sick in bed. It doesn't feel like what I remember of the bed of my childhood. I am aching for the kind of motherly, soothing care only *the* mother can provide for her child in pain. And I know she is dead. Even in the universe of dreams she is dead, murdered in Bergen Belsen.

The door opens, exposing to a bright gentle light my whimpering body. Not the body of a child, but that of a person who *knows* he could never grow into adulthood. Framed in morning radiance, there stands my mother. Vigorous, calm, young. I freeze in silence, wondering if this isn't a practical joke, a cruel prank perpetrated upon me by who-knows-whom, perhaps by God.

She enters the room that isn't my room. The closer she comes, the smaller I grow and the taller she seems. She sits on the edge of my bed. She does not touch me with her hand. Her smile, whispered onto her face, is caressing. Her smile is a blend of the tenderest love and the most luxurious playfulness, with a hint of feigned mockery. Then she speaks two velvety sentences that have not stopped living in me ever since. Theirs is a double reality: a dagger in my flank and an expert hand removing the intrusive weapon while healing the wound. "What's the matter, my big boy?" And she glides her weightless yet almighty arms into my direction. "Come to momma, I will take care of you."

And I wake up with torrents of howling pain oozing from my entire being in an endless flow of hopeless tears. And rage.

For forty years I have been hurting and no one has asked if I was still alive. No one cared to hear what an orphan's pain is like. But, most of all, for forty years I have not been anyone's "little boy". I never had a chance to grow into being mother's big boy!

Since then I have gone to sleep every night praying that she will be waiting for me at my bedside waiting to consummate the maternal embrace never extended to me in the empty years between December 1944 and this miraculous dream. I exhort God: "This is your chance to at least decrease your debt to me. You have had her all these years when she should have been nurturing me. You are a cruel donor. You toy with the heart of a child without caring if it can survive the loss of maternal love. Why did you have to take my mother? Why did you let me come into this life anyway if all you intended for me was eternal abandonment without the embrace of my mother? Now is your chance—now, now that you have teased me in my dream, let her come to me for a short while. Just enough time for her to soothe whatever ails me, just enough time for her to tell me her tale." But, as usual, God remains silent when I demand his answer, when I need his presence. "My God, you are not my God any more!" I hear the child in me pout in disappointment and rejection, as if he were speaking to a nasty friend: "I'm not your friend any more, I'll never play with you again."

I have never seen my mother again. Instead, my dreams are inhabited with souls who want *me* to take care of them—to promise them deliverance from their eternal roaming in search of peace, in search of a suitable resting place.

In my waking hours, as I roam in strange lands searching for a familiar sound, for faces from the other side of the flame, her sweet voice lulls me into a cruel dream. Always the same. Always a dream. Its reality is as lavish as the awakening is desolate.

Possessed by the obsession of the fantasy I dialogue with a phantom who seems so palpable, so rich, that the texture of poverty that covers my existence is not even noticeable. I make my mother perform miracles for me from beyond the grave she has never known. The somnambulant reality and the haunting dream interweave into a shelter at times reminiscent of the dark dampness in whose bosom I mourned her absence. At other moments, when wearing my forty years of "orphandom" as a lead mantle becomes too much of a burden, I ache to break out from the captivity it forces upon me. Yet I don't want to give up the hallucination. It's not a matter of giving up the murder of my mother and the vacuum her passing has dug into my life. At one moment I run toward the beneficial mirage, at the next I try to escape the mixed effect of its reach.

What is so extraordinary about that fabulous dream is that, for once, she came alone. For ever since that December morning when she marched out of my life to the tune of harshly shouted orders and insults, I have not been able to separate her sombre yet deeply maternal face from that of the murderer who ravished her from my side. For years and years I have avoided the face that gave me the gift and the curse of life for fear that once it would be the *other* who would appear, alone, having done away even with her image. The more I struggled with the obsession, the less I dared to even think of my mother as a memory that was once as real as my own flesh. What took its place was the steel mask of the murderer on that frozen morning. For years and years, every time I needed the presence of my mother, the vision of that last morning has rushed to my mind. With its life span of one skeletal hour, it wipes out eight and a half years of history, the history of my life on my mother's lap. Why has time turned on me? Why did it become the murderer's accomplice? How can all those years bursting with the wealth of sweet memories disappear like the air that vanishes from a pricked balloon?

For years I have been tormenting myself with the bitterness of these questions and the void that comes as the only reply. And every time I succumbed to the temptation and to the weakness engendered by the solitude of an abandoned child, it was he who first emerged from the shadow world. Without life in his eyes, his glance cut my face with the indifferent aggression of a pair of bayonets. His cheeks protruded with the chilling cruelty of a butcher's cleaver. He seemed to have metal bars instead of lips. Not even a fake smile escaped those lips to indicate some commonality with his victim. The more I struggled to destroy this intrusive presence the more I felt surrounded by him. First just him, then he seemed to have split into identical twins who continued their proliferation at the same rate as I frantically sought an exit from the horror of it all.

From the other side of this circular wall of terror, I could barely perceive my mother's sobs. I didn't hear them, I felt them in the dry emptiness holding my stomach captive. In the despair of the child who has lost his sanity in the futile struggle, I began to wonder. "Are you their partner in torture? Did you leave on purpose to punish me for the suffering I had caused you while you carried me in your womb? Are you getting even with me for the scream of your flesh as I thrust toward the light? Am I the initial torturer, a crime for which I deserve to be repaid in the language of madness?"

The further I strayed from the object reality of my mother's deadness, the deeper the grooves of confusion dug into my moment-to-moment reality. To protect myself from the empire of delirium I called less and less for the soothing memory of what I tragically mistook for a mother's omnipotence. Until one day when I awakened to the numbness of the realization: I can't identify my mother's voice, I can't summon her face onto the screen of my remembrance. My mother is so dead I don't know if she ever existed! The only thing that was more real than her total absence from my memory was the inviolate wholeness of that December morning. But it seemed as if I had never lived through it, as if I had been *told* the story I had witnessed and endured. With sad resignation, I accepted my banishment from my own life. I no longer seemed to be a participant in the tale of how our thick, well-endowed family album had burnt in the flames of darkness. Instead I had become a spectator.

From a forgotten corner of my childhood, I recall a story that didn't make an impact on me when mother originally told it to me. I have a floating fantasy that I must have heard this bizarre, premature tale often enough for me to be able to unearth it today without effort, without will. It seems to be paying a surprise visit as if to say: "Listen to me, I'm a messenger from beyond."

In a Transylvanian village, a solitary peasant, a simple man, was callously betrayed by his neighbours when he needed them to save the life of his horse, his only companion. In his sorrow, in his anger, and in his determination not to be caught in the web of human evil, he burnt down his house and forsook the company of men. He went to seek solace and to rebuild a life without speech in the bosom of the forest.

One night, after many years, his mother appeared to him in a dream. She urged him to return to the village and to tell his story with whatever language he could invent. "Your tale must be told, mostly with your heart. It must be told so that the children can be saved from the evil of their elders."

Shaken by the dream, and amid great trepidation and anxiety, he decided to obey. He returned to the village, covered in animal skins, sporting an unruly beard and dishevelled hair. Without the faculty of speech, he attracted the attention of his former neighbours. Gesticulating and grunting, he compelled the villagers to witness the recounting of what had happened to him. The stunned village folks, recognizing him, could not extricate themselves from the spell of his indicting pantomime. Some of the children covered their faces in shame, others grew angry, and still others were disdainful. But they all understood the selfish, evil act of their elders.

When he was about to tear his tongue out of his mouth to demonstrate his refusal to commune with his fellow man, miraculously, the simple man's voice rang out clearly in front of the muted community: "I left your company for a life of silence but I have been ordered to come back and save your children. They must learn from my tale—*our* tale—that true brotherhood knows neither conditions nor exclusions." Uttering these words, he began to shed tears of joy, for he recognized that his voice was speaking a new language, the language of hope, a language only the children could really understand. Then he realized that having discovered the language of hope, he could cope with the old inner sound of pain. He was again ready to take a chance on living the life of a simple man.

Now I know that it is my turn to tell my story. If I want to live to keep my children warm, to raise them to strength and love, I must recant the sad lament. A voice inside n.ᵉ—maybe that of my mother—whispers more and more frequently: "Tell the story and you'll benefit from its magic: as it unfolds out there, in the company of the young, it will hurt less and less. The harshness of the ice will change into a soothing warmth in your children's eyes. Tell the story so that it can become once again *your* story. Without a tale a man has no past, and without a past a man is not a man. Come on, tell the story, don't be scared. To be sure, it will never leave you, but it will be easier to live *with* it than outside of it, or worse, *in spite* of it. Tell the story. Go, tell it."

With a great deal of hesitation, I started to speak. It was more in the nature of thinking out loud—as if it made no difference whether or not I had an audience. Silence has been my medium of choice for communicating for so long! Now that the shell was cracking and sounds were making their way slowly to a world in which I was an outsider, I felt an immense detachment from what I had to say. I approached the invisible voice with words whispered in the manner of a parent not wishing to awaken a child. Each utterance made me more aware of my fear of *really* being engaged in a dialogue.

The men had been taken away months ago. Only mothers and children remained. Life was limited to being awake and to being awakened by the commanding howl of air-raid sirens. There were no other sounds but wails, sobs, and explosions. I was always afraid. I slept as deeply as was needed to avoid the horrible questions: will I die today? Will it hurt to die? Will I die with my mother to guide me wherever we go after we die? Or do we go anywhere? I can hear the women—mother and Aunt Sari—whispering words that have something to do with who will take care of the children if mother is taken away. Oh, my God, will they take mother, too? They have already taken dad! And what about my sister, Agi, will she have to go also, wherever they all go? Who will take care of us, the little children? Who will look after *me*? Who will make sure that I have food to eat and that I don't get hurt? I'm so scared, I have never been so scared in my life, not even when they beat me up at school for being a Jew! Maybe we all will have to stay with grandmother. But she is too old, too fat, and she doesn't really like any of us, except for Tibi. Perhaps because he is the fattest of us all and she only likes fat people. There are so many things I don't have the answer to and dad is gone, and now maybe mother is going to go also. Why do they all have to go? Why can't they tell the soldiers that they can't go, that they don't want to go because they have little children to look after? They can't *want* to go, because they all look so gloomy when they just talk about going, so why don't they fix it so they can stay? It's not fair! I want to tell mother that I don't want her to go and that it's not fair. But I'm afraid to say anything, they all look so sad, maybe it would just make things worse if I said anything.

The adults are always either silent or whispering. I think they have something to hide that they don't want us children to know. This is awful; it would be better to know what they are hiding. It's so terrible to be a child, especially when the grown-ups seem to be in trouble. They don't know how to reassure us. There is no one I can turn to. Even Agi, who is thirteen and who knows a lot of grown-up stuff, seems confused and scared. She hardly talks to me, not even to be nasty. And that's not usual. She always has time for teasing me. I wish she at least paid attention to me—after all, we are brother and sister, we have to stick together; we are both children. But lately she looks so old. Her body is still small but her face is just as serious as mother's and Sari's. What is happening to all of us? Won't somebody tell?

I guess I just have to be quiet and hope that mother will notice that I, too, am in trouble. I could fake being sick, that always works for attention. But somehow I don't think that would be right this time. Mother is so sad-looking that I *can't* trick her. And Tibi is only three years old—he doesn't know anything; and Zsuzsi is only two, she knows even less. She doesn't even seem too bothered to have been left behind by both her mother and father. She just sits, plays, eats, and sleeps. She doesn't even cry as much as she usually does. Come to think of it, nobody is doing what he usually does. This sure is a weird time. We hardly spend any time at all outside, we never ever go to Liget, the most beautiful park in the whole city, maybe the whole world. Nobody ever thinks of playing with the children any more. We don't even have school any more even though it's winter. And we have to wear these yellow stars on all our jackets, shirts, sweaters. I don't know why we have to wear them when most of the people I see out in the streets don't wear them. It's got to do with the fact that we are Jewish but that's all I know. Why doesn't mother explain to me what wearing this star means? She says she *can't*. Why can't she? And if she can't why doesn't she try to find it out so we can all understand it? I think she's not telling truth, she just doesn't want to tell me. It's really too bad because I'm very embarrassed to wear it; sometimes kids in the street make nasty jokes about me being Jewish. If I didn't have to wear that stupid star, no one would know that I am Jewish. After all, I look like anybody else. I don't wear those weird clothes the orthodox in Dob Street wear. Even the kids. I don't have *payes*, or a *kipa*, or the *tales*, so how could anyone tell I am Jewish?

Besides, I wish someone would explain to me what's so bad about being Jewish. Everyone seems to think that it's wrong to be Jewish. The Christians attack us, beat us, lock us in special Jewish houses, take our fathers away, make us wear these ridiculous stars. I even overheard a couple of grown-ups whisper in the air-raid shelter that in some place with a foreign name they are killing Jews! What is so bad about Jews that they are treated with so much nastiness, so much violence? It is as if everything was the Jews' fault, as if the whole world hated us. Even the Jews mustn't like being Jewish. Everyone we know has converted to being a Catholic or a Protestant. I don't really know what difference it makes that we went across the street in an air-raid shelter and learned a lot of Catholic prayers by heart and make the sign of the cross a lot. I got into a lot of trouble with the priest because you're supposed to use your right hand and I'm left-handed. He kept yelling at me that the right hand is the arm of God and the left is the arm of the Devil. And that Jews were all working for the Devil, and if I keep making fun of God, he'll tell the Germans and have me taken away where all Jews belong, to hell. I was scared all the time we went to those lessons that he would send me to hell. Luckily, the course ended. I was baptized, whatever that means. I was given the name of a saint, Benedict, and it was supposed to make me into a good person, a Catholic person. I don't really understand what that means. I always thought that children were always good even when they misbehaved a little. And we never did anything *really* bad. Besides, how could a few prayers and some gestures change someone from bad to good? I don't feel changed at all. The only change I know is that we are less and less free, we have less and less to eat, and people around me seem more and more scared. But we are still the same. They may have given me the name of a Catholic saint, but I still have to wear the yellow star. Mother says, "Never mind, all that matters is that in the end, being Catholic will be good for us." But she doesn't explain why or how. Maybe she doesn't really have an answer, either. Maybe she just says it to be less scared.

I hate it even more when mother is scared than when I am scared. I am often afraid of things that I know are silly, like the dark, the man dressed up as the Devil in the movies, and things like that. But when mother is scared it means that there is a good reason to be fearful. Like during the bombings. Those are terrible times. It sounds like the sky is going to fall on us and crush us all. Now that is a good reason for being scared. I am so terrified of the bombings that I have no other place to hide but in dreams. I sleep through most of the air raids. But even in my dreams I *know* that bombs are dropping all around me and that they make big holes in apartment houses killing everyone in them. Even in my dreams I *feel* the terror of the whole building falling on me, burying me alive, not being able to breathe, breaking all my bones. But in the dreams so many other things happen that are fantastic that I can tell myself that the bombings are just one of those unreal fantasies. But when I wake up on my mother's lap and I feel her knees shake under my body, then I know that the dreams can come true.

Only grandmother seems untouched. She either sleeps or munches on something. Or plays cards with another old lady. Every-one else's eyes shine so much from fear that they glow in the dark, like hot coals in the stove. We just sit and stare, no one daring to say anything. I guess we all must be thinking the same thing: when will this nightmare end? Will it ever end? How will it end? Will we ever live in the light of day again, free in the streets, in the parks, in the stores, without yellow stars?

No one knew the answers. No one even posed the questions out loud. We just seemed to live them.

The next morning, I was awakened by an unusual noise. Not completely unfamiliar, but unusual: the clanging of the superintendent's bell. He sounded it when there was some official announcement to be made concerning the residents of the building. Usually to announce that the water was going to be shut down for several hours, or the electricity, or a new curfew, or some other change of rules concerning Jews. I was fully awakened by the shrill noise it continued to make. But I knew whatever he had to say wasn't directly my business; the grown-ups would learn the new rule and I'd learn it from them. It was just too cold to get out of bed in the unheated apartment. After all, it was already December, past St. Nicholas' Day. I just pulled the down blanket over my head to have my entire body covered with the secure warmth of the old eiderdown.

Seconds later, Agi tore the cover off my face. She looked waxy yellow. She was never given to speaking loud, but this time her whisper was scarcely audible. She seemed to be trembling with her whole body. She began to shake me: "Get up, get up, they are taking all the women, they are taking mother, they are taking mother."

I wanted to jump out of bed, run to mother, clutch onto her legs and not let her go. I wanted to protect her against anyone who wanted to take her from me. But I was frozen in my panic. My legs wouldn't move, my arms didn't seem to have the strength to push my body away from the bed. I just kept thinking stubbornly: no, they can't take her, I need her, they can't take a mother from her children. I wasn't even thinking. Had I been thinking I would have known that they had taken Aunt Boriska, Zsuzsi's mother. And that they had long ago taken my aunts Manci and Ila. But I couldn't think, I was blinded by my obsessive panic: they can't take mother, if they do, I'll die. I wasn't even thinking of her at that moment. It didn't even occur to me that if she were to go, she might very likely die or be badly hurt. After all, I heard her say many a time how unwell she was. She never said, "I'm sick, I don't feel well." She always said, "I am unwell today." She would never speak of hurting. It was probably one of those things she referred to as "not before the children". My dear mother, who always sheltered us from unpleasant thoughts, they want to take you away now. No one will protect us from anything from here on.

I wanted to run to her, shower her with kisses, begging her forgiveness for all the times I made her unhappy, angry, or nervous, all the times I used to think she was cruel, that she was tormenting us with her threats of calling the police on us for misbehaving. Now, I knew, she was not the cruel one—I was, for pushing her so far with my bad behaviour. I also knew now that she would never have abandoned us anywhere. I wanted her to know and to believe that I was very, very sorry for having been such a bad boy so often. I wanted to convince her to stay. As if she had a choice!

One moment my mind was racing with fantastic schemes to save my mother, to make it possible for her to stay with me. The next I was seized with terror. My sister Agi just sat in a corner mumbling her words, maybe prayers, staring into nothingness.

Then mother came in. Very calmly she sat next to me at the edge of the bed. She took my hands gently, but firmly. She first smiled at me very faintly. Then her face grew sombre, the face of someone who has bad news to announce.

"My little big boy, the superintendent has just announced that all women under sixty must report in the courtyard within thirty minutes with a day's food and three days' warm clothes. I think I may have to work somewhere in the provinces for a while. Sari and grandmother will stay to look after you. Grandmother is over sixty and Sari is going to have a baby, neither one can work. They will care for you as if I were here to do it myself."

At this point, I noticed two teardrops in her dark eyes. I knew that what she said wasn't true, that no one could take care of me as she did, but I couldn't let her know that I didn't believe her. It was hard enough for her to go, she didn't need me to make a scene and make it even more painful for her. Besides, I was now fully aware that nothing I could say would change anything. I had to make sure that she wouldn't worry about how I took the news of her departure for destination unknown. I just hugged her as hard as I could, for as long as I could, and I kept saying in a very serious tone:

"Don't worry, Anya, don't worry, we'll be *all right* here, don't you worry, we can take care of ourselves. Just come back before my birthday, in July, or even sooner if you can. Don't worry, Anya, don't worry, you take care of yourself."

My heart was drowning in all the tears I was swallowing so that she could be spared having to deal with my fear, my sadness. But a mother always knows. She hugged me back, with trembling arms.

"I love you my little boy, my little man, you are so brave and I am so proud of you. We'll be all right, we're strong, stronger than they are. You take care of the little ones, you know you are the man of the house. And don't worry about me, I'll be just fine. I'm sure I'll be back soon, sooner than you think. And so will daddy. We'll move back to our place, just the four of us. We'll go to the amusement park, and the Liget, the Island, and take the boat up the Danube, and daddy will bring you chocolate cups from Hauer every Saturday as he used to. And we'll buy a new bike for your birthday. And I'll make you a brand-new outfit, a special one for your birthday. My handsome little boy, eat well, sleep well, listen to what Sari and grandmother say, they love you very much, as much as I do, well, almost as much. And listen to your big sister, Agi, too; you take good care of each other, you need each other. Whenever you have something you'd like to tell me or daddy, you just whisper it to Agi, she'll keep your secret until we come home. From now on, you are not just brother and sister to each other, but also mommy and daddy. That's a really big job but I *know* I can rely on you, that you can do it, my little man, my little boy."

She turned her face away. The rhythmic heaving of her body let me feel her hidden sobbing. She was still embracing me but I already felt the distance growing between us. We were already talking about the future, this deep, dark hole without a bottom. We were already too busy trying to convince the other that everything would be all right, that this was just a very temporary interruption of our normal life. Neither one of us really believed it with much certainty.

Agi was sitting in the corner, speechless, determined in her face to carry out some decision she must have made while mother and I were saying goodbye. Her jaws clenched as if they were ready for a street fight. Her eyes were fixed on mother, trying to hold her captive.

"I must go down now, children, or we'll all get into trouble. Come, walk me downstairs, we'll say goodbye at the gate. But before we go, I want to have a word with your aunt in the kitchen. You just wait for me here. You know, some boring grown-up stuff."

Agi and I looked at each other in silence. I reached out for her hand. It was cold and clammy but it was still my sister's hand. We looked at each other and we both nodded in silence. We dropped onto our knees right against the kitchen door with our ears glued to the wood. The door was not completely shut. We could distinctly hear the sobbing voices of our mother and aunt.

"Sari, my little sister, take care of my babies, love them with my heart, safeguard them with your body as if it were mine. And if I don't come back, raise them as if they were your own. I know I'm asking a lot of you. After all, you have your little one and the one on the way, and no husband to lean on—not to mention mother and Susie. I pity you, my dear Sari. But you are the last one of us; without you, they'll perish. My little Sari, swear to me on your child's head that you'll love my children as if you had borne them, swear to me in a hurry for I must go down."

"Leave in peace, my darling sister. I would rather die than let anyone harm your babies. They will miss you of course, but not because I won't have done my best to cajole them, to nourish them, to protect them. From here on there is no 'your children' and 'my children' or 'Boriska's child'. Only 'our family's babies, our family's survival'. God bless you and keep you on your journey. My heart will be with you wherever you go. May you come back to us in good health. Be careful, you are not a well woman, take the best care of yourself. Don't volunteer for anything, just try to blend into the crowd, try to not let them see that you are there. That's the only way you can survive the forced labour, the hunger, the cold, the loneliness. Don't trust anyone. These days everyone is struggling to survive, to alleviate his lot; you do the same. Only you count from here on for you *must* come back to these two kids and to us. So few of us are left, we must prevail at whatever cost. Go now, my big sister, take my heart with you, and let the knowledge of your children's safety and comfort guide you wherever you go."

They embraced very fast, and mother hastily turned toward the room to fetch us. We were ready. Our hearts had sunk to unknown depths. Now we knew the full truth: dad wasn't likely to come back and neither was mother. I felt the chill of being an orphan throughout my body. My sister grew even more morose, her eyes reflecting a wall she must have erected between her pain and the outside world. She seemed almost dead, just like a mask.

We walked down the three long flights of stairs. It usually took forever to reach the ground floor; now time just flew away with the furtive haste of a moment.

The courtyard was already full. There were about twenty women with knapsacks, small suitcases, handbags. All of them appeared a lot fatter than usual: they were wearing as many layers of clothing as they could fit on their bodies. Accompanying the women were their mothers, their little children. Every resident of the building congregated in the frosty courtyard on that December morning. Everyone except my Aunt Sari.

In the front of the courtyard, by the superintendent's apartment, stood the super himself, his frumpy wife, four German soldiers with submachine guns, and four Hungarian Arrow Cross men in leather coats with guns. At the back, near the staircase, right in front of the apartments nearest to the front gate, stood another line of Germans and Arrow Cross men. All immobile, all silent. They seemed to know the routine ritual as if they had performed it on countless similar occasions. I remember looking at them, one after the other, scrutinizing their eyes to see if there was any hope left for my mother. What I saw was indifference in the Germans' eyes and hatred in the Hungarians'. "There is no hope left with these people, they want to take them all, they won't see in my mother the simple housewife and mother of two little children, they just keep seeing in her the image of the enemy. My mother is nobody's enemy, she likes everybody, and everybody likes her." I looked at Agi, and she sensed that I was going to speak out, to do something unwise, for she put her hand across my mouth, gently but firmly. And she shook her head, warning me against any foolish behaviour. I felt totally resourceless. I just dug my nails into my mother's palm as if I wanted to get under her skin so that we couldn't be separated.

"All women step up front. You others, stand back, leave an empty space of at least five metres between the women and the rest of you swine," sounded the order from the mouth of one of the Arrow Cross men. Mother looked at me with a long, tender, penetrating look, one that was meant to nourish me forever.

"I must go now, my little boy. Remember what I said to you upstairs. You'll be well taken care of, loved and safe as if I were here. Your Aunt Sari swore it to me. And I'll be back sooner than you think." She kissed me gently on both cheeks. She left a line of tears on both sides. She then turned to my sister. "My big girl, you take care of the little one, and of yourself. Remember, I won't be far from you. I'll be carrying you in my bones, in my heart, wherever they may take me. Goodbye, my children."

She stepped forward toward the front of the courtyard to take her place in the group of women. Suddenly my sister bolted out of our line, tearing her hand out of mine, and ran to join my mother. She stood very close to her, erect, as if she wanted to appear bigger than she really was. "What is she doing? Does she want to go? Does she want to leave me behind?" I thought, terrified. Mother seemed to be in a daze, shocked by Agi's presence by her side, in the group of the damned. One of the neighbours wanted to push her away but she stood strong, holding onto my mother's arm.

The Arrow Cross man in charge noticed what was going on: "Just let the young lady stay, she is old enough."

I was alone with two little cousins and my grandmother, who didn't seem to comprehend anything of what was happening in front of her eyes: the eldest of her seven children, and *her* first-born, were about to be taken away by men full of hatred, armed to their teeth. I wanted her to do something: "Grandmother, bring back Agi, she isn't a 'young lady', she's a kid, don't let them take her, she's just a kid." I was tugging at her ample coat, nearly hysterical. She looked around, scared, to see if there would be any repercussion from my loud behaviour. Then she put her heavy, warm hand on my head: "There is nothing I can do against the law and these men, with guns and all the power behind them. I'm just an old woman; if I open my mouth, they'll kill me or take me with them. Now surely you can't wish that to happen, my little boy, can you?" she spoke to me in a hurried whisper. No, I didn't want to lose her, too.

"Now, I'm going to call the roll of all those Jewesses registered as residents in this building. When you hear your name, you'll answer by a loud and clear 'present' and stand to the left if you are healthy and fit for hard labour. If you are sickly, suffer from some chronic illness, you stand to the right. Anyone whose name I read who is not present will be searched for and, when found, will be shot on the spot. This is your last chance. If you know someone in the building who is not here, signify it by raising your hand."

This was delivered again by the Arrow Cross man. He sounded and looked as if he really would shoot anyone disobeying him. "Please God, make my mother obey this man, and all men like him all the time," I prayed without a sound. Then I felt a razor-sharp flash in my stomach: Sari is not here, she is hiding, she will be found upstairs, and they will kill her right here in front of her mother, her son, and the rest of us. "Should I call out her name, or should I keep silent?" I was delirious with confusion and fear: if they find her, they'll shoot her for sure. If she is given a last chance to come down on her own will, she may be spared.

"Mrs. Graner, Ilona."

The first name was called. It was too late for me to do anything other than just stand in silence.

"Present," sounded her answer, and in spite of her robust, youthful stature, she went without the slightest hesitation to the right, the side indicated for the unfit.

"Mrs. Hirsch, Roza."

"Present." Mrs. Hirsch, a woman of my aunt's age from appearance, stepped forward, and *she* joined Mrs. Graner with a decisive stride.

The Arrow Cross man continued with the list. All those called were present and stood on the right side of the courtyard. There were already about a dozen women, when I heard:

"Mrs. Stein, Piroska."

"Present." I heard my mother's faint voice. She sounded as if she were about to lose consciousness. With halting steps, she was the first to step to the left. "Why?" I screamed inwardly. "I don't understand, there's a mistake, she must have forgotten that the side for the unwell is the right, not the left; if she didn't make a mistake why would she lie, she *was* always unwell? Why?" I was very confused seeing my mother alone while all the healthy-looking younger women huddled on the other side. Mother looked very small all by herself. She was fidgeting as if she felt uncomfortable with all the eyes on her. As if she were naked. She even moved her arms in front of her chest to cover, to protect herself. I wished with all my racing, aching heart that I could change places with her. "I am stronger than she is, I can work hard, I am not unwell. I am well fed, they should take me." But I just stood there in awe of what was taking place in this courtyard. The very unripe wisdom of my eight years of life could not wrestle to the ground the enormity of reality. I wasn't even sure this wasn't a nightmare.

"Mrs. Schonfeld, Malvina."

"Present." This was the old lady from the second floor. "What is she doing here, she's older than my grandmother?" I asked myself. I was just further mystified. Even more so when I saw her take a place next to my mother.

"Mrs. Weisz, Sari."

My heart stopped. I thought I was going to be dead the next moment. I waited for a miracle, for someone to yell out "present" and for some strange woman, my aunt's guardian angel, perhaps, to materialize and take her place on either side.

"Are you deaf, Weisz, Sari? Where in the hell are you?"

The silence that dominated the courtyard was broken only by a barely audible whisper by one of the Arrow Cross men in the ear of their apparent leader. We couldn't discern his words. A mocking grin appeared on the leader's face, and without a word, he made a gesture with his pen that seemed to me like crossing her name off the list.

"Mrs. Klein, Emma." He called the next name. I couldn't believe my ears. My aunt Sari *does* have a guardian angel, they didn't start searching for her, she is allowed to stay, to live.

What a relief! And what an anger, what a rage: why couldn't the same mysterious power protect my mother as well—how was it that her sister would be spared? What did my aunt have special that my mother didn't have? She was just another simple Jewess like my mother, so why the preferential treatment? At that moment, I hated my aunt, I wanted her to be discovered and killed. "If my mother can't be allowed to stay, her sister shouldn't be privileged either." I was overwhelmed with hate when I heard the Arrow Cross man call out:

"Well, that's the lot. You, girl, join your mother, whichever side she is on. First, the right column will march out in a single file, without a word, then the left column will follow. I want perfect silence. Those of you staying behind, keep clear of the women departing. You'll join them soon, don't worry. You will all be united in due time. Attention; march!"

Again, I was torn by the confusion of what was happening. Should I rejoice about what he had just said about being reunited soon, or should I be dominated by the immense sadness and panic I felt when I saw my mother getting ready to leave? Also, why were there only two women and Agi in the left column? All those other women—they must know something my mother and Mrs. Schonfeld didn't know. This was so excessive for my young age that I was no longer able to feel or think anything, as if someone had turned off the electricity inside. I felt nothing but darkness. I ran to the side, next to the steps by Apt. 2. I hardly noticed the line of women going, I just wanted to see for one last time my mother and sister.

First came Agi. The lady from Apt. 1 (rumour had it she was over a hundred years old) grabbed her by the arm with her bony hands, giving Agi a powerful yank (and making all claims about her advanced age incredible). Before anyone could say anything, she threw my sister across the threshold of her open door. "You're not going anywhere; you're a little girl. Let them take me if they want a woman." With that they both disappeared behind her door. I was stunned. None of the armed men seemed to have noticed, or, if they had, none of them made a move toward the old lady's apartment. "My sister's safe," I rejoiced. I caught my mother's glance: she smiled with relief, her face looked brightened, as if the sun had got up to shine just on her. Then she waved at me and blew a kiss the way she used to when I was a very little boy.

That's the last image I have of my mother.

And now I am alone again. Still, emptied, disappointed. Having told the story that I have safeguarded as an extraordinary treasure, I find myself humbled. The exclusive access to the void left by the loss of my mother consoled me at moments. Now that it's "out there", an object with its own existence, it seems more and more distant from me, less and less the account of a private tragedy. I can almost see it float further and further from me. It's no longer just my pain, it's no longer the tale of *my* mother's disappearance in the night. By its telling it has been transformed into an object available for public scrutiny.

Why should that matter to me? How does it detract from the pain of my premature orphanhood? Why does it make any difference at all that people "out there" hear my words? No reaction will change the facts of the tale. The voice had promised an uplifting solace as the reward for disclosing the solitude etched in my entrails. I expected a soothing peacefulness upon freeing the tale. In my most modest calculation, I was persuaded to unburden my heart to permit my back to straighten up after all these years of journeying with the awesome weight of that memory.

The fact is that I hoped that by telling my story, *our* story, as the voice had urged me to do, I would regain my mother, that the nightmare I have been living for so many years would come to a sudden end. I'd wake up in my little bed in our modest apartment in Budapest surrounded by my parents and my sister, all of us young and very much alive and in love with the simplicity of our ordinary life. I hoped for the true gift of rebirth, a second chance, a fair one this time. After all, I was ripped off coldly and cynically by whoever is in charge of individual destinies. My mother was robbed of decades of existence, of motherhood, of partnership. We all deserve to start over at the very point at which the cloud of madness collapsed on top of our lives, dumping upon our destroyed family a deluge of death and suffering. And that is just what I am left with now, after having told my story. I don't even have access to the melancholic resignation I shared with my secluded memory. What an emptiness! Generations to follow may learn history from my story and from the stories of others born in death and solitude. So why doesn't this knowledge soothe the *malaise* brought upon me by the telling of the tale? Why do I keep posing the same question, year after year, never receiving even an acknowledgement, let alone an answer?

The more I am aware of words, inadequate words, the more deeply loneliness settles inside me. I want to escape into the world of dreams, to be lulled by a vision that forbids me to speak, a dream that invites me to whatever a benevolent unconscious offers me as distraction from the cacophony of words. I close my eyes and let my attention drift toward realms beyond an indefinite horizon.

There is a universe of turmoil on the other side. Light doesn't shine in this land, yet indistinct shapes and movements can be perceived with ease. I am not aware of seeing so much as piercing the air around me with an unfamiliar, new sense. Whatever travels through this space penetrates me rather than meeting me at a safe distance. Somehow I am informed that what creates the busy traffic around me is a reciprocal fervent search for friends, parents, children, enemies. The number of searchers is so phenomenal that the probability of finding the person sought is minimal, which enhances the frenzy of the quest.

I feel intimidated by the speed of the tumult around me. I haven't acquired the skill to dodge the silent movement. A constant flurry of sharp winds blowing in all directions tosses me about. I sense myself being sucked into the eye of a hurricane. There is an occasional decrease in the intensity: it corresponds to a fortunate meeting of searchers. I don't know whence I gathered this information. Just like everything else in this extraordinary universe, it has penetrated my consciousness without my being aware of its point of entry.

I become agitated, feeling the urge to move about at the same time as I experience an indefinable attraction from the outside. I allow myself to drift with the flow of the bewildering magnetism.

The experience is totally novel to me, yet I don't feel the need for caution or worry. The pull of whatever draws me is now so intense that I have a sense of flying through great expanses of space saturated with dense energy. I still don't see anything, yet I haven't collided with anything, either.

My heart is pounding as if it were sending a message in Morse code. Now, I begin to yield to anxiety: I am in a realm where mysterious forces that I can't see or hear have irresistible power over me. What if they are malefic? They may want to destroy me, to do harm to me. What if I am going to be tortured? Panic takes hold of me and I can't find the strength to extricate myself from its grip. I am falling faster and faster toward what seems to be my doom. I don't know how but I learn that I am about to be engulfed by it. I am about to experience my ultimate destruction when I shatter the world of silence with my shriek of agony: "MOTHER! HELP ME!" I find myself lying, invaded by pain, when I hear a voice without seeing its source:

"I am here, my little boy, don't worry, I'm by your side. I'm the spirit that animates you, that soothes your pain so you can live with it. What can I do to make the hurt more bearable, my little boy?"

"You've let me down so many times, I'm scared to trust you. You can be just as cruel as you are loving. Do you know the difference between the two, mother?"

I don't actually *hear* my voice utter these words. My lips are not moving, my mouth is sealed into one concrete mass, yet they ring clearly in the crisp air that envelops my body. And she must hear me, as well, for I can hear her gentle sobbing as she begins to articulate her answer:

"Don't blame me, my son, I've done what I could do. I've encountered experiences for which life did not equip me with knowledge. I made mistakes that cost me my life, and you your mother. But, please, understand and believe me. Whatever I've done was inspired by my love and concern for you. If I abandoned you it's because I didn't know how to stay. If I asked you, urged you to lighten your burden by telling your tale, to inspire the young to protect themselves against evil, I hoped that you'd be less lonely, less tormented by the weight of solitary knowledge. If relief didn't follow your telling the tale, don't hold me responsible. I hated to see you go through life with a bag of cadavers on your back.

"I was wrong. I was wrong the entire time I tried to understand the world with the mind of an uneducated seamstress. No one groomed me for the decisions I had to make. And luck did not visit me as often as I needed it. It stood by me, however, when I left you in Sari's care. She did what she could, but I knew that the task was too big for any ordinary Jew. And yet, you survived, your sister survived, and, to some extent, your father survived. All those lives spared. I like to think that it was not fate or God who intervened, but luck and your mother's prayers. God abandoned us long ago; there was not much to expect of Him. And fate is just another mask of God. I learned to be wise about these matters the hard way. I gave my life for this cursed wisdom.

"My son, my little boy who is so old and so uncared for that it pains me more to be with you than to take leave, I will stay by you to undo whatever is not too late to undo. What can I do for you?"

"Tell me your story, answer all the questions that have been burning a hole in my life ever since you crossed the threshold of our house forty years ago. Illuminate this darkness with your answers and maybe then I can rest. Maybe the inevitability will be easier to accept coming from you, who lived it against your will, against your heart. Mother, why did you leave? Why didn't you come back? All those women who were healthy and strong but stood on the side indicated for the sick and the weak came back that same night. Every one of them. They all survived. You and Mrs. Schonfeld were the only ones who were weak and unwell, and you were the only ones to lose your lives to the murderers. Why did it happen this way? How could it end up like this? If nothing else, just answer these two questions. I imagine that just the knowledge that you didn't abandon me purposefully will alleviate much of the eight-year-old's pain. Help me free that little boy. Even if he can never have his mother again, he can at least put her to rest, and, finally, he can permit himself to rest. Perhaps. I am cautious, you see. I have been disappointed too many times. Enthusiasm doesn't come to visit me too often. There is too much bitterness in me to provide a hospitable reception for uplifting movements of the heart. You may offer me a taste of peace. It's not yet enthusiasm, but it's no longer haunting pain, either. Will you tell me your part of the story?"

"Of course I will, my little boy. I fear, though, that you may be disappointed. It's so banal, so stupidly banal that no one could ever think that in fact the enemy would build its empire on the victim's refusal to consider it as a possibility. My story is very simple: I fell into the trap of my own ignorance. This is what evil was erected on for millions of people like me. It doesn't help *you*, of course, you need the 'story' of how this was true for me. Well, I'll unveil the picture of my ordeal in front of you.

"Months before that December morning, I had already known that it was just a matter of time before we would fall prey to the Nazi monsters. We had heard about what torments Jews had suffered in Poland. Our hearts were shattered by the insane rumours from which we sheltered the children about the cruel deaths of my sisters and their families. We hung our heads in resignation when a stranger from the East sought us out to reveal the tragic details of how your little cousins, Vera and Tomi, had been burnt alive in an infernal pit deep in the bowels of the Ukraine. My gentle sisters succumbed to impersonal bullets. They died a lonely, desolate death: the assassins denied them the comfort of collapsing into the pit holding hands with their life's companions. With each word of his sinister tale I felt myself slipping closer to the bottom of the night.

"Helplessness alternated with despair in my heart. Sounds and images from our childhood obsessed me. My two little sisters, always so gay, so innocent, and so hypnotically drawn toward the marvels of nature, now were rotting, unburied, under hostile Ukrainian skies. Every time my attention turned to their children, panic inundated me: that tiny little ballerina and that angelic little boy could have easily been you and your sister. 'My God, they are going to kill all of us, even my children.' First I mourned the waste of our family with sorrow no human can describe in any language. Then the lament was eclipsed by the bowel-wrenching anxiety about our fate. My mind was racing hysterically, searching for an escape route for all of us, but at least for you children.

"Your father, a man of subtle passions and timid demeanour, was possessed by the demon of silence; he abdicated his will and his urge to commune. A morose fog tightly wrapped his mind and his soul. He was already preparing for the road. Don't judge him, my boy, your father was the personification of the loving parent. But he never learned how to shelter himself and his little ones from flames. Like a man fearing that he might do more harm than good, he let Providence take over where the knowledge of an ordinary man couldn't serve as a guide.

"And one day, a cursed spring day, he had to go. He looked so frail, so childlike yet so anciently old under his backpack. He said: 'Mother, take care of the little ones, love them for the both of us, take care of yourself until I come back.' His eyes said 'Farewell, my beloved, this is where our common journey ends and we each go on our separate ways. We shall never meet again, we shall never rejoice again in raising our young ones together. We have to go to die. You alone, and I alone. I love you forever but the words to reveal the unique blend of my love and sorrow don't exist in my simple vocabulary. Farewell, we'll meet in Heaven.'

"I knew he was right. Soon after, we had to move into the Jewish house. It was so hard to explain to you why we had to abandon our own home, all our belongings, and share a crowded apartment with what was left of our family. Not being clever with words, I opted for short elusive sentences: 'We have to move in with grandmother and Aunt Sari for a while, the law requires us to do so, and it will be just for a while, everything will be in order soon.' I knew that my enigmatic statements uttered from behind a poorly fabricated mask of calm composure and confidence added to your confusion, to your fear of the future. So many changes, so many hostile words and actions around us, how could you believe that *anything* would ever be all right again? I ached for all of us and I knew how impotent I was in the face of the inevitable. And yet, overcoming my fright and my melancholy, I was ready to make decisions, to search for solutions, to look for rescue plans. But alas, my son, your mother was never a woman of the world. She was most at home in the realm of her household. I had no idea how to prevail on well-intentioned but overwhelmed officials who possibly would have helped a verbally more agile woman. I lacked the finesse and the funds to secure us a shelter in one of the foreign protectorates.

"What I did excel in was making the best of resignation. My face seldom betrayed the despair of my heart, the solitude of knowledge. For none of you was allowed to be harassed by futile thoughts of impending doom. I carried the burden of certainty under the austere cloak of frail health. No, my son, I wasn't very sick, I was tired from being overloaded with the burden of a dying family. When you heard my periodic complaints about being 'unwell', it was more my soul that was suffering than my flesh.

"And I never gave up trying to save you. When I overheard, in my scattered gallopings through the dishevelled city, about the possibility of being exempted from deportations if one converted, I abandoned without a moment's hesitation the faith of my ancestors. I thought: 'If there is a God, She must be a mother, She must understand and welcome my trading the pious history of my forefathers for a possible future for my children. If God doesn't understand my choice, God doesn't deserve the love of the pure of heart. Besides, what difference can it make to God whether we worship in a synagogue or a church, as long as we worship? At a time like this, the most godly behaviour is to save the children. If I were to lose this priority from sight, I wouldn't deserve the love and protection of God, anyway. I'm a simple, uneducated seamstress and according to the wisdom of sages I may be erring from the sacred teachings. But for me there is nothing holier than the life of my babies. God's love must inspire in every mother the desire to raise her little ones to maturity. Should man or any other force attempt to meddle with this holiest of all dedications, God must punish the pervert. And if God remains silent in the face of evil, can God be anything else but another version of evil?'

"So we went to seek out the services of a priest officiating from the temporary local parish installed in the basement of the building across from our own. A hostile enemy of God, he was, this divine servant. He looked at us, branded with our shameful yellow star, as if we repulsed him. His face became distorted with spite and disgust as he ogled us as one does with a fascinating abomination of nature.

"'Well, look what mud dripped in from the street! The stray

lambs finally found their way home, after two thousand years of rolling in filth in the company of swine. No wonder they don't want to eat pork, it's like eating their best friend. Well, come on in, this is the charitable house of the Lord, He forgives you, even if I don't. Don't be so sheepish, you haven't completely forgotten how one behaves in human company, have you?'

"With that he extended his hand to me. It took me a few seconds to recover from the haze that fogged my numbed brain. 'He wants me to kiss his hand,' I realized. 'Is this part of being Catholic,' I wondered, 'to kiss this cruel man's hand, to further humiliate myself in front of my children? Could he be the true mediator of God on earth for the Catholics? Do all Catholics have to suffer his arrogance or is the Church not exempt from the disease of the times either? Who cares, I'll kiss his dirty feet if I have to as long as he leads my family to safety. I'll pledge eternal obedience to him, to his God, to his entire world, just show me the corner of a dark shelter where I can hide with my children until the night dissipates.'

"I kissed his hand with fervour. 'Father, we come to become good Catholics. It took these terrible times to lead me to the light of the true God and I don't want to go on living in sin, nor to continue raising my children without His blessed teachings. Father, please convert us to the true religion, I beg of you.' I don't know where those words came from, I hadn't been accustomed to making such speeches, especially to strangers. Every time I'd go to our family doctor, before I could tell him what was the matter, I had to rehearse before I would dare to open my mouth in front of this 'learned man'. And even so I stuttered and stammered and blushed while I squeezed out of me the simple words describing my discomfort. How did I learn to make such a speech before this hostile, hateful priest? This is one of those questions to which no human can find an answer. Was it the grace of God, was it a hidden reserve that contained a stock of wisdom for moments like this? I don't know. However, my seemingly sincere enthusiasm must have reached him because the hard mask of spiteful anger on his face softened to a more tolerable expression of mockery mixed with sympathy.

"'Well, that's fine, of course, you all have just seen the light, the

Germans had precious little to do with your sudden zeal, had they? It's either the Catholic Church or immediate and certain hell for you folks. Am I wrong? No matter, the Lord is not picky; He forgives all the sinners, all the time. But it's not so easy and not so fast. First, you have to take catechism lessons, all of you. You must attend church every day, and you must be baptized. I'm not sure you have that much time. Come back this afternoon for your first lesson.'

"I was at first ashamed of having been so humiliated by this heartless man. Next, I was aware of panic: 'What if there isn't enough time to finish the catechism and the rest? Oh, my God, please give us the time to be saved from the human hell!' By the time we reached the street level and stepped outside, I again felt invaded by despair. 'It's no use, the children will perish just like their cousins and thousands of others.' As we crossed the street, I spied a group of young hoodlums, armed with guns, their sleeves clad with the dreaded Arrow Cross insignia. 'This means instant torture, we must run with our hearts, kids,' I said to you in frenzy and I grabbed each of you by the shoulder and I carried you while running as fast as my legs would transport me. Again, where did all this strength come from? Normally I could hardly pick up one of you with two hands. This time I was able to summon up enough power to lift you off the ground and dash with you. Would anyone believe in the extraordinary strength of a mother? Under the relative safety of the doorway, I noticed the expression of terror and disbelief on your pale faces. Your sister was silently sobbing and shivering. From that well I drank a limitless gulp of hatred for the evil savages. Again, I felt I was beaten: I, alone, against a whole world grown thirsty for my children's blood. What was I to do? Who was going to hurry to my aid? I shook my head in a sadly conceived conclusion: this is a time to hurt, to kill, not to rescue. The few who risk their own lives to save others' are just as mad as the rest of us. May they find reward in a more just world than this one. And certainly there aren't enough of them, and there are too many assassins. My children will die with me.

"I lived in the mournful company of this premonition as the days followed one another. Each one brought with it a new humiliation, a new threat, the news of a new death. My sister Sari and I, so different in temperament, in social habits, drew close to buttress one another, to prevent the other from falling into the trap of depression. 'We are needed; mother and the kids deserve all we've got,' she'd say. And I would respond: 'We must do what we can, and that's not much. Even hope has been deported to the edge of life somewhere in Poland.'

"At other times, I would be the one attempting to pour some life into her: 'Sarika,' I'd say, 'where are you, come back to your usual optimistic self, you've your son to live for; there is another baby in your belly oblivious to the evil ripping our lives apart; that baby needs to be nourished with love. And to love that unborn life you can't neglect your own, you can't let these human monsters turn you into your own enemy.'

"She'd look at me through an indisguisable cloud of fear thickened by fatigue and discouragement: 'You believe, don't you, that struggling will help us out of the trap set by a time outside of history, a place created just for the damned? Is clawing the walls of this Jewish house going to make the big yellow star on the gate disappear? What chance does my baby have to be born as an ordinary human being? I am weighed down by the absurd curse that I cannot help but leave to my children as their unshakeable legacy. Is there a way to remain hopeful with this reality burdening my heart? Wouldn't it be better just to die fast, without pain, in peace?'

"I knew she was right. But can a mother carry out this dark deed no matter what? Doesn't she become just another monster?

"'No, we can't succumb to what seems to be the easy escape; we have been chosen by God and nature to carry the future in our flesh, we have no right to extinguish the light to alleviate our pain. We are breathing, right? Well, as long as there is a lungful of air in our bodies we must fight for our children's chance to live, to blossom into adults so they can add a link to the chain that connects us to eternity. We must live to see the defeat of evil. We must live because we were born.'

"Where did these words of wisdom come from, I would wonder; some of them were not very clear even to me! Who was speaking through my voice? For what mysterious power had I become the spokesman? As usual, there was no answer to my questions. How much easier it would have been to endure the torment had I had a sinister and reassuring knowledge that our deaths were needed in the scheme of the universe to safeguard the future of God's creation, the knowledge that all this horrible existence was not in vain. It would have been so much easier to find a resigned solace in the promise that our lives were not being wasted as a no longer usable common object. This relief, just like all others, had been denied to us. On the contrary, I had the sense that as one day died after the other, our lives had less and less meaning.

"Then came December, with its finite chill. Moments of strength scarcely ever visited me. Madness was my new friend, constant companion. It was a quiet madness allowing no room for howling. Our dialogue was limited to whimpers and whispers; rage and fear turned inward, running rampant in my bowels. It was a madness that secured the tenuous balance between the urge to throw myself into the flames and the desire to extinguish them with my bare teeth. My faithful companion permitted me to summon my waning maternal instinct every time the air-raid sirens began to howl....It would rush me to your bed, leave me just time to steal a normal mother's glance at your peaceful sleeping face, without granting me another moment to linger, to savour the joy of watching your sweet face at one with the insane world. It would force me to act mechanically, to gather you in my arms and run down the interminable steps to the spurious safety of the dark air-raid shelter. With each explosion, I felt released from and burdened by horror. 'Thank God, my children survived this bomb,' I would think, and then wonder: 'Oh, my God, will the *next* one kill them?' 'We have made it through this dark tunnel so far, thank the Almighty,' gave way to: 'We'll perish ignominiously, buried in this immense grave, all of us, mother and child. I can't take it any more, let it come right now! Curse the name of the God that permits this senseless massacre of the innocent.' This is the portrait of your mother on that December morning as moulded by her merciless madness.

"And then, our slowly agonizing existence switched to a diabolical pace. What I feared more than starvation, cold, torture, disease, death, finally happened. They came to take me away. When I heard the shrill, urgent sound of the super's bell, I knew with a certainty not usually given to humans that this time the bell tolled not for water or an electrical emergency. I knew that this time the habitually indifferent gong was animated by the super's gleeful enthusiasm at purging the house of us, 'human insects' as he used to refer to the inhabitants of the building.

"No, I was not ready, how could I ever be ready to leave my babies to what seemed to be an insufferable fate? Should I poison them immediately? Was Sari not right when she entertained sinister projects of communal suicide? How is it possible to live with the relentlessly haunting obsession: 'What is happening to my children? Is anyone looking after them to feed them, to shelter them, to protect them from bombs, machine guns, grenades? Is there anyone to gently caress their tiny heads bursting with the horrors of war and orphandom? Are they still alive? If not, did they die a horrible death?' No, it's just not possible to live under the yoke of such torments. This is a version of madness no mother can be expected to endure. Kill me right here, I want to die before I am swept off my feet by the whirlwind that robs me of the last remnant of decency and sanity, before I become a will-less, naked puppet manipulated by a demonic torturer. I am already teetering on the edge of the bottomless pit. How can I do anything but end the struggle at once?

"Before I could act on my despair and release us all from the clutches of impending terror, your faces, your tormented little faces appeared to me, as if pleading for mercy.

"I was half unconscious in my confusion. 'I can't abandon my children to the hands of the slaughterer and I can't end their young existence with my own hands, either. Help, somebody help, I don't know how to make a decision that would make any sense at all, that would allow me a moment's peace, that wouldn't rob my children of their precious lives. Help, mother, save me, save my babies, mother do something for your first born!'

"But your poor grandmother seemed to have shrunk in size and in age. She seemed just as scared, as disoriented, as pleading for her life as the other children. There was no help forthcoming from her. No one could do anything for me. I was already half-way in the grave.

"You must get ready, say goodbye to your children, go or you may bring greater trouble upon your head. Don't worry—how absurd I must sound to you—I'll do my best. As long as I live, your children will have a mother, they'll be fed, sheltered, and loved. But go now before it's too late.' My sister Sari, the practical one, the one who always bounced back onto her feet like the proverbial cat, brought me back to the reality at hand. In fact, she was right. I had no choice. I had to go and put up with the absurdity of what was waiting for me.

"'I'm going. But swear on the head of your child that you'll keep my children in your heart as if they had been sprouted in your flesh. Swear that you will save my children.'

"We hugged hastily. The embarrassment of the one who had been spared chilled our last embrace. The shame of survival settled between us like an infectious disease. For her, I was already on the other side, the other, the one who must die. No, I'm not bitter, nor was I then. I had no anger for my sister, she was as much a victim as I, two miserable marionettes on strings held by the cruellest hands ever formed in a human womb. No, I had no bad feelings for my younger sister. She was correct in placing me outside the rank of ordinary people. I myself felt the transformation in me: I already sensed the distance between the living and the doomed. Of course, we all die one day, but when I was singled out for untimely, wasteful death I experienced a rigidity in my entrails that could only be the sign of a premature and coerced end to my earthly life. I *was* now the *other*, the one whose life can be taken with the shrill sound of an indifferent bell while, one way or another, life continues to limp on.

"I said a painfully short farewell to you. I was afraid of you; I expected your scorn, your hatred, your indomitable fear thrown in my face for what you might have perceived as a cowardly exit. I was more terrified of your fear than of your hatred, for what kind of a mother must I be if I can't loosen the grip of fear around my child's neck? But my little boy of eight precious years grew a century old right in front of my very eyes. You looked so wise, so resigned, so strong, as if you had endless resources to draw on. I was grateful then to God for sending you this gift of wisdom which allowed you a measure of protection against the evil of unsoothable pain and fear.

Now, and since then, I curse the Almighty for having created man so powerful that he can rob an eight-year-old of his youth in a second.

"With my heavy heart scarely beating, I went down to join the women assembled in the courtyard. Don't ask me what thoughts went through my mind or what feelings filled my body. I was completely numb, as if I were prepared for surgery on my whole being. I stopped seeing you and Agi, I stopped feeling my own pain, maybe for a few moments I was dead and then reprieved.

"The Arrow Cross man's orders brought me back into the cold reality of standing in that December courtyard: sandwiched between a row of indifferent and hateful murderers on the top, and my tiny, panic-stricken family on the bottom, I and my neighbours stood in the solitary silence of the damned, those already outside the community of men.

"'The sick to the right, the healthy to the left,' was his command. Of course, I knew that this decision was to seal my immediate destiny. If I opted for the right, they would probably march me off to the Danube and shoot me into the icy river. If I went to the left, I might be taken to hard labour that would kill me slowly but surely. How diabolical of them: we had to make the decision! Not the decision between life and death, but between two moments of certain, unavoidable death.

"How was I to decide, my God? What if the sick were, for once, given a reprieve, and they killed the healthy as a more powerful enemy to be feared? How was one to make such a decision? What human knowledge informs such a decision that must spring forth from a wisdom located in the heart and not in the brain? How is an ordinary seamstress to make life and death choices? 'My God, help me make the right choice, I have no other wisdom but the ultimate trust in your goodness. Help me opt for life, Almighty Lord, help me find the way back to raising my children, *your* children!'

"'Mrs. Stein, Piroska.'"

"I had abandoned all intentional thinking. I allowed my legs to take me to whichever side they seemed to prefer.

"I ended up on the left side, all by myself! God, oh my God, could it be that you'd answered my prayer and you had decided to save me, just me, while you let the others go to their fate? Maybe they didn't turn to you in this moment of need, maybe they remained so angry with you that you lost interest in their destiny? Or could it be that I am the only one you are cruelly abandoning while lavishing the gift of survival onto the others, *all* the others? What have I done to deserve your ultimate scorn?

"I felt naked in my total solitude. A sense of modesty possessed me. I covered my body in a clumsy attempt to become invisible. Mrs. Schonfeld joined me. 'Is this a good sign? Is her presence by my side an ill omen? She is almost as old as mother, how can they seriously take her as a healthy woman while a dozen or so young women, younger than I, are huddling on the other side feigning to be decrepit? And if they don't give credence to her choice, will she discredit mine? Mrs. Schonfeld, you could be condemning the two of us to immediate death! Mrs. Schonfeld, you are an assassin! Mrs. Schonfeld, you old liar, you are robbing my children of their mother; I should call the Arrow Cross man's attention, I should tell him not to lump you with me. You are over sixty years old, and I'm only forty-two. You are diabetic and I am quite well, except for some stomach ailments and dizzy spells. You can't work, Mrs. Schonfeld, you can hardly see, you yourself have been complaining to me that the diabetes is robbing you of your sight, that you can no longer even thread a needle. I am a qualified seamstress, I can do valuable work for the Germans. Mrs. Schonfeld, damn you! Let's pray God we both make it, I can't point the gun to your temple. I'm not a murderer.'

"No one else joined us. They all reported sick, unfit for work. What did they know that Mrs. Schonfeld and I didn't? How did they all end up together? 'Can they kill all of them, after having gone to the trouble of coming here and rounding us up? They said they needed hands for hard labour! Can it be that only the two of us will be judged unfit for work, regardless of our claiming to be well enough to bear the rigours of hard labour? Can it be that this poor old woman and I are their only victims this morning? What do they really want? What will really happen to me?'

"We were marched out of the building. Thanks to old lady Katz, Agi was saved. God had abandoned even my young child; but this ancient woman had pity on her tender age and, risking her own life, she rescued my baby. I took a last look at your face. You were white as the Sabbath tablecloth. My poor little boy, you already had the appearance of an orphan. Your eyes were sunken in, they seemed to be mourning already. That was the last impression of you that I took on the road with me. Your beaten little face was to accompany me on my journey however long or short. The darkness at the bottom of your eyes settled in my heart with the weight of two lead bullets.

"'I must survive, I must come back to chase the night from my son's eyes,' I swore to myself.

"'A futile self-deception,' said Mrs. Schonfeld to me, guessing my thoughts. 'We'll be shot in a matter of hours. Spend the time like me, praying the Almighty to welcome you into life everlasting. We're done with this existence. Why do you think I chose this side? I knew they would never believe that I'm a well woman. You don't have to be a medical man to see that life is only a visitor in this old carcass and no longer a resident. I want it to be short and painless. I'm not fit to bear the rigours of a long march, of beatings, of starvation, of harsh labour and even torture. Since the end is inevitable, let's get it over with quickly. But why did you opt for the side of death, Mrs. Stein? You're young, you have little children. Why didn't you do like the others and report sick? They'll come back, every one of them, because it's too late for them to bother otherwise. They are losing the war, you know, they are now desperate and in a hurry. If you're useless, they kill you immediately. If you can be useful, they'll put you to work for them, hoping beyond hope to turn the flow of events. You made a dreadful mistake, Mrs. Stein, your time shouldn't be up yet.' With that she turned inward, her lips moving at an incredible speed as if she wanted to repeat every single prayer she had ever learnt to ingratiate herself with the Lord.

"I knew she was right. But it was too late. The healthy ones had been rounded up from other buildings also; they were standing across the street in a small group, about thirty of them. We had to join them. The others formed a much more imposing column. 'Of course they are the ones to be taken to Germany to do slave labour for the Nazis.' I was the youngest in our group. 'I made a mistake, a mistake that will lead to my death in the rigid bed of the river.' I didn't even have the energy to rebel, to feel anything. I was drained by this exercise of playing God, by the months of fear that this might happen; I was exhausted by life on the periphery of the living. Death would come now, soon, and it would be over. I could no longer fight. My guilt for having failed my children was the last vestige of humanity left to torment me.

"'They deserve a mother, they have the right to grow up in a home, sheltered by their mother and father. We both failed miserably. I should have hidden them in the country somewhere. So many others succeeded, simple people, without connections — why didn't I? How could I let those poor youngsters down? How could I be so selfish and not think of them no matter what? But now it's all over for me. I can't do anything for them. I don't even have the tears left to weep for them. May Sari keep her oath and provide those two orphans with all that a child needs to grow and to grow up into a strong adult. May their lives blossom into rich flowers even though their roots are planted in blood and ashes. Farewell, my darlings, farewell.' With that I sank into emptiness, having lost all care for my life. The darkness of my son's eyes guided my feet.

"And the journey was long. It didn't lead to the Danube, as feared. In fact, it led to the railroad station. Those from the other column, the 'sick ones', went in another direction. We had no idea to what destination point it led them. We were certain that they would be spared. Our fate? In the cattle wagons, piled on top of each other like so many logs of dead wood. Without windows, without contact with the outside world, we lived in a self-contained universe, the planet of the damned. Judging from the railroad station and from common sense (which lost its meaning altogether), we were heading west. This could mean Germany or Austria. In either case, we were intended for hard labour after all.

"'We're not being taken to our immediate death,' Mrs. Schonfeld whispered to me feverishly, 'we'll be working in a camp, where they'll have to feed us, shelter us if they want us to do work. That means we'll be spared. Praised be the Lord, He listened to my prayers. You didn't think for a moment He was going to let us be gunned down in the Danube, did you? I knew it all along, the Lord watches over the innocent. And who is more innocent than this group of weather-beaten old hags? Mrs. Stein, you, too, can praise Him for having had mercy on your life, on your little ones. Don't forget the lesson: where men abandon their fellow men, where men massacre their fellow men, the Lord intervenes on behalf of the pious, the most faithful of His children. Don't forget, Mrs. Stein, the Lord is the only one who cares for the poor Jew. And we're the living proof of His love of the poor, the weak, and the old, blessed be His name.'

"I remained silent. I hadn't made my peace with the Almighty.

"We arrived in Bergen Belsen. The Almighty had never been to Bergen Belsen. How can I forget that?

"My little boy who grew so old, so tired forty years ago, you have the soul of the child in the wrappings of an ancient sage. The endless flow of words seems to have deafened your heart. For so many years I have been calling to you with the plaintive lament of a mother's soul. You remained unmoved. I thought you scorned me with your back turned in defiance and hatred. Now I know the truth. Your heart had drowned in a sea of endless dialogues. Your speech was marked by the alternation of torrential soliloquy and futile silence. Do you hear me now, my poor son? Your mother is here. I have just told you my story, the one you have been aching to hear for so long, the one you hoped would explain my desertion of you, the one I hoped would put your restless soul to rest. Where are you now, my little boy, my gloomy little boy? Show me the light in your eyes."

"What happened to you, mother, why didn't you come back from Bergen Belsen? Others, not many but some, did come back from Belsen, so why didn't *you* come back? For years I have not allowed you into my dreams. I have banished you into the deepest corner of my unconscious, not permitting you to surface except in fantasies that you were still alive, in Israel or some other place, and that you had suffered amnesia and that's why you never gave a sign of life, that's why you never came back to me. So where *are* you, mother? Don't stop your story now. Without an answer to my question the story is of secondary importance, it's only a story. The answer will determine the rest of my life. I survived as I survived without you. But now that I hear your voice with my ears, my heart is becoming a trifle more daring. I want to open it wide for you to make a triumphant return, a regal procession into this minute kingdom. So mother, my dear, beloved stranger, reveal your secret: where are you?"

"The end of my story is banal, the most trivial of all stories written in the night. There are millions of tales that have the same ending. We have become the most redundant nation on the tired back of the earth: ours is the nation of the unburied dead, population six million. I am only one of its ordinary citizens. No, my little boy, I didn't live to see the light of day again. I shall spare you the senseless details of my journey through the madhouse at Bergen Belsen. I did end up working for the Germans as a seamstress. Every day was like the other: each of them spent in the knowledge that this would likely be the last one. And every day I died. The next day I didn't resuscitate, I just died once more.

"This language is of course absurd to you, but what else can I tell you, my son—the truth, at least my truth, is beyond your grasp. I can't tell you about the ordeal of my neighbour, for she lived hers with words that she needed to invent, and I lived mine with my private language. You can never understand another man's pain, it flourishes in the uniqueness of his body, his soul. So if I tell you that to have died one final time, after so many moments of death, is one of the most ordinary experiences in this cursed nation of the unburied dead, you must understand the meaning of my words with your heart and not your intellect. The life and death of a mother or of a son can't be communicated through articulate speech, it howls in your heart, one moment like an Arctic wind, the next like an all-consuming flame. The death of a mother or a son has no beginning, no middle, no end: it just is, with a finality that always amounts to pain. But I sense that you *need* to know the details: was I killed by a bullet or the gas chamber, or did starvation ravish me from life? Was it the son of a man who ended my days or was it a beast, a demon, or even the Devil?

"I died a simple and vile death. While no man subjected me to an instrument dispensing certain death, I hold the slaughterer responsible. 'But which one, what is his name?' you will wonder. He had no name. The entire community of men was my assassin: the Germans and their partners for setting up the Kingdom of Death, the Jews for not learning from their history, and the rest of the world for allowing the Nazis to produce corpses the way one might manufacture goods. And God? Well, my son, I leave that one to you, I have enough on my heart as it is.

"My son, what extinguished the whisper-like flame in my body was a bout with typhus. The disease enjoyed a cheap triumph over my moribund shell. Typhus is one of those illnesses that sees the light of day only with the willful collaboration of men. It cannot be blamed on nature. Millions of unburied souls lost their bodies to this relentless assassin. But, my son, don't ever forget that the illness was only a reflection of the much graver disease that had infected man's heart and robbed him of a conscience. Beware of that disease, my son; its seduction is without escape. And even the innocent can succumb to it if he is not vigilant every moment of his life. How do you protect yourself against it, my son, my bitter, enraged little boy? By keeping a pure heart, free of hatred, free of revenge, animated by a strength that pumps blood into other humans rather than sucking it away from them. Keep your heart available for the call of the weak so that no mother of a victim in another corner of the earth can ever accuse you of having idly allowed the massacre of *her* son.

"Now, my little boy, I withdraw from your presence, you have a new life to begin, a life restored to a tolerable state of health. The pain will never go away, but the illness has been controlled for the rest of your days. You do have many days ahead of you. Go, my boy, enjoy them one at at time, in spite of the pain. Do not continue to endure them as if the pain were the aim of life. Know that I'm never too far, and no, I'm never close enough. This can't be changed, but then, neither can my love for you."

Her words were followed by a new type of silence. Gone were the invisible searchers, or, at least, I was not aware of the winds blowing around me. I felt still and somewhat grounded. I opened my eyes expecting them to reveal a familiar world to me and not the shadow kingdom I had just visited.

Indeed, I find myself in my home, at my typewriter. My fingers feel tense and tired, as if they have been working for endless hours pouring millions of letters on paper. Could it be that I was attempting to commemorate every one of those unburied dead with whom my mother shares her eternal journey with a letter? This is one of those questions to which I shall never find an answer. And the rest has all been said.

"Farewell, mother!"

"Welcome, mother!"

Dialogue with a Spectator

"*I*HAVE BEEN ROAMING for many years in a world peopled with gentle souls fond of parading in front of one another in a succession of historical moments. They delight in erecting monuments to martyrs and heroes. Some are carved from rigid mineral able to withstand the vicissitudes of changing times and prevalent stories. Others flow endlessly, displaying lofty theories, self-assured ideologies, and new metaphors glorifying the moral superiority of their creators. Their commerce is so alluring, so intoxicating, that I easily succumb to the attraction of their charm. How irresistible for this superannuated ghetto flower, who grew up in the shadow of the yellow star, to be a member in the fraternity of the just, the wise, and the powerful! Their generous hospitality and gallantry toward me, a being who bears a sometimes awesome, sometimes counterfeit resemblance to ordinary humans, is irrestistibly enticing. A survivor, yet not a conqueror; a victim, yet a survivor; what can I be to this assembly of vigorous optimists and narcissists? How can they satisfy their favourite pastime—of classifying all that their well-heeled intellect has so elegantly gathered in a surrounding *fond de tableau* to their supreme status in the rank of men—when their eager gaze is arrested by my awkward stature? Constantly navigating between the shadow world of the pits and the boisterous realm of the jubilant I present a blurred image to their indiscreet, arrogant glass eyes. And yet, in a sleight of hand unfathomable to my confused mind, I have fallen through their meticulous inspection as well as through my own reluctance to belong. I find myself a member in a community in which everyone is a stranger.

"Lately in my journeys I have sought the company of men of evil. You and others, I know, have delighted in wielding conclusive words at this undertaking. You gleefully lavished on me an arsenal of polished labels ranging from 'clinically unfit' to 'socially insane'. What informed these mystical snippets of your wisdom? Could it be your lack of familiarity with any knowledge which does not spring from the lofty intellect? Could it be that knowledge born of the scream of the flesh and the roaring upheaval of the soul is so foreign to your tweed consciousness that you recoil from it in anticipation of some doom? Does my acquaintance with torture disturb your contemplation of a flawless conscience?

"And yet, when I unwittingly unveiled before your eyes the portrait of a whole generation's pain, you rushed to expropriate it as one does a secretly discovered treasure. Little did I suspect that you, too, would be fuelled by the pressing urge to find the vulnerable spot in the tissue of my tale. Just before absconding with your bounty, you cleared your throat, fixed your gaze on a point in the distance and proffered, with stern politeness, your discomfort in the presence of my raw humanness:

"'This,' you said, 'of course must be examined in the nonpartisan objective light of established and prevalent theories. Without such rigorous scrutiny, your data cannot transcend the boundaries of fiction inspired by either madness or calculated prevarication. One detects a dubious cluster of intentions in your most regrettable tale: to inform, to prosecute, and to indict a whole civilization's moral edifice, its conscience. A rather ambitious enterprise erected on the unstable foundation of an emotionally overloaded biography. Who can ascertain the underlying motivation of such an extraordinary enterprise? It is not in the realm of the formal analysis of human knowledge to take pragmatic stances in the face of undigestable data. Our task is to generate such knowledge, not to implement it.'

"For forty years I have kept my distance from human discourse. If my words did not reach my mouth, it doesn't mean that no speech was born in me during the span of more than a third of a century. A multitude of voices vied to be heard. One had grievances to air; one was blindly lamenting the loss of a lifetime, again another demanded rational accounts for the endurance of senseless suffering. There were voices, accusing voices, clamouring for revenge against man and God, squared off with the internal expression of a trance-like panic. Some begrudged the past, others howled for direction in their labyrinth of pain, and some condemned mankind to eternal indebtedness to all children for the ravishing of one innocence.

"No, indeed, the silence did not attest to the cessation of life within the struggler. My silence was a timid hint at my confusion: I didn't know who was out there listening. In the kingdom of darkness we learned that when we speak the language of truth it doesn't necessarily blossom into knowledge in the mind of our listener. Emerging from that world deprived of light, with my mouth filled with the clotting words of death and torture, has taught me to distrust truth. Who would guide me toward men of true intentions of brother-hood? And who would lure me to the lair of the cruel traitor masquerading as a lover of truth, especially a truth born from ashes? No, indeed, dealing with a mysterious world with a hidden face was not within my means. Now, after a long quest for a cleansing fire, I can finally see the heart of the flame.

"Your world has never seen the need to hide its face. You have never had to rush under the cloak of an unlit doorway for fear of being unmasked as the murderer's accomplice. On the contrary, you hastily learned the rewards of parading in the triumphant sunshine bestowed upon the saviour. You taught me that there are two kinds of survivors: those who struggle with memories and those who have nothing to remember. And I saw no reason to question the inevitable.

"Now, my heart beats to the cadence of a different truth. I discovered that you have so many faces that it strains the eye beyond its means to discern just one. You have so many tongues that the point of bifurcation is invisible. You have so many lies to forget that you have no use for memory. I can now speak to you. Having found the key to your enigma arms me with a wisdom that unlocks my throat. I don't have to listen to my own words, I don't even have to exercise caution in what I bestow upon you. My words are given to me, they flow from a place so familiar that only the limits of language can mask them. Instead, I listen to your heartbeat, I watch the colour of your iris, the quiver of your lips, while you endure my discourse.

Your response to me identifies you, sketches the clearest portrait of who you really are.

"Little by little, every time I open my mouth to tell a dark tale, I make the acquaintance of one of your countless visages. What betrays the undeniable commonality among all of you is your urgent need to convey to me, your self-appointed inspector of conscience, your ultimate innocence, your outraged disavowal of any knowledge, any blood that would link you, however precariously, to the murderer, to the torturer of little children. What you fail to see is the spotlight you shine on your own face in your ceaseless confirmation of your immaculate heart.

"Whom do you wish to convince so desperately? Whose tranquil sleep are you attempting to safeguard? Whose history book are you intent on rewriting? Whose questions are you petrified to answer?

"I imagine that this new language leaving my mouth—with you as its sole intended recipient—is an unwelcome novelty to you. 'The victims should continue to have the decency not to display their lugubrious collection of pictures unfit for one's squeamish conscience.' I have elected to linger on the edge for so many years that now you find my presence intrusive. After all these years, when you have finally learned to breathe again without looking over your shoulder, I appear with a whole exhibit of images of whose spurious existence you have successfully convinced yourself. I come, arms loaded with a rich basket of information to bestow upon you as a belated but well-deserved present. Mind you, neither do I expect to receive nor will you be inclined to offer the reward of your gratitude.

"To the eager and the self-righteous in you, the one who proceeds with the unquestioned strength of his conviction, the world exists only to the extent that it lends itself to be explored, analysed, and interpreted. To those of you guided by tepid sentiments of compassion and pity, I present an infinitely deep well from which to replenish your shallow hearts. For you whose horizon grows imperceptibly dark beyond the flimsy fence of your private heart, my hollow profile fails to challenge your blank myopia. Thus it no longer surprises me that on so many encounters with such an awesomely rich crowd of evil portraits I never recognized you on the road. You see, I am not only fallible but also severely bounded. And I am blinded by the mournful knowledge that recognizes only those evil eyes whose stare already visited me during my nocturnal sojourn.

"I had heard of you in hastily whispered laments, in outbursts of despair from beyond the wall of the endless shriek of souls. But you remained unreal to me until I emerged on this shore of the abyss. You were waiting for me there with tearful eyes made to measure by ritualized protocol. You extended your generous hands toward me: clutching Hershey bars in one, you held impatient questionnaires in the other. You came to meet me as do intrusive anthropologists who approach exotic natives of unexplored lands: with bribes.

"Starved for human attention not modulated by the explosive chant of bullets or by the muffled thud of a felled life, I welcomed your trinkets wrapped in hypocritical smiles. I was eager to see in you an honest attempt to redeem the fruits of evil carved out of my besoiled existence. You seemed so convincing, so inviting, and, above all, so harmless, that without effort I began to see in your constant generosity the essence of all that I so desperately needed to attribute to man as his genetic parcel. I hastily discarded my bitter caution and threw myself without reserve at you for a fraternal embrace: 'No, evil is not the sole occupant of man's heart. Good is so well installed in there that even after this absurd hibernation it awakens with a boisterous and bountiful spirit. It is vigorous, and it is available to the voyager of the night.'

"But my exuberant internal monologue was short-lived. The embrace was not forthcoming and the Hershey bars grew rarer and rarer, leaving the space open for questions sounding increasingly like accusations and suspicions. Wherever I turned for refuge from this brand-new form of torture I met the gaze of the brute. The mantle may have been new but the eyes were unmistakable. They were demanding death for the indiscreet who didn't have the decency to die, death for the one who could unmask the villain. And since the new order no longer approved of blatant assassination to isolate the mighty from the just, the eyes commanded silence.

"Even if nothing else had led me onto your tracks, the fact that with such short delay you tossed before me the obstacle of an absurd paradox would have clearly pointed the finger at who you really were.

With the face of a brother and yet with bloodstains in your eyes, with the chant of a comrade and yet with the rasp of barbed wire on your teeth, with ancient psalms in your soul and yet with indifferent whines on your well-fed lips, to me you appeared as a monster not to be trusted any more than the master of the night.

"With cautious resignation and bitter self-preservation, I joined the fraternity of silence.

"I spent many years in the mute desert I constructed in your midst. With an undying quest for the tiniest oasis, I roamed the earth. The rewards were always the same: treacherous mirages vanishing the moment I thought I had arrived at the term of my voyage. And yet it was not all in vain. While I haven't discovered the tranquil garden to be shared with a community of friends, I did amass a pirate's bounty about your true essence. Thanks to this wisdom I have become your equal in strength. Now I can tell my tale, now I can confront every one of your faces that came to meet me with the sharp saliva of your contempt. Open your ears wide, let my words reach beyond the shelter of your masks. I'll tell you only one tale, and I'll tell it only once. You see, I want to promote the infamy of evil men, not their fame.

"By being confronted with the story, you'll see a face for the first time: your own. Under the protective layers of disguises, there is real skin harbouring your vulnerability. It is from that boundary inward that you and I are brothers; it is to that audience that I address my words.

"I'll withhold from you the minutest description of life in the company of the torturer. I won't disclose to your eyes (eyes that prefer not to see anyway) the close-up portrait of suffering. Not because I wish to spare your sensitivity or your frail conscience. Quite the opposite: I would discharge my mission more faithfully if I unleashed on you the entire herd of vicious memories. Only thus would you be in position to place your sugar-coated, cleverly disguised acts of cruelty into proper frames. Only thus could you discover the meaning of your selective indifference, your all-intrusive egoism, your counterfeit empathy, your evasive abstractions, your self-serving incredulity, your jealously guarded greed. I won't disclose the memories to you because doing so would be futile and even hurtful to *me*.

"In case you wonder how I came to dress this nomenclature of evil, I'll reveal to you my sad source: what you have before your curious gaze, sheltered by a brow raised in distrustful suspicion, is an album of your different portraits. I gathered them in the exile of silence over the last forty years. I met every one of them, many times, in many lands. I know them so intimately that I don't even have to open my eyes or lend my ears to be certain of their inclement presence: a woolly rush of vertigo, a slimy touch of solitude, or any number of similarly alienating sensations accompany our periodic encounters. Yes, I know all of them well enough to have made the decision to break the seal of silence, to introduce you to versions of yourself you have never allowed to appear in decent company.

"Oh, I harbour no illusions about your stance on the auspicious occasion when you finally come face to face with your own humanity. I would be a romantic fool given to Messianic delusions if I expected to see you fall on your shameful knees repenting for the harm you have been inadvertently afflicting on me and on other poor devils emerging from any corner of hell. No, I don't expect your admission of guilt or even shame. I am prepared for aggressive denials, sophistic rationalizations and justifications; I am also ready to encounter your indignant accusations. So be it.

"We must have this confrontation even if the flame of my anger leaves your virginal conscience in its habitually immaculate state, even if you end up projecting all your guilt and shame upon me. Because years of distant contemplation and silent tracking have taught me that at some moment of solitude, in some corner of seclusion, a voice from within your bowels will address you, demanding that you account. I won't be there, of course, but you will be. It is in that instant that the painful rage and the endless sorrow contained in my words today will clearly resonate throughout your memory. You'll not only remember this encounter, you'll also let my voice penetrate your elusive heart. It is this certainty that urges me to speak to you even if your sole reply is silence.

"I feel your presence, I hear your participation in this seemingly one-sided dialogue: I pour out long-winded memories from depths unknown to you, and you store them furtively in nooks and crannies reserved for your exclusive access. I am soothed by this tacit participation as much as you feel weighed down by its discomfort. And yet, you stay. Well, then, hear my words this once. Hear them as they leave my hesitant lips. You may, one day, welcome this intrusive mosaic, for it may serve as the founding stone of the edifice you'll wish to erect to shelter your offspring's undisturbed dreams.

"To spare them (and not you) I'll glide over the images of horror. There is another reason for this surprising discretion. There is a new breed of horror mongers that blackens the already dark horizon. They peddle tales born in the shade of the gas chamber, in the swollen bellies of children starved to death, in gentle mothers violated beyond the confines of their wombs. They traffic in mournful chants in a bazaar spanning the electronic globe. I shall not compete for your attention with these pirates of suffering. To do so would desecrate graves that still demand to be dug. I will not sandwich my mother's decomposing memory between one commercial message exalting the merits of a brand of sanitary napkin and another one boasting about the superiority of Coca-Cola. I shall not parade my gallery of beloved dead so that the reflection of their wasted lives can be added to the tumult of fictional horror so popular in our movie theatres, in our libraries, in our very own bedrooms.

"The tale must be told in an unadorned inventory, without the habitual *maquillage* of aesthetism. The art of atrocity must not be allowed to exist. No, I won't wed 'art' and 'atrocity', and let them give birth to a new face for entertaining, pleasing, or otherwise distracting the human soul from the most naked truth of all. When an artist gives expression to his experience in the grip of atrocity, what reaches our hearts is not just the record of his pain or the full howl of his torment. Instances of the art of atrocity are more eloquent attestations to the survival of art than to the experience of pain.

"The only respectful echo for my struggle to breathe beyond the atrocious is that inarticulate howl. The rest inspires a profound suspicion and lately, more and more often, a fearful indignation. All the generous words offered to exalt the triumph of human dignity in the most squalid quarters ever visited by men is just another one of your devious façades. The heart of the truth is much less edifying. The grip of horror, the torment of hunger, the echoes of death demanded the undivided attention of the victim, not permitting a moment's respite to contemplate his dignity. Another bite of stale bread, another gulp of watery soup, another moment of warmth in the belly of safety and I would have agreed to any bargain with the Devil. Posterity will take care of the reconstruction of human dignity and other Utopian fantasies developed in the lap of luxury. Yes, the strugglers were right. In their newly found wisdom they learned to attend to the merciless priority of the hunger pang ravaging their entrails, to ignore even their own fright. They knew implicitly that they could count on you."

"'Humanity has paid a great price for its survival. We have before our tearful eyes the undeniable proofs of human gallantry not tarnished in the guilty light of its own enemies. We have just emerged from the darkest tunnel of our history, but the most important lesson we taught to future generations is that we *did* conquer the densest darkness. Our heads are bowed in sorrow and mourning for the fallen comrades for the countless victims of this horrible war. But let me assure the world: their death was not in vain, it will teach any future nation that the aggressor can never win, that the aggressor is always wrong, and that the brotherhood of the just will always triumph over the fraternity of evil. Destruction and death swept the human community with such a tidal force that none of us survived its passage without being touched by it. We are all losers, we are all mourners, even if we stand on the mighty platform of the champions of justice and human rights.

"'For every Jewish life shed, there is a commemorative candle burning in every Christian heart. For every Jewish survivor there are tears of pride, compassion, and brotherly love in every Christian eye. Your valiant defeat of the most powerful enemy mankind ever knew is a victory for all of us. You endured the pain of hunger, cold, torture, and above all, the shame of dehumanization. We shared with you along your Calvary the weight of the burden. Now we extend to you our hearts in our mighty hands, with our arms stretched out to embrace you. We welcome you back into the bosom of the human community. We shall build together a better world for Christian and

Jew alike. After all, we are children of the same God, aren't we? Our common heritage commends us to work together, in mutual respect and harmony.

"'Just as we didn't allow the Nazi beast to devour our Jewish brothers, we shall never permit any other people to finish the terrible work of the Germans. We pledge our eternal support to the surviving children of the house of Jacob, Isaac, and Abraham. May the Lord bless us all and find us in the same fraternal embrace that He is witnessing today.'"

"Do you recognize these grandiloquent words? Do they please your ears? Do they correspond to your feelings of universal love without regard to race, creed, or religion? Do they fill your heart with the fulfillment of a lifetime's efforts toward the achievement of moral superiority? Do your veins bulge with proud blood upon savouring such uplifting thoughts and oaths?

"Of course you do. They are *your* words, *your* feelings, *your* solemn promises. How could you extract yourself from the spell of such magnanimity?

"Or for that matter, how could I? I am no better than you; remember, we have been carved out of the same tree of life. My eyes were blinded by the new dawn. My mouth was still full of the taste of innocent blood, but my lips already parted timidly to drink in the new air. My ears still retained the staccato rhythm of bombs exploding around my tiny shelter, yet they were already eager to delight in the vigour of words proclaiming the inauguration of a new life. Your words had the charm of an irresistible magnetism for ears no longer remembering the sound of solidarity, the song of freedom and plenty. Your high-flying oaths committing your soul and might to the defence of my people still cowering under the yoke of the ignominious yellow star were saturated with the healing balm required by our bottomless wounds. Oh, how I threw my forty-pound existence into that nurturing lap! And yet...it took you a lot less time to vanish than to appear. How quickly I had to learn that those words were hollow masks. Except for the articles of canned sustenance distributed like alms to destitute beggars, or the occasional hand-me-down pieces of clothing generously shed by a self-righteous New Yorker bartering a used jacket for a hastily appeased upheaval of conscience disturbing one night's sleep, or the ubiquitous Hershey bar, I never experienced your presence. You had no intention of receiving me in your bosom. Just as you failed to find room in your vast lands or in your tiny stony hearts for the damned cargo of the *St. Louis*, you opened your door wide enough to allow only a trickle of homeless strugglers into the sunshine of your wealth.

"You lied to me! You told callous lies to an eight-year-old who had to scrape together the energy to believe in you, to feel enthusiastic about you, to trust you, to see in you the embodiment of the kingdom of light! You never cared whether or not I lived, you didn't waste one of your precious cents, one of your brave soldiers just to come to rescue me from the claws of that dark coal-storage room threatening to bury me alive under the weight of one of *your* bombs. You took three years to make the journey of one day. You allowed the live incineration of my little cousins in the hateful Ukraine, and you didn't come. You allowed the murder of my entire family in efficient death camps, and you still didn't come. You allowed the enslavement of my father and the loss of his sight. And you were still not coming. You watched the agony of my mother in the clutches of typhus in Bergen Belsen, and you were not moved to come. You watched the brute rip my flesh to shreds but that didn't speed your steps. So what is this shameless bragging about the price you paid for survival? If humanity paid a high price for it, then you are not included in the ranks of the human.

"While you basked in the comfort of your inviolate land, you found it inconvenient to put an end to the industrial murder of my people in Auschwitz. While your luxurious trains rushed you effortlessly to seaside resorts, you found it inconvenient to blow up the tracks ushering millions jammed into cattle-cars for torment and massacre. While men you elected chose not to save the lives of ten thousand Jewish orphans in the name of your family-oriented history, one million children were robbed of their right to blossom into maturity. So where is the logic, where is the authority, where is the truth that allows you to make this counterfeit use of the plural? 'We' don't exist, and never did when the antecedents were intended to include Jews. I resent this perversion of language put to the despicable task of covering up your shameful failure to give proof of your commitment to your own humanity. Like so many uninvolved spectators, you watched the air get more and more saturated with ashes where communities used to flourish.

"You almost succeeded. For years this face didn't materialize before my eyes when I entered into your presence. The other, the one not born by human mother but prefabricated by the same professionals who promote the virtues of soap and beer suds, dominated the screen. I was disturbed by the amorphous malaise each and every time we met. It took years and years of stubborn determination to unearth the source of dissonance. But paying close attention to your deeds as well as to your words bore its bitter fruit: you present one face to the world to safeguard the other. Your speech bleeds so that your conscience can remain inviolate. Your hands wave toward the wretched who need your powerful support so that in the privacy of your communities you can pat yourself on your own shoulders for a gallant humanitarian comportment that is not any more real than the reasons you invented for your shameless passivity.

"You made a crucial mistake in creating the mask. You counted on our numbness to last forever. You banked on the heavy fog that settled into the victim's heart never lifting from the survivor's spirit. You wagered on that silence to blanket our existence from our liberation to the grave. You never expected that some of the ambulant cadavers would one day start asking questions again.

"One of the cursed bequests of the night has been a faithful companion—from the ghetto, to the awesome surf of California, to the vast frozen expanses of insipid Ontario: my lack of trust in people who pose as benefactors. This burden prods me at all times to question, to ferret out the flaw in exalted speeches. You have fallen prey to this obsession. I curse the night for this destructive inheritance, just as I curse you for proving it useful and necessary.

"Know that in my heart you are a murderer's accomplice. Though you kept at a distance from the barbed wires so that the executioner's hand could never be mistaken for yours, you are as guilty as if your fingers were inseparably intertwined with his. When the savage devours human flesh by the million, and you wield pens, typewriters, and printing presses as your most involved weapons against Zyklon B, you, too, are accountable for an act of mass murder. When you aim your camera at the victim rather than aiming your gun at the slaughterer, you are an inextricable partner in murder. There are times when only the roar of bomber planes will be heard by the murderers. He who silences that roar is a murderer in deed. So you see, there is no such thing as being an uninvolved spectator. There are only different types of participants. In the drama that unfolds on the stage the spectators in the audience play the indispensable role of active audience. In the tragedy that ended on a stage littered with six million cadavers, it was the audience's commitment to life to prevent the bloodshed. By failing to risk a fall into the pit, you stained your hands forever with my blood. By making a mockery of my survival with pernicious lies you lost the right to the respect owed only to the innocent and the just.

"My mother was never your comrade. Your head, bent in sorrow and mourning, was but another pose among the many you sport to gain admirers for your counterfeit virtue. Your humanity is subject to relentless scrutiny: anyone piously claiming that the death of harmless men, women, and children was not in vain fails the test of moral qualifications for membership in good standing. If only one child dies for the sake of teaching a lesson to generations to come, we are in the face of a senseless murder. Such a lesson is not worth learning at such a price. But as long as 'victor' continues to mean 'just' we can expect that such a wasteful version of pedagogy will prevail.

"So don't masquerade behind the pompous face of the hero. You saved lives not out of a genuine movement of heart but out of strategic and economic contingencies. Let's speak the clear language of naked truth, for once. You have conquered the kingdom of night. It doesn't earn you the title of 'just'. It bestows upon you the awesome responsibility to account for not having done it sooner. In the crassest and the most sincere words, I say what your lips will never utter: saving Jews, millions of them, was not worth the effort to enter into war. To save markets was much more worthy of your attention. What do you know, then, about justice and human rights? Do they include the Jew or are we forever relegated to the rank of the stranger, the intrusive visitor, the *other* upon whom you can project with impunity all that you hate about yourself?

"Our defeat was not valiant. There is nothing valiant about having to endure the thrust of the rapist, the theft of my mother's life, the extinction of the light in my father's eyes. It's not a victory for humanity that I have emerged alive from that abyss. On the contrary, it is an ignominious shame, it is an indictment of all who perpetrated these evils as well as of those who failed to prevent it. Your victory rescued the shreds of what was, only three years prior, a thriving community of peaceful Jews. Your victory is the tragic memento of all those lives you failed to save.

"These are harsh words, words devoid of any make-believe generosity, any respect for the embarrassment they may cause or for the blemish they expose on your traditionally immaculate physiognomy. They don't contain even a hint of gratitude for saving my miserable skin. Damn you, you owed it to me to save me! I was a child in the merciless grip of giants. You, the king of free men, owed it to me to come to my rescue. That, too, is part of the tacit pact you so frivolously flaunt under the abstract packaging of terms like 'humanity' and 'brotherhood'. If you are not your younger brother's keeper, in what way do you qualify for the title of man? No, I am no more thankful to you for the oblique way in which you opened the gates of hell than you are to me for pointing my accusing finger at your cleverly disguised face. You have never included me in your private community. For that I *am* grateful. Its seduction would have robbed me of the clarity required to confront you today."

"Alas, I am weighed down with the memory of another one of your portraits. This one is so much more painful to carry around wherever my quest takes me, because this face resembles mine. He answers to a name not unlike mine. He, too, worships the God of Israel. He is one of your most diabolical identities: he is a kind of New World Jew!

"Disheartened by the futility of hiding from guilty memories, there came a moment in the struggle to escape them when despair was overwhelmed by insistent promises, seductive offers. They allowed glimpses at a world seemingly untouched by the weight of jackboots, where the air had never been punctuated by machine-gun bullets. They afforded peeks at a community at peace with its own past, confident in its present. Most of all, by means of a clever sleight of hand impossible without my participation, I was mesmerized by a treacherous mirage: you presented the face of unconditional brotherly love. Jews live in the invigorating sunshine of California, in majestically soaring skyscrapers in the heart of New York City, even in ardent rural hearths on the endless plains. How could I resist the call of a shadowless sky? How could I not succumb to the charm of a land without ashes? How could I not run to embrace you, you who were holding in both hands the blueprints for a new life?

"With hesitant feet, I stepped onto the planks of the massive ship that promised to whisk me to the finer shore where you would be waiting to bestow upon me the map to those New World marvels. They were magical treasures endowed with mystical powers able to coax me away from the silent company I had been keeping for nearly twenty-five years. I waved a guilt-ridden farewell to the earth that shelters the records of the nocturnal horror. With ocean winds already tugging at my coat tails, I turned my back on the graveless cemetery.

"My heart was glittering for the first time ever. That *Atlantic Queen* could have been sailing toward the Garden and I wouldn't have been more firmly in the possession of hope.

"And yet. As if a benevolent guardian angel had been trying to alert me to the spurious nature of your earth-bound Eden, to pierce the dangerously thin veneer of my trusting euphoria, restless waters disturbed night and day the journey that led me to your threshold. My heart was neither able nor willing to heed the upheaval of my entrails. Wrapped in a thick mantle of fog, your welcoming face wasn't radiating with a hospitable smile. On the contrary, the harshly chiselled contour of your jaws, your impersonally thin lips uttering commands instead of exuberant words ushering me into the warmth of your home, confused me. I began to suspect a harmless error, an innocent quid pro quo.

"But then I saw your eyes.

"The grey February mist petrified me. I wanted to stop my blood, I wanted to arrest my duped heart. Those eyes! Those chilling, lifeless blue eyes! I had known them all my years spent in the pit. Those eyes stabbed me with detached indifference. They saw in me the outsider, the stranger, no, not even that, the *Ausländer*! In the whirlwind of a moment, I felt the unequivocal metamorphosis from cherished visitor to superfluous object, from the much-expected new member of your community to the bothersome, intrusive *other*.

"Your voice snapped my name aloud with the brisk violence of a horse whip.

"I nodded from the depth of an incredulously sinking heart. This is not the Land of the Free; I've been duped! This is but another abyss! Let me out, I want to scurry back to the belly of the ship to hide from the blades of these steel eyes.

"'How much money do you have?' came another crack of the frozen whip. The inclement retrieval system of my memory thrust into my awareness the image of the rapacious wooden bins on Klauzal Square initiating us into the world of the ghetto. No, this is a cruel practical joke! Or a ritual whose meaning escapes me. Any second now the banal face of evil will be replaced with a large crowd of jubilant welcomers yelling an enthusiastic 'surprise!'

"I looked around as if hoping to spot some sign of another reality.

"'How much money do you have?' You sounded more impatient. Your raw voice conveyed unequivocal urgency. I just stood in complete silence. Beyond the shocking novelty of my arrival to the New World, the only word I understood was 'money'. Not feeling securely grounded to this confusing soil, I grumbled hastily with a shrug of my shoulders:

"'*Je ne vous comprends pas, je ne parle pas anglais.*'

"An impatient rictus indicated to me your displeasure with my response.

"'*Hast du Geld?*' Your next probe slapped me with a reality that I had sought to abandon upon setting out on my journey. No, anything but that! Don't tell me that the language of evil is still the tongue that dominates under the mask of the more palatable, more trustworthy

English? I never wanted to hear the speech of the torturer again, and yet, he is my host! No, this can't be! I expected to be received by a gentle, effusively warm New World Jew, not by this unmistakable twin of a Nazi interrogator. Or could it be that evil had triumphed even more thoroughly on this shore of the waters than on our truly dark continent? Did Jews take on the persona of the torturer without even knowing it? This would be the ultimate victory of the house-painter.

"I don't want to believe my ears, this Jew born of the same ancestry as I couldn't be my usher into the diabolical realm of pain unveiled by a hastily dissipated mirage. What of the heart-warming letters promising me a life enriched by friendship, togetherness, membership on equal footing? What of the exalted offers of scholarships, opportunities to thrive limited only by biologic endowment and my determination? What of the sweet oaths attesting to spiritually and culturally rich communities animated by the vigour of commitment to the bearers of the torch from beyond the darkness? Are they not any more real than the showers, the relocations to Eastern communities, the postcards heralding good health and impeccably humane treatment? If this is what survived of the Jew in this modern-day Canaan, I'd rather take my life with my own hands, to toss it in the face of the despicably mocking God before offering my support to the Other committed to toppling Him in the heart of His own creation. Could it be that He can't rest without inventing new forms of inflicting horror? Could it be that as soon as some succeed in piercing the secret of His underworld, He opens the gates disclosing a new depth, one which needs a further effort in order to rise above its unknown pits? Just how many dragons can one ordinary man be expected to slay? Just how much slaying must one perform before becoming a dragon?

"But wait, I feel a new flame inside me. A new light, a new warmth; the blood is flowing again. The grey drizzle is replaced with a red flow. I am not afraid of you, I whisper to myself, I am strong, you have no power over me. Should you reach for my life, I'll rip your stomach out of your banal existence, I'll ventilate your dark viscera in the lofty air of the New World before enduring once more your weight crushing my life. I have emerged from the stupor in which pain kept me prisoner for all those years. Pain can also invigorate a violated body. The tortured has nothing to fear, he has seen the ugliest face there is. He has defeated the cruelty of torture by keeping its taste in instant readiness next to his salivary glands.

"I match your annoyed, impatient gaze. From the deepest depth of my presence I summon the grizzliest chill onto my face, into my myopic eyes:

"'*Ne me parlez pas en allemand, c'est la langue de la mort et moi, je suis venu en Amérique pour vivre. Engagez-moi en silence, si vous voulez, mais pas en allemand. Les mots me parviennent mais je ne leur permets pas de signifier.*'

"You held my gaze, visible anger hardening your already rigid facial muscles. But I knew that I had derouted your aggressive thrust. I was tired from the five-day struggle with the restless waters of the February ocean; the unexpected turn that my arrival to the Land of a Thousand Dreams took drained whatever little vigour I had left. And yet, I have never felt so mighty. Indeed, I began to pierce the fundamental mystery of the New World: people were perhaps just as evil as they were in the most cursed corner of the moribund old order, but the vast land secured sufficient space for anyone who wished to confront others eye to eye and not from the humble posture of one's knees. The air seemed saturated with the undrainable wealth of courage able to transform the meekest victim into a mighty pioneer. The impetus had to come from within, springing from an endless commitment to one's life. On that February morning in the mist-clad pier of New York City I found in my body that generous source.

"You took off your dark grey hat. For the first time, you looked down, your confused fingers scratching your uncovered head. You were obviously discomfited. Then, with a brusque energy signalling an upsurge of arrogant impatience, you muttered: 'Oh, shit!' You replaced your sad hat on your head, and with one crisp flick of your bony finger you ordered me to follow you.

"We didn't speak again.

"You didn't even care to walk by my side as we penetrated the hustle of this metropolis I had so much longed to explore. You frayed the way amid the rushing flow of hurried humanity much as an ice-cutter clears the water of any obstacle threatening to impede its willful passage. I had a hard time keeping up with your pace and trying to soak up glimpses of this extraordinary land. In fact I remember nothing, I saw nothing. Pressing through the streets at that mechanical pace robbed my eyes of any target other than your rigid back.

"You had navigated me through a murky sea of offices, some obviously Jewish, some obviously not. In each encounter with a man or a woman behind a desk, your disdain for me was apparent. In the reality which you and the bureaucrats of New York were jointly constructing of my identity, my essence as a newly landed member in your midst was brilliantly clear: another mouth to feed, another body on the employment lines, another messenger from the world of void. You all saw in me another morbidly dishonest attempt to milk the generous nipples of the great American cow, another hand aiming to hold onto the tail of the Golden Calf. Little people with pebble hearts, you saw nothing in me but the poor Devil making an absurd appearance in the Land of Enchantment with a small suitcase. Had you known that it contained only books, and nothing but literary works, your spite would have ballooned to even more impressive dimensions. You looked so well fed, so comfortably clad, your facial skin so free of the furrows of endless pain, your eyes so unencumbered with the reflection of an ashen sky! Of course you had no affinity with this gloomy bearer of tales. You had spent twenty-five years in the cool shade of a well-reconstituted conscience: why would you want to endure a presence that would rattle an otherwise unshakeable edifice?

"But why did you bother to lure me into the bosom of your suburbs, into the warmth of your circle, into the light of your study rooms, into the heart of your life? Why take the risk of contamination, of sleepless nights spent creating plausible defences to my inevitably probing inquiries about your silence? Why invite me to spoil the contemplation of your innocence and generosity (to which massive cheques endorsed to Israeli bonds pay loud tribute every year)? Is this part of the ancestral curse of never allowing yourself the luxury of going through a perfect day without enduring a paradox? Is a stirred-up night a monument to the vitality of conscience? Do you need me to provide a point of contrast against which to measure the length of the road you have conquered—from the flatness of Nebraska to the glittering heights of Beverly Hills or the enchantment of Forest Hills? What do you want from me?

"We spent that endless day in a version of togetherness characteristic of spouses who, for decades, have had nothing to share but the curse of an ancient oath. We saw the setting sun from an airport teeming with humanity. Your mandate was to deliver me to the airliner, which would take me to the end of the road, Berkeley, California, and free you from further contact with me.

"I had already reconciled myself to the new reality. You were not my New World brother, you were my silent guide into a life I had imagined differently. I no longer expected any interest in who I was. You gave me a day from your life; I thought that was grounds for some sharing to mark the crossing of two lives. I was naïve: what immortalized my presence in your life was a cheque rewarding you for your endurance and patience. I was not a presence. I was an assignment. It took an apprenticeship of several months for me to comprehend this dubious but indispensable wisdom.

"And yet, you didn't leave me shrouded in tacit spite. Just as I was about to sit down in the departure lounge, to rest until boarding time, you grabbed my arm just a little harder than was necessary to attract my attention. You placed your face close to mine, your chilly eyes agitated with some emotion I couldn't identify. You had come alive. Then you started to speak to me—in sometimes a halting, sometimes a pressed manner—as if to say: 'I don't know how to say this but I want to say it before it's too late.' Owing to my linguistic ignorance, I didn't understand your words. But the grip on my arm, that varied from a light touch just securing the contact you obviously sought to the strangulation of a vice intended for total submission of the object, was quite eloquent. Yes, indeed, you harboured some strong responses to me that February day in 1959. Your breathing was so shallow that your delivery trickled to a whisper. You must have needed to vomit out the contents of your soul to rid yourself of me, and maybe, just maybe, a part of you, a part you didn't really want present in your everyday existence. Perhaps you wanted me to take it to the other end of the continent—to let it float out with the mist of the Pacific.

"While the meaning of your words has never penetrated my consciousness, their taste has become familiar. Based on that unsavoury knowledge, I have concluded that your parting soliloquy was the expression of a hastily pieced together apology for the person you had become while the rest of us searched the walls of the night for a hidden road to your heart. Perhaps you were saying something like:

"'Don't condemn me. We are not worse than you or anyone else. In fact, we have never soiled our hands with unnecessarily shed blood. You resent me for my obvious lack of altruism, for my commitment only to my own family. You line me up against the wall with the murderer for not having rushed to your rescue. What you have suffered must have blinded you to the reality of other lives. The world cannot stop in every household because tragedy is flowing in red river beds ten thousand miles from the pressing concerns of my wife, the whooping cough of my son, or the merciless expectations of my bank. I know those are mere trivialities to you when you are nose to nose with the torturer. But how far must I deny the oath I took to my bride, to sustain and to honour her, in order to live up to the expectations of every devil struggling for another breath before hell swallows him up? How often do I have to risk the life I owe to the Creator so that a stranger can thrive in the village next to my foreign grave? Is it a just brother who demands that I die with him if I can't save him? Must I rush into the uniform of this land, which blessed me with its horn of plenty under a free sky, to right the wrongs of anciently evil people whose company my ancestors left in disgust and in terror? Didn't their gesture of farewell to the reign of evil exempt me from any bond with those who chose to remain under the yoke of the torturer?

"'My words must sound cruel to you in their assertion of my moral right to safeguard the integrity of my home, my own life. Had I been there during the era of oppression, I would now be standing in your shoes pointing an accusing finger at the proponent of lukewarm excuses for allowing the slaughter of my people.

"'I am never going to quarrel with your justified anger and distrust of me and the rest of American Jewry. Will *you* reciprocate with a similar movement of heart in respect of *our* daily reality?'

"'*Il y a des moments où le monde entier doit s'arrêter,*' I heard myself articulate out loud, forgetting that I was in the passive company of dozens of strangers waiting for boarding. Some turned toward me. One even addressed me, looking quite solicitous, but I didn't understand him. Those internally projected words cut me to the most sensitive depth. I have not felt as alone for a long, long time as I did in that New York airport surrounded by people who were strangers to me not only because I didn't know them but because they all spoke a language that totally excluded me from their ranks. Vulnerable to pangs of alienation by nature, I became aware of actual physical pain as I imagined your lame justifications. I was not moved by your predicament.

"'No, sir, you do not have the right to sleep in peace while children are being raped, maimed, and massacred only a continent away! And even less if you share with them the bonds of common ancestry, however distant. You trespass over the boundaries of humanity when you limit your humaneness to your own flesh and blood. And even that becomes suspicious: a man who doesn't jump to his feet and rush to the defence of martyred children is likely to remain frozen when his own progeny face the pit. Just where do you draw the line of demarcation? How close does the murderer have to come to your house before you grab the nearest weapon? How can you be so blind as not to see that, when you prevent the murder of a distant man, you are safeguarding yourself, your own future?

"'How can you be living in such isolation from your Jewish brethren that the shriek of their agony doesn't reach your soul? By what right do you continue calling yourself a Jew? When you gather your family for Seder, what do you tell your children about the new meaning of Exodus? How do you do justice to their questions about your part in perpetrating the darkness? Are you so certain of your innocence that you are absolutely free of anguish at the thought of an eventual request for accounting? Or, to the contrary, is there a meticulously hidden spot of self-doubt in your soul at which you wish to take critical peeks in the indirect light of your children's confusion?

"'What do you answer them when they aim inevitable questions at your conscience, questions which accuse more than request information: 'If it is evil to kill, isn't it just as evil to permit murder?' 'What

does distance have to do with evil?' Do you remember the age-old
question: 'Just because we are not in the forest does it mean that
falling trees make no sound?' When humans fall like trees do you
have the right to pretend that it is not happening because you don't
hear the scream, because you don't see the glazed eyes of the victim?

" 'Go back to your suburb, agonize over the invasion of your
backyard by evil crabgrass, tend to the aches and pains of your wife
and children, turn on your radio to regale your soul with the beauty of
music. Then go to your Brotherhood meeting and utter meaningless
words of sympathy and even anger over the cruelty against innocent
Jews and discuss how we can't go on tolerating atrocities in the name
of human solidarity, in the name of the God who chose us all to be His
children. Then go home, turn out the light, and retire for the night
with gratitude in your heart for the fulfillment of all your spiritual
needs.

" 'But don't call yourself my brother! I saw the disdain in your face
when you and your *real* brothers assessed my miserable appearance
in the light of your opulence. I doubt if even you see me as wholly
human. After all, I carry in my bag and on my back all my earthly
belongings, my family history, the ordeal of a nearly extinct people. A
grown man without a piece of earth to call his own, without a hand to
hold, without a family to gather! Just what gives me the audacity to
claim full membership in your private club? Right? How do I have
the gall to come to this land, the land made to flourish with your tax
dollars, with one meagre suitcase and demand to be accepted as one of
you? Right? I am nothing more than a necessary blemish on the
otherwise perfect portrait of your achievements. If it weren't for the
wretched like me, there would not exist a counterpoint to your success
by which to measure your outstanding accomplishments. I am the
black shadow in your white paradise. I am the living memento of how
tragic life can be. Elsewhere.

" 'You need me to come over for dinner once a year so that when I
leave the opulence of your home, you can make didactic object lessons
to your naïve family: 'Appreciate the life I offer you. Think, you could
have been a poor devil like him. Stop rocking my boat because you
may fall into the waves of boiling waters that scathed *his* heart. How

would you like to have to spend the repast of a High Holiday on loan to a real human community, out of charity for the wretched? Just remember him the next time you feel dissatisfied with your life. You could have had his. Praise the Lord for who you are, thank me for what you have got.'

"'Yes, I condemn you for the version of solidarity with which you and your neighbours entertain each other, convince each other of your moral integrity. No, I don't resent you for your lack of altruism. I resent you for your unwillingness to see that when you let me suffer, you are soiling, you are desecrating, your home as much as you permit the destruction of mine: you not only rob me of a future free of ashes but you abscond with the innocence of your own children.

"'I want you to know that I have proffered these same indicting words to my very own torturer. Draw your conclusion from this dubious company. No, what I have suffered didn't blind my eyes to the reality of your life. You blinded yourself when you chose to delineate it in such a myopic way that what happens on the other side of your picket fence is so blurred that it no longer seems to concern you. Would you worry if a neighbour's house were on fire? Would you think, "I'd better lend a hand to extinguish the flames or else the fire may spread to my own home?" Does this strike any chord at all? Would you have similar thoughts if the fire were two blocks away? What's the difference? If you can't find it, follow the track that begins with your tragic lack of human perspective. Have you ever done anything on the strength of a movement of heart leading to "I have to get out and help, I just can't live with the knowledge that someone in my community is facing a tragic demise?" If you have, what is the difference between your neighbour's plight and mine? What's the difference between him and me? Yes, the world *must* stop in every household while thousands are being massacred in any corner of the globe! That's our only hope to survive, to really survive. Every time a people is being slaughtered wholesale, we reinforce our own will-ingness not just to do evil but to become thoroughly evil.

"'I am not exempt from this solemn warning. My hands have bloodstains that will blacken my horizon for the rest of my days. Worse: my children will inherit them along with the tendency to baldness and myopia, and the talent for music and foreign languages. With each massacre the spectator's genetic make-up is altered. Until one day it will be impossible to distinguish between murderer and spectator. The foundations of the bridge between them are already laid, the road to existential evil is nearly completed. You have contributed more than an ordinary share to its completion.

"'I am not better than you are in this respect. But I am more honest. Twenty-five years ago, you failed to see the road from your door to Auschwitz, to Bergen Belsen, to Budapest. Today you are still lost in the same dark labyrinth. So dark that it doesn't even occur to you to look for your heart. Mine was scorched by the flames. I know how much of it is charred, how much of it still beats. I know when I am guilty of passive massacre. The image of all the murdered children in South-east Asia, in Africa, in South America, is burning in my viscera with such heat that often I feel incinerated. If I were produced before a tribunal of war crimes and charged with mass murder, I would plead "guilty".

"'You stupid, dishonest fool, we are *always* guilty. The innocent are always massacred, they are never here to plead "not guilty"! Only distances and colours change, the destruction goes on interrupted only by a change of scenery. But you have constructed a wall so high around your heart that you can't feel even its own beat. Your tongue has learned only words of wishy-washy apologies. Mine speaks with the authority of the guilty, for only he knows what he has really done and how much remorse he feels. And this is what digs the trench between you and me so wide that we can hardly even hear one another: you are stubborn in your counterfeit innocence and I can never stop feeling responsible. Your sleep is never interrupted either by memories of another version of life or by the tremors of a conscience forever jolted out of its innocence. I, on the other hand, always remain awake for fear of encountering my horrible old acquaintances or of making new ones.

"'You ask me if you must break the oath you swore to the companion of your life. I am not in a position to make such decisions for you. As for myself, shutting my eyes and ears to the plight of a child in the strangle-hold of an assassin would mean that I allowed—

no, that I invited—the flames of evil into a yet untouched corner of my soul. As the vital area is shrinking, the less I have left with which to sustain and honour myself, let alone my bride. If she wanted to bind me to her anguish on the lap of safety, I would have to tolerate my guilt for the bad choice I had made in the selection of a mate. If she didn't stand by my side in the struggle to save the children, my loneliness would be complete, equalling the solitude of the grave. Each time I fail to risk my life for the sake of a child, it loses a bit of its value. When I have lived long enough to have totally devalued my life, it will be time to say farewell to it. I'd rather leave my children as orphans than force them to endure the darkness of an existence hiding from its own guilt. These are rules by which I attempt to conduct the course of my journey in the company of men. I don't have the arrogance to prescribe them, to coerce them upon you. But, in exchange, don't expect me to stamp your forehead with the fraternal kiss of love or to warm your heart with an all-accepting embrace. You chose not to hear your brother's scream, you chose to see in him a stranger, you chose to draw the frontiers of humanity where your backyard ends. As far as I am concerned you can continue to live in that Lilliputian world animated by a heart proportionate to its horizons. Just don't expect me to bleed with sympathy and compassion for your dilemma.

"'And yet, you are a Jew! This sad realization distresses me with the burden of a life lost, with the awe before a murdered brother. Yes, looking at you, I see endless lengths of barbed wires encircling the globe, I smell decomposing lives again howling on the coat tails of millions whose ashes have just cooled off. Looking at the tense harshness in your jaws, I see bayonets again followed by faceless men in uniform. A man without doubt has no face. A faceless man cannot see the face of the victim. A man who can't see the face of his victim is forever the enemy of men.

"'And yet, you are a Jew....

"'And yet, you are a man....

"'But so was the German *Bürger* who nailed his gaze to the indifferent asphalt while his own son deported the family doctor who had helped his mother give life to him. And so was the Polish peasant who swallowed three guiltless meals a day in the shadow of the chimney stack at Oświęcim with his taste buds riveted on the flavour of the world-famous Cracow ham. It was thus natural for him to attest to his innocent ignorance of horrors committed in his midst.

"'Or maybe you are not really a Jew.... No matter. In either case I want to stay away from your company. I don't trust you any more than I would trust a rabid dog. Don't you see the link that binds your passivity to the selective blindness of the German or of the citizen of the cursed Polish village? Don't you know that your choice of willful detachment not only amounts to a tacit permission to perpetuate the carnage but also to the justification of starting new ones? Don't you see that turning your gaze inward was an eloquent statement of acquiescence? Don't you see that your all-exclusive concern for continuing business as usual could be read as an invitation to continue the industrial-scale murder *in your behalf?* No wonder I see you more and more clearly as a murderer and less and less willingly as a spectator caught in an absurd dilemma coined by evil. I want to leave your company now and I never want to see you again.'

"I closed my eyes to you and kept them closed hoping that the dark silence would efface the record of our meeting from my nascent career in the new world.

"But I felt a tug at my arm sending electric shock waves to my bowels and below. You were there, before me, insistent, your eyes narrowing to two slits beyond which tiny flames of anger were raging. Your stone-like jaws were even tighter—as if you were gathering energy in them for a colossal bite. Your hand held me with a cramp even you didn't seem to be able to undo.

"'How dare you sit in judgement over me, you sanctimonious little parasite! How dare you equate me with the monster that sucked the blood of millions? How dare you draw for me the confines of my conscience? You are very clever, but I see through your preaching pseudo-humanism. You refuse to tell me what would be right for me to do, but you accept as morally admissible only your own comportment, thereby expelling me from the rank of decent people. I did what I did not out of a snivelling coward's fear but according to the world's most powerful nation's interpretation of right and wrong, feasible and unfeasible. If rescuing you had meant the annihilation of six million and one Americans and their allies, it would have been morally impermissible to get involved. If the men in whose wisdom we trusted, by electing them to their high offices, chose to descend upon the Nazi vulture when they did, then they did intervene at the right time. *Right* not in relation to your plight, but according to our chances of decapitating the monster, not just wounding it.

"'Who the hell are you to tell me that my heart was not filled with indescribably bitter pain at learning the truth about the destruction of our people? I, too, had lost in that pit a whole history; after all, where do you think my roots are, in Long Island? How dare you blacken my face in front of my children! They have learned from me the respect for human life, but they have also learned a respect for the order of the land of which we are proud citizens. You drag your pitiful, nomadic bag from one hospitable land to the next and will never know the fulfillment of living in a country in which your vote is of equal weight to that of a Presbyterian or a Catholic. Our address is not marked with the Star of David. My children's future is determined by their own ambition. You can't know the security of being a free citizen in our land. Before I sacrifice all this for the martyr's lot, before I orphan my children, I'd seek aid and asylum in a mental institution. And if you point your condemning finger at me for that, you are just as arrogant, just as cruel as the very people from which you are seeking refuge in this vast country of ours.

"'I know that your plight has embittered you, that it has taught you a language and a demeanour without which you couldn't be here today. But look around, listen and look around: you are in an entirely foreign land. We speak the idiom of tolerance and freedom, we respect our neighbour's right to be different from us. Discard the bile that deadens your heart and poisons your tongue. You'd better learn today: this is a land populated by proud citizens who feel and act like me. We have only a reflected knowledge of your shadow world. If you want to find peace and respect, you will start afresh. And that means focusing on today with occasional glances at the past to commemorate our fathers and mothers but never wallowing, never soiling the purity of the moment. Your tales of terror are yours forever: don't flaunt them. Your judgements smell of a rotting continent: chuck them in the garbage prior to boarding the aircraft. Lighten its burden and yours. If you want to achieve full membership in our society you must stop seeing in every man and woman over forty-five a moral monster. You have a choice between importing your private hell and learning that ours is a language free of guilt. Above all, learn that your personal history does not entitle you to moral superiority. Surviving doesn't earn you the distinguished medal of "righteous man". And neither do I deserve condemnation for having acted on a moment's meaning indigenous to our history. Well, good luck to you in America! You'll need it!'

"You released my arm, numbed by the violence of your anger, and vanished from my vision as if you had never been near me. Obviously, you weren't expecting an answer. Pity. For I would have liked to thank you for the integrity of your feelings, for trusting me enough to let down the mask, even if only to unleash a torrent of rage at me. I would much rather endure your ire than your whining, sneaky request for absolution. And yet...and yet, I would have liked to tell you how much you frightened me by your blind submission to the 'wisdom' of your elected officials, as if they weren't men just like you, just like me. I would have liked to point out the striking similarity of your words to the murderer's self-righteous 'not-guilty' plea on grounds of patriotic fervour. I wanted to call your attention to those moments when we all must act on our private consciences freed from nationalistic or ethnic constraints. For conscience is a most trust-worthy adviser, concerned with us as unique human beings yet aware of our sameness in terms of the basic rights guaranteed by our human birth. I would have liked to thank you for your valuable advice concerning my initiation into the New World. You were right in warning me about my arrogance, but I would have liked to share with you that it was not a haughty survivor's speech that you heard but that of a bitter, skeptical victim. Finally, I would have liked to explain that what you mistook for a victim's moral superiority was really a survivor's indignation and pain. It would have been better if the two of us could have parted as potential friends rather than as disapprov-ing antagonists.

"There is so much we could have learned from one another! And yet, how could I *not* tell you that I see in your blind nationalism a New World version of a ghetto Jew's stance: instead of huddling in self-imposed ghettos or *shtetl*s, you assimilate out of gratitude for not being persecuted. Or could it be that you weren't persecuted *because* you abdicated so much of your Judaic culture that you remoulded your persona to have no trace of Jewish vulnerability to the mystical attraction to paradoxical existence, paradoxical reasoning?

"On further reflection, though, you *are* my enemy. As a pre-condition of entrance into your society, you wanted me to disown the person I have become, not out of choice, but out of necessity. If I failed to do so, you'd be among those who would brand me as an undesirable horror monger, polluting the spurious purity of this continent's conscience. No, I don't want any commonality with you. But I would have liked to have a chance to tell you all this."

"Seven months later my wish was granted. Though your face was clad in a somewhat different mask, I recognized your harsh voice, pelting out guttural words uttered from a vacant space where most of us shelter a vulnerable heart. That crisp, unequivocal delivery trained to order rather than to invite, to interrogate rather than to greet, can't be masked. I was not happy to meet you again.

"I had endured long months of solitude. Each day built on the loneliness of the preceding one, imprisoning me in the depths of isolation. The New World seemed new only by chronological comparison to the one I had left on the other shore. I maintained my existence on a diet of nostalgic day-dreams that resulted in inevitable comparisons and ill-fated judgements. Throwing myself at the one escape that never failed me—work—I studied with an obsessive fervour. I learned English quickly. Whereas in the process of acquiring an intimate knowledge of French I discovered the intricate soul and impeccable creativity of an awesome nation, in learning English I found only superficial commonplaces, vulgar truths, and an exemplary predilection for hypocrisy as the main social cement. Later I learned the absurdity of such a self-indulgent smoke screen. Behind it I hid my fear of a nation of blond giants self-assuredly playing in the endless sunshine of California. The more I became familiar with this playful generation of young Americans, the lonelier I felt. My puny body had not been nurtured on a shadowless beach. On the contrary, it had been squelched by the shadows of a sunless basement existence. While they romped naked in their exuberance, exhibiting flawless expanses of skin, I hid deeper and deeper in unlit places where my solitude was guaranteed.

"Then came the first eve of Yom Kippur in my adoptive land. I had not entered a synagogue since the memorable day before my Bar Mitzvah, when, coming home from my last lesson preparing me for the Big Day, I discovered a tombstone in the temple garden erected to the memory of 5,000 Jews murdered in the ghetto. I was so overwhelmed with shame and fear that I immediately swore never again to set foot in a synagogue, never again to be a Jew. And I kept the first part of my sad wager. The latter was, of course, out of my reach. On this late September day, ten years later, tormented by my loneliness as a Berkeley student, I stumbled onto an unknown need: 'I want to go to Yom Kippur services, I want to say a prayer for my mother.' It hit me with its abrupt appearance as much as with its relentless stubbornness. 'I must find a temple.' To my great surprise, on my way toward the centre of town, I discovered that I lived two blocks from a congregation, directly on my way to campus. I had been walking in front of that temple for months without noticing it. 'How can a synagogue blend into a cluster of residences?' I wondered. This was my first contact with casual Californian Reform Judaism. It aroused my curiosity and thus the load of anxiety grew lighter. The less formal the religious practice, the less I'll have to account for the ten-year hiatus. The less I feel gagged by guilt, the more probable that the prayer will flow from my heart.

"Then I met you again. You were standing by the door of this large family residence converted into a sanctuary. You stood inside, in shirt sleeves, with your head uncovered! My confusion and curiosity increased as I approached the door. Inside, I saw dozens of worshippers all with naked heads, women and men together, children running around on tricycles, a guitar-playing young rabbi in front of the Ark. Before entering, with an atavistic gesture, I covered my head.

"'Your ticket, please,' you said, looking at me with curiosity.

"'Ticket? Do you need a ticket to come to pray on Yom Kippur? Isn't being Jewish sufficient condition to gain admission to the sanctuary?'

"Your reply slapped me with its dry impersonal anger:

"'Don't be funny, boy, today's not the day. Now, you want to come in or not? If you do, show me your ticket. If you don't have a ticket, you can buy one. So what'll it be?'

"I couldn't believe what I had heard. But then I recognized the horse-whip quality of your voice. I flashed back to New York: '*Hast du Geld?*' and I was sure of your identity. But this was not the right time. I wanted to lose myself in the warm tears of the traditional prayer for one's lost loved ones. I hadn't felt that urge since the birth of shame in me. Now I didn't want to lose the feeling that could free me from that self-inflicted wound.

"'Please, let me in, I'm a student at Cal, I've just recently come to this country, I have hardly enough money to eat and pay rent. Today *is* Yom Kippur, can't I pray for my mother?'

"With a shrug you pushed me aside.

"'Don't you have ears, boy? You can't just want to come in and not pay on a High Holiday. Who do you think you're kidding? I know you wise guys! You think U.C. students can just walk in without paying like the rest of us? Now pay or beat it, it's twenty-five dollars for the Holidays.'

"Twenty-five dollars! That's two week's rent, almost a month's food! For the privilege of praying in the company of people who make a business of praying, of people who push and shove one another on Yom Kippur, the Day of Atonement! I was overwhelmed with that old shame again, but I quickly realized from the hard stumping of my heart that, this time, I was possessed by rage and not shame. I looked you in the face to find the centre of your eyes so that you could see clearly the full expression of my fury. There they were again, those lifeless, uninvolved blue eyes. One glance at them and I knew that you had nothing against me personally. You were uninvolved. You had been told to check tickets and you did so with greater devotion than you probably had when you prayed. I have seen this self-effacing submission to duty before. But never at the threshold of a temple on Yom Kippur. 'Another triumph for Hitler' flashed through my mind. However shamefully cowering Jews may have been, the gates of the *shul* were always wide open in Budapest to anyone who desired to enter. The soul of the congregation reached all the way to the street in front, travelled as much by busy Gentiles as by pious Jews.

"Where was *your* soul that September day? Was it assimilated like the rest of the congregants, who looked more like Methodists or Presbyterians than Jews to me? I wanted to hate with fervour that evening. 'But I can't hate you,' I thought with discouragement, 'a Jew must never hate another Jew, that would be anti-Semitism.' I didn't want to succumb to the same evil atraction that robbed you of your spirit, replacing it with the idolatry of assimilation. Your pitiful little synagogue was camouflaged to fit in without attracting attention. Our synagogues in Europe were proud edifices surrounded by gardens or elevated on pedestals to rise above ordinary buildings. This tiny sanctuary cowered, surrounded by tall hedges and luxuriant bushes, with a minuscule sign on the gate. No wonder I hadn't noticed it before. One had to really look for a temple to find this one! It 'fits in'. Mostly it fits in with the need of the Jews to blend in as lizards disappear into the foliage. And you reminded me of a lizard that day.

"'I don't have twenty-five dollars, I don't have five dollars, and I want to pray for my mother's soul. She was killed by the Nazis in Bergen Belsen; surely that entitles her to the prayer of her son on Yom Kippur, doesn't it?'

"'I don't care if your mother is the Prime Minister of Israel, no one goes in without paying, can't you understand that, jerk? Now beat it, you've tried my patience long enough. Beat it, or you'll learn a lesson they failed to teach you in the ghetto.' And you shoved me again, but this time hard enough for me to lose my equilibrium, physical as well as emotional.

"'You son of a bitch, you are worse than the Nazis, you threaten me, the orphan of a victim of Nazi terror, with violent lessons? You should be ashamed, you fucking anti-Semite, you murderer! I spit on your temple. If this is a congregation of Jews I don't want to be Jewish ever again! You make me sick.'

"The last words escaped my mouth almost choking me with a rush of tears. Yes, there was a lot of anger in my mouth, but the old shame was also rekindled. In Budapest, I inherited shame for my Bar Mitzvah. In Berkeley, I learned a new reason for shame: the cruelty of one Jew toward another. But the explicit threat of finishing the job for which the Nazis ran out of time would have made Hitler's heart smile in awe before his own achievement: a Jew born and raised in California, on the eve of Yom Kippur, threatening to teach a survivor a lesson he hadn't learned in the ghetto! Yes, indeed, Hitler was in your heart that day. And that day, for the first time in my life, you inspired hatred for a Jew in my heart.

"And I spat on your mezuzah.

"'How dare you call yourself a Jew—the same word that you use for the millions killed—while you act at being Jewish as if Judaism were a melodrama. You're Nazis, all of you, the worst Nazis ever, for you started out as Jews. You have turned not only on your humanity, but also on your martyred heritage, on one million Jewish children. If that's what it means to be Jewish in California, I spit on your synagogue, I spit on you. I learned *that* in the ghetto. No one will ever teach me lessons for which the Nazis didn't have the time. You'll have to kill me first.'

"By then I was surrounded by a group of your friends, your sad alter egos, outraged at my outburst, bewildered by my audacity. Two of them picked me up under the arms and carried me into the street as tavern bouncers would eject an impertinent drunk interfering with the patrons' quiet enjoyment of their stupour. Their strong fingers dug deeply into my flesh. 'Here we go again, I'm being violated again, my body is again being handled like meat. They might as well hang me on a meat hook like a side of beef.' In the middle of the street they tossed me on the pavement like a dirty rag.

"'Get lost, bastard, and don't ever show your dirty face around here again; take your ghetto arrogance to Brooklyn.'

"I am indebted to you for this lesson; and I'll never be able to make good on what I owe you. You have taught me how easy it is to hate anyone, no matter whom; you just have to find his Achilles' heel. That day, a bit more disdain, a dash more humiliation, just one more word desecrating my mother's memory and I would have taken arms against you and would have killed you without remorse. Who needs such hideous evil masquerading in the skin of Presbyterian Jews? No, I am being injurious to Presbyterians, they would probably never stoop to throwing one of their brethren into the street for reason of poverty, let alone with such sad credentials. No, you were special, you had walked over the plank that bridges the ever-narrowing gap between spectator and torturer. Your father may have been a passive spectator of Jewish deaths by the millions. You joined the vicious ranks of those who assault Jews. You would have been right at home in Bavaria on *Kristallnacht*! You already highlight your spite and superiority when compared to the Brooklyn Jew faithful to his faith, his ethics, his God. That day you taught me to avoid Reform Jews with the meticulous fervour with which one avoids the plague. That day I fell into the Nazi trap of seeing in your face the identity of countless communities. You planted in my mind and in my soul the seeds of prejudice based on the mythical reality of stereotypes. You stole from my eyes the memory of Jewish individuals and replaced it with the counterfeit portrait of a monstrous hybrid, the anti-Semitic Jew. How can I not hate you for this diabolical trick?

" 'I told you in New York to learn the idiom of the New World. You didn't heed my advice, offered to you free of charge in a land where you don't get anything for nothing. Instead you learned it the most painful way. In America we don't bow our heads before anyone, we need to be strong against subversion. We can't afford to get sucked into the whirlwind of tepid compassion for the victims of yesterday. If we do, we'll be next in line. If you want to be one of us, you must act like one of us. And none of us would beg his way into temple to avoid having to pay. If I didn't have twenty-five dollars, it would never occur to me to rely on charity. I'd rather not go to temple. Some of the younger fellows are excessive in their commitment to the new ideal. But who is to bear the blame for their excesses? Your example was so intolerable to our American pioneer heritage that we had to erect new models fast. Our children should never experience the dizzy spell caused by crawling for one's life, for a piece of bread, or for a seat in temple. They had to learn before you spectres came to fill their hearts with guilt that there is another way to be Jewish. You must admit, we have succeeded in creating a new breed of Jews. These lads would rip to pieces any Nazi wanting to burn their houses down. For that, at least, you must give me credit....'

"'Enough, I don't want to hear more! Your dishonesty, your sophistic rationalizations fill me with nausea. No, I don't give you credit for raising Jews whom I can't tell from the Devil. No, I don't praise you for creating another version of human monstrosity as a counterpoint to the gentle pacifism that led millions to the crematorium. No, you hypocritical brute, I don't believe that you speak with the authority of a community of Jews, I don't believe that any rabbi would give you the mandate to eject a Jew from temple on Yom Kippur. You self-hating wretch, you want to exorcise the *shtetl* out of your suburbanized soul so eagerly that you are willing to parade in the invisible mantle of the executioner.

"'You won't dupe me into taking you for the voice of the congregation. I have never seen you inside, you always malinger on its periphery. I have never seen your head bent in prayer, I have never seen your eyes moistened by your sorrow for the countless generations of martyred Jews. You are a Jew-hater trapped in the body of a Jew. You spread your evil venom that poisons your shameful existence among the unsuspecting. Your pay-off? You provide the confused with reasons to look down on us, to justify the waste of lives, to perpetuate the myth of Jewish inferiority, the myth of the innate asocial character of the Jew, the morbid greed of the Jew. Everything that you fear to be true you project onto innocent millions just to gain acceptance into that spurious paradise of white Anglo-Saxon Protestants. Don't you think they see you for what you are, for who you are: a self-hating subversive, a tragically harmful outgrowth of Hitler's master plan? You, too, are a victim without knowing it, without allowing yourself to know it. For your cruel way of showing your affliction I feel more rage than compassion. You have succeeded in reaching my vulnerability: I disown solidarity with your pain, for it can only thrive at the expense of your young, at the expense of the survivors, at the outrageous expense of the victims. This should never happen. I feel tears of fury inundate my face, I want to hurt you until you scream for help, the right kind of help. Help to chase the venom of self-hatred from your veins, help that would prevent your unquenchable thirst to cause pain from surfacing in the company of the weak. I have to hate you, or else I end up afraid to look in the mirror. Oh, my God, when will you close the gates of hell forever?'"

"As if to answer my desperate query (to which I really didn't expect any reply) you came to meet me again. This time we met in the enchanted gardens of Beverly Hills. I found myself in your home without seeking to be there. Sometimes I think you arranged meetings with me just to continue to torment me. And then I realize that you live in many hearts, in many places, and at many moments. Our meeting this time was at least more sophisticated, if not less painful. You slit my throat with Beverly Hills finesse, with Beverly Hills cold, literal cruelty.

"Your daughter had rescued me from the abyss of solitude and depression, my two faithful friends after our last encounter. She was a gentle woman, with a simple soul oozing with compassion for my visibly solitary existence. She was also a victim of the hypocritical Jewish ethics prevailing in your circles in the late fifties: sizzle with the forbidden passion of lust, but deny its satisfaction until the blessings of holy matrimony give permission to depravity. I was touched by her tender offices. With the madness of a man stumbling on an oasis while travelling through the desert without water, I threw myself on her generous person. I was driven by a desperately honest intention to found a family with this modest woman so inclined to heal my wounds. She was dressed in clothes scarcely distinguishable from rags; I believed her to be of humble lineage. She had alluded to a home in Beverly Hills, but her lifestyle helped me conclude that she was an offspring of a chambermaid and a chauffeur. To my great surprise, I met you behind the wheels of the family limousine on my first visit to your palatial dwelling. Your face was more relaxed than in our previous encounters. You smiled at me, you called me 'my boy', you broke bread with me at your genuine Sabbath table. I didn't even recognize you until the Sunday morning when you had learned in the privacy of your library from the eager lips of your first-born that she wished to link her life to mine.

"I recognized you at the breakfast table. The wall behind your eyes, the steel-cold rigidity of your jaws, the upright stiffness of your chest were the carbon copy of your physiognomy on the New York pier back in February. I already knew that you had passed judgement over me. Just the way you *ordered* me to pass the jam disclosed eloquently your spite for me. What did you find objectionable in me? That I was poor? Or that I wanted to marry your daughter? That I tried to infiltrate the tribe? The fantasy of me being a fortune hunter? All or some of the above?

"I didn't have to guess for long. You were not a millionaire Beverly Hills businessman for nothing. Procrastination was not one of your vices. Again, you *ordered* me to take a walk with you. Why is it that you always appear to me with the military authority of the executioner each time you meet me? Does it make you feel powerful that you can bully me for a while? Or is this the only way you can deal with your fear of becoming soft? I was really in the dark about you. For the first time, I felt sad, for I had really learned to like you. Your home was warm, your Sabbath simple and elevating, your daughter unassumingly humble for a princess raised in royal luxury. Your wife reminded me of my mother's quiet, severe charm. I could have become your son without effort. Until you showed me your other face.

"'So, Fran tells me you two want to get married. Well, I'd have nothing against it in a year when you both can make some money,' (somehow money is always a topic in our conflicts), 'and live modestly on your income. Because I wouldn't give you two a penny. If that cools off your passion we can stop this meeting before we get into the meat of the matter. It doesn't? Well, you're more clever than I would have guessed. All right, let's proceed and not waste any time. I don't believe for a moment that you *really* love my daughter. Or that she really loves you. You have filled her gullible head with horror stories about your family massacred by the Nazis, children killed in cold blood, your sick mother deported to camp, your father blinded in a labour camp. You have paraded in front of her innocent, unsuspecting eyes a whole procession of dead lineage to reach her heart and implant yourself as my heir. Of course you don't mind living modestly for a few years

when you expect to inherit four million dollars. I don't even blame
you for that. That just shows that you have greater ambition than
energy or talent. I wasn't really significantly different from you: I was
poor when I married into Fran's grandfather's millions. But I find you
the most despicable creep, the most unscrupulous mercenary of
horror for not finding another road leading to a woman's crotch and
purse. I have heard of leeches like you. Being a firm believer in the
good in all men, I always dismissed such tales as fiction. Now you
make a liar out of me, you rob me of my optimism and you seduce my
daughter with a pile of crap about a tragic fate at the hands of the
Nazi monsters. You are a monster, you know. There's been ample
proof that the whole Nazi murder of Jews was fabricated to a great
extent to entrap us rich American Jews to act on our so-called guilt
and make amends in hard currency. Well, my boy, you found your
match in me. You're all creeps sucking the blood of vulnerable young
girls, toying with their well-known gullible emotionality! My daughter
just *thinks* she loves you. She feels compassion for a mythical misera-
ble victim of war crimes she can't even fathom. Such a victim doesn't
exist, of course, except in your calculating rotten imagination....'

" 'Shut up, you bastard, shut up! I've listened long enough to your
blasphemous attacks on my family's memory. I have endured long
enough the poison of your shameful ignorance: no Jew, especially no
wealthy Jew, should have the audacity to deny the horrible truth you
allowed to be perpetrated. If you don't believe the authenticity of this
crime without appropriate name, go to Europe, visit camp after camp
until you finally aren't able to stop yourself from vomiting, until
you have so many nightmares populated by glassy-eyed ambulant
cadavers that you'll never sleep again.

" 'You are of the worst I have yet met. To buy yourself peace of
mind, you soil your daughter's love for a stranger. If you had kicked
me out as a fortune hunter, I would have thought that you were acting
out your stereotypical destiny. If you had barred my entrance into your
family because a man without lineage behind him is suspicious, I
would have resigned myself to the curse against which there is no
remedy. But to accuse me of a mythical verbal matricide is the most
depraved cruelty I have suffered in this New World paradise! To have

pulled the veil of darkness so closely around your face that a mere fifteen years later you can't see the pile of ashes and soot reaching to the sky is a new atrocity. And to top it all, you soil the purity of your own home by promoting the germ of hatred! What kind of man are you? Or are you a man at all?

" 'Don't you fear the relentless blows of guilt for having listened to the lament of millions with the same detachment that you afford to a mystery novel? Is your conscience so deeply indebted that even piles of Israeli bonds and rows of trees planted in kibbutzim don't let you rest? Do you need to kill the passion in your daughter's heart, to prevent the conception of a new lineage, to keep the massacre far enough from your reality that you can live within your skin? Do you need to sacrifice once again six million people just for your very own private fantasy of a peaceful world?

" 'But even you can't push me to become the enemy of man. I spit on your ignorance. I love your daughter with all the tenderness left in a partially charred heart. That's more than the counterfeit thrills a plastic Beverly Hills son-in-law will ever produce. I pity your daughter, for you not only rob her of the partner she chose for life but also you have just destroyed her little-girl fantasy about an ever-loving, unerring daddy. You will never to able to cover up that double murder. Go, count your money, it's Sunday.'

"I have not met you since that Sunday in 1959. I'm sure you continue to haunt the hopeful, the vulnerable, the unenlightened. But there are a lot fewer of these potential victims to catch in your guilty trap. The disabused, timid beggars have grown into a mighty fraternity of accusing storytellers. We don't need to tote violent guns spitting death, in your neighbourhoods. Instead we tell our stories countless times. The more people we reach with our stark tales from the edge, the less room will remain for you to play your shameless masquerade of brotherly solidarity.

"Oh yes, in case you wonder, we still suffer every Passover when only our skeletal families populate our Seder; we still writhe in the clutches of nightmares filled with memories that millennia could not wipe from our souls. I still whimper every time I feel the solitude of the orphan. Yes, I still ache with bitterness every time I hear a grown man speak to an elderly angel, calling her 'momma'. But don't let my unquenched sentimentality twist your lips into a crooked smile of disdain. Next to that never-fading pain, there is now the throb of a heart strengthened by four invincible children, my children, the children you denied to your daughter's womb. They are learning every day the indispensable knowledge that will show them the true faces of evil. Yours occupies a prominent location in this cursed gallery, right next to the murderer, the torturer, and the other merchants of death.

"You see, you, too, lost. No, I didn't triumph at your expense. We all are defeated by the guilt of evil. But the children will at least have a chance to bask in a future sun cleansed of ashes and blood. Farewell, my wicked brother, may I never have to walk in your shoes."

"Twenty years have passed since that encounter. I have lost my hair, my illusions, my blindness. I have managed, somehow, to navigate my tiny vessel through the treacherous waters without running into any sharp obstacles. There has been the occasional jolt, a vicious storm now and then. But I did find some time to rest away from the maddening crowd of memories. I can't say that there has been enough energy or free time to master joy and elation. Or even the satisfaction that rewards an artist, a musician, or a habitual bridge player. No, I never have been introduced to the pleasure or the pride with which so many are rewarded for the achievement of a lifetime.

"I work ceaselessly because I don't know how to do anything else. I work because the task always has to be done. I have accepted this diet without complaint. The survivor has no right to complain, he has unfinished business to complete, messages to deliver; he is the postman of the dead. What I did hope for was a select company of magnanimous and wise scholars who by the very commitment of their lives to learning would agree to accompany me on this road.

"I was wrong. I was wrong to have expectations at all. But above all, I was wrong to mistake the knowledge of academic sages for the necessary flame to warm our souls on this frigid journey. I was wrong to expect that wisdom opens people's hearts to let in the kind of humility that can't be measured, quantified, categorized, typified. I was wrong to trap myself in a foolish hope that one day, when the tale was told, my academic entourage would pierce the enigma of its language. I was wrong not to have realized that they would turn their ears to happy stories rather than learning the idiom of gloom.

"I was wrong to usher my peers into my story. They thrive in the cajoling security of two-way mirrors and windowless laboratories. These busy minds harbour no evil or malice. They are just busy and detached, for without that protective distance their hearts could be touched, their eyes could water. And that would fog the clarity of their vision. It would dilute the vigour of their pen. Their reality is the safest of all realities. It is also, for that reason, the most seductive to someone like me who has grown cautious of fires burning in the street. I have even succumbed to the charm of the artificially but clearly lit library stacks and scholarly dialogue.

"I hurried to learn the sheltered language that grows under the spurious light of fluorescent tubes. Until one day my heart broke under the weight of too many pages of silence.

"And I discovered you on the other side of the street. You were sticking your tongue out at me. You called me names you believed would demean me by soiling my academic cap and gown. You pointed mocking fingers at me: 'You lyric journalist', 'You dilettante story-teller', 'You wishy-washy humanist'.

"I failed to recognize you at first in your colourful disguise boasting of wisdom acquired at Oxford, Cambridge, Harvard, the Sorbonne, and other unforgettable bastions of pure knowledge. You sounded different, as well. Your accusations were not aimed at the tormented past painted on my face as in your earlier impersonations. No, this time you whirled stones at my newest physiognomy, at the mask cautiously etched over a twisted visage. You were not disgusted by the blood trickling from my veins; no, you were appalled by the blood dripping from my words. There is no human more anemic than you, there is no human more afraid of blood than you.

"No, you and I can't walk on the same side. So you let the busy traffic of life separate us. From the safety of that distance, you lecture me. It took me ten years to feel the madness of your soliloquy. It took me ten years to recognize that the voice I heard was not a monologue but a chorus in perfect unison. You used it with such authority that it didn't even occur to me to question how many voices were out there or what they were *really* saying. In the mesmerized process of listening, I failed to recognize your face, your message. You no longer aimed at discrediting my past, nor did you wish to put me in the box of the accused. You were not intent on expelling me from your faculty clubs because of the victim's stench, nor were you given to extracting unpayable membership fees at the campus gate. No, your logical minds didn't find fault with my survivor's pain. You found a web of holes in my way of telling the story.

"The story, in fact, fascinated you; the language of the teller, however, was not worthy of your respect. And since one of your favourite axioms is 'to name is to interpret,' you ejected me from your libraries, your printing rooms, your scholarly salons. I spoke the unwashed words of pain which lacked the objectivity required of all interpretations aspiring to enter the sacred halls of academe. I, too, have an axiom. It was taught to me under the gloomy doorway which led to a cursed hall of knowledge: 'to name is to accuse.' A plague of an axiom! Who wants the company of an obstinate prosecutor? Who would want to tolerate a speech that coerces the listener to an unavoidable examination of conscience? It is so much more reassuring to theorize about conscience, to dissect it as if it were a laboratory rat. So I remained alone with my dark tales from the edge.

"But your words linger in my mind with the clarity of a bell that tolls for the unburied:

" 'You've been walking on two roads at the same time. How many times have I advised you to desist from such a rigourless and futile exercise? As a social scientist, your commitment must be limited to the observation of what actors do and say and how they make sense of these processes in different settings. Your guiding beacon must always be *objectivity*. You, the private person, as well as you, the researcher, must be absent from your scrutiny, your analysis. You must take a distance from your subject of interest to ensure that episodic details of your own biography won't cloud either your method or your interpretation of the phenomena at hand. Your typifications must include all information except that with which your personal history provides you. Otherwise you must abdicate the illusion of "doing social science" in favour of the more abstract and totally subjective activity of producing fiction. You can't do both at the same time. So don't be surprised if we frown at your ambiguous endeavours before we shy away completely from endorsing them.'

"As in every other endeavour, one is responsible for making choices. Mine centres on the priority of conducting my quest in a manner respectful of the enormity of suffering that bleeds through the pages of meditations. I owe respect to six million murdered Jews forming a cursed nation as well as to six million individual victims. To speak of them as 'subject' and not as 'martyrs' would inevitably and shamefully result in losing that very respect that guides every step of my halting journey. I can't know much about their experience other than what can be observed from my edge of that unbridgeable gap. They each had one body, one history, one soul. I can steal furtive glances at their ordeal only through the familiar tissue of my own body, my own pain, my own mental and psychic shutdown. And yet, you expect of me a divorce from that amorphous collection of raw memories while I pursue my detached studies of human suffering on an industrial scale. You present me, therefore, with a sad dilemma, the outcome of which casts me outside your circle: to earn and keep your respect, I must disregard the one I owe to six million open graves. To bask in the sunshine of your illustrious fraternity or to hover over the pit: some choice! The clearer my commitment to the call from the edge, the further I drift from your ranks.

"I have spent many hours in therapy sessions, countless moments in dialogue with people who didn't hear, who couldn't hear my story. My gloomy tales about the kingdom on the edge led to a sad conclusion: in fatal collaboration, you and I have relegated the bearer of ill-tidings to membership in a fraternity of outsiders. Our solitude is grounded in the indiscretion of enduring the torturer and in telling the tale that led to our survival. The merciless consequence of this indecorous comportment rests in our status as 'strangers'.

"But there is more. We are outsiders for being born into the skin of the Jew at a time when to be a Jew was equal to an existentially-guilty-of-their-own-birth verdict.

"My membership in this absurd fellowship of fools is further supported by my autobiography. A whole gloomy chapter in it revolves around the violent penetration of my body and the pain that has been seeping from it years after the scars have disappeared from the surface of my flesh. This grotesque identity has been sticking to me like an incurable skin disease, a blemish that can be camouflaged but not hidden. You would have been less categorical about our expulsion had we exposed our wounds quietly and only before appropriate tribunals. But parading our naked honesty was an indiscretion which interfered with your search for and appreciation of knowledge.

"Did you ever stop to muse about the knowledge that paralysed our lips for so long, about the knowledge beyond which there is only the void? In a language more familiar to your exigent ears: the existential awareness, the empirical memories of the ultimate torture, the rape of the sovereignty of human flesh are outrageous instances of knowledge as burden. Endowed with this hideous outgrowth, the only choice I saw available was to slither in the periphery of light, crawling along the edge of a horizon populated by monsters in whose howl I recognized my own silent litany.

"We were a gruesome bunch of spectres, an embarrassing sight in a post-war health-oriented culture. While the world busied itself with renaissance, reconstruction, living the rites of a new spring, we, the half-people, withdrew into the protective cloak of self-doubt, psychosomatic illnesses, and a neurotic fear of intimacy.

"Your label 'journalist in a lyrical mode' was intended as a condemnation. My crime? I chose to unveil the eye of a personal tornado in which a solitary candle-light has been burning with commemorative discretion as a tribute to the death of the child I was until the ninth year of my existence. You exiled me from the ranks of valid social scientists for speaking of rape in the first person singular. But rape, my dear colleague, is the curse of a lifetime. Long after the flesh wounds have mended and the body has forgotten the taste of its own blood, there lingers on the outskirts of every experience an amorphous bitterness, a dry tear shed for the knowledge of having been spoiled; spoiled and branded as meat of a dubious origin.

"With an impatient shrug of your shoulders, as if to say, 'Some people just don't grasp the meaning of tactful discourse, one must be blatant with them. How uncouth!', you left my presence.

"Of course I understand your indignation. There is a malaise and fear at the bottom of that irritated well. If I am permitted to fuse the personal and the public domains of experience, you may fall under scrutiny for not being willing to lift the veil of discretion about the private person you are. If I am not sanctioned for dragging my cursed history into the classroom, on the inviolate pages of sacred social scientific texts, the clientele may demand accounts about the sterile silence of the illustrious halls of higher learning. They may request personal data from you: how did it happen that you allowed the university to degenerate into a breeding ground for indifference? Of course, I am a threat to your well-heeled ivy-clad conscience. Of course, my language violates the grammar of modesty and propriety. The syntax of academe excludes the arrogant use of the first person singular.

"As a social scientist I learned that you, my colleagues, don't have access to the meaning of my words. For I use different words even if they sound familiar to you. To you and your entourage my words make sense only in the light of your life experience. To dissert about the cause and effect of a pool full of dead women and children inertly swimming in their own coagulated blood means something only if you are authorized to hear the words as metaphors, as dark poetic symbols, as quotes from the demented nightmares of a madman. When I offer this sequence of hitherto unlinkable terms as an instance of eyewitness testimony, they weave an obtrusive tapestry whose content is not available for deciphering. Hence, you relegate the words to the bin of semantically meaningless statements.

"After months of starvation, the first food I ingested was a large quantity of onions and navy beans pickled in vinegar and water. How can I give you access to the meaning of words such as 'after months of starvation' in the context of that violent gastric assault? How will you, the student of language and meaning, generate data from the pain that ensued from ingesting *that* poison in the context of *that* starvation? How can I communicate and interpret the pain and the panic that resulted from the threat of something as mundane as bean salad? How can I bring to your consciousness the bitter and violent regurgitation of that unwelcome foodstuff? Or the sense of defeat and hopelessness that overwhelmed me at the realization of that maddening reversal of meanings, the reversal of what seemed to be the natural order of things: food is supposed to nourish and not to invade the body and threaten it with annihilation. Was this really a meal or a mockery of it? What answer can you, the social scientist, offer to my dilemma of how to proceed with eating from then on? Indeed, I was beyond the sphere of expertise, and you, you are still in the dark when it comes to making sense of my confusion. With the bankruptcy of language we must pay tribute to the passing away of academic knowledge. It is exiled to soar in the thin atmosphere of abstractions.

"I want you to understand my words on this subject more than on any other. Because, for once, I am not speaking to you from my heart but from the privacy of my knowledge. I am willing to lift the veil of sorrow and anger for a brief moment so that we have a chance to understand, for once, what happened before the darkness totally engulfed us all. This version of the tale is less mournful than the preceding ones. I am making a one-time effort to decipher the absurd.

"The more you amass knowledge of the same substance, the less access you'll have to new ideas. As such, you may end up as an erudite beggar panhandling for spare change who is in the dark when someone bestows upon him a gold ingot. If you want to secure for yourself the tranquil conscience required for restful sleep, open your ears to hearing all kinds of new stories. In the end, they will add up to one wisdom: mortar and bricks for building the edifice of your own tale. And yes, what you allow to reach your heart could very well keep you awake forever. You see, you'll have unmasked one of the central lies of our world: that a clear conscience buys us a verdict of 'not guilty'. Nonsense! Nobody is pure enough to earn the platonic badge of 'clear conscience'! We are all somehow participants in the perpetration of some atrocity. Our consciences can be clear only if we isolate ourselves from truths that inescapably pierce the myth of innocence. Those who choose this willful avoidance not only soil their consciences, but they discard them altogether.

"So, my dear colleague, I invite you to open your home for a brief moment to this social scientist speaking with a voice born in the ashes. Let me rearrange somewhat your abode. Then you may want to ask me to explain what I did and how. Or you may throw me out without regard. But at least you and I will be able to look into each other's eyes and find the cleansing reflection of having uncovered an alternative horizon. You will have gained one more insight into the intimate mosaic of your dwelling.

"Beyond this initial step on our journey, we'll engage in a philosophical repast: we'll break the bread of our ideas and offer small, digestible morsels to each other. This would be our first truly joint activity as brothers in the academic family.

"'Our world is said by some to be divided into two classes of objects: those objects which we want to discuss and those which we use in order to commune about them. These handy little objects would never speak about themselves. Their material existence is totally irrelevant beyond the design of the masters they serve in *being about* something other than themselves. In other words, not having a tale of their own, they have to be resigned to eternally telling the tale of others. What a sad version of existence! Never to be in the limelight except as a mask! Do you hear the ominous consequence hiding beyond my words of lament and sympathy? Our total lack of concern for the man who wears the clown's costume and his prefabricated smile, our farewell to the shrouds of the dead without feeling the gap at the passing of a cherished one! In a more cruel vein, it teaches us that the murderer is not *about* himself as a ravisher of life, he is only a banner flaunting the supremacy of an abstract order, or the arrogant prevalence of his country over the sanctity of each private life. He cannot be held accountable as a responsible member of the human family, for he is only the uninvolved vehicle of an insane ideology. How cruel; how guilty!

"'This sad wisdom also intimates in an underhanded manner that the world is composed of two realities: one that we experience and the other that usurps the place of experience. There are those that *just are*, and those that *are about*. These latter are handed down to us by generous, unsuspecting elders as guidelines for assembling the unruly pieces of the mystical puzzle of the elusive reality that *is*.

"'Do your eyes perceive the blueprint for a master and slave relationship? Are your Cartesian ears able to hear this Cinderella story without a fairy godmother? Most important, is your heart affected at all by the evil inherent in this version of speech? Is there sufficient light in any corner of your "objective" mind to discern the true face of cruelty hidden under the impersonal cloak of a seemingly uninvolved theory?

"'What does my dead six-week-old cousin's tiny cadaver lost in the dark wilderness "stand for"? What does the emptiness left by her vanishing from her mother's breast "symbolize"? Didn't all symbols die the moment the chimney stacks began vomiting human smoke into a guilty sky? Can you close your eyes and see that smoke as a column of soot without discerning the interminable procession of blank faces outside the gas chambers?

"'For you, only the tale is real, the teller's pain is not unless there is a tale to record it. But is there a language for telling the story of pain on the edge?'

"I looked into your eyes. My question was born so many years ago that I feared its sharp urgency was no longer perceptible to the untrained ear. I was filled with eager expectation. I watched you squirm; my lengthy tirade had obviously taken you off guard. I realized without effort that, at that particular instant, your soul was more violently involved in the struggle than mine. Through a novel twist of experience, I witnessed within myself the growth of a fence between you and me. I also knew beyond doubt that the flames were absent from both my gaze and my voice. I was possessed by the demon of ambivalence: I craved the wisdom animating your answer, validating the truth intrinsic in my indictment of the word; I longed to have you embrace me as your ally, your confederate. On the other hand, possessed by anguish, I hoped to avoid your answer for fear of learning that you, too, were committed to the well-travelled road that secures an open vista on your innocence. I dreaded learning of your refusal to 'own' your spectator-guilt, a pernicious malaise of which you would ache to be purged by a resolute commitment to fight passivity with the might of your academic chair.

"An unctuous smile appeared on your face. I saw more clearly the filter of haze than the upward movement of heart that a smile tends to promise. 'He is about to begin a bout of shadow-boxing with me,' I thought with resignation.

"'My friend, I have listened to you carefully, not neglecting a word of your colloquium. I was genuinely moved by the pathos of your critique of language, the foodstuff indispensable to the survival of any social scientist. I almost succumbed to the seduction of your elegantly dressed plea for what I interpreted as a new version of silence or a new version of speech. However, I was troubled by an unidentified nagging voice inside whispering to me: "There is a moral trap somewhere in this labyrinth." I have been sitting here for quite some time attempting to discover the flaw in the marginal wisdom of your tale. I am convinced of its existence, only its essence escaped me until the moment I found the source of the malaise: you disclose a universe whose ugliness shouldn't be disputed even by the blindest demagogue. You indict the world of science as its co-creator, an accessory before and after the fact, so to speak.

"'But you don't have the right to disclose and to accuse at the same time. You are violating all the rules of respectful scholarly procedure. Your prosecuting voice morally binds me to defend myself for my primary commitment to science, rather than to free me to subject the substance of your propositions to the purity of rational analysis. Had you couched your exposé on the bankruptcy of meaning and its interpretation in a context that didn't require my moral participation, I would have been able and willing to continue the dialogue. For example, had you done empirical research on the unpredictability of meaning in a setting such as the Fun House at the Amusement Park, we could have been in agreement about your stance. But this way....'

"I turned my eyes inward, *wanting* to see the darkness triumph again. Can we both be sane, you and I? Can you be suggesting a possible substitution between the edge of the labyrinth of evil and a frivolous spot devised for innocent naughtiness? Can you make this diabolical trade and claim sanity? How can I entertain any credible notion about my own mental health if, indeed, you are permitted to offer such a deal within the impartial walls of our institution of higher learning? One of us must be the *other*, the one whose words bounce aimlessly from wall to wall....

"I am overwhelmed and bitterly amused by your effort to search for the flaw within my words. Your critical inclination suggests a deeper gap between you and me, between you the academic spectator on one side, and me, the naked victim, the dirty survivor, on the other. Your inability or unwillingness (only you can assign the accurate label for the stance you exhibited in response to my words) signals to me with sad clarity that our worlds share no border. How can I erect my edifice of meaning without the record of my forced visit to the edge? How can I exclude from my taciturn version of knowledge the inescapable reality of your passivity? To what sort of wisdom would I contribute if I failed to dwell on the truth which warns us of moral responsibility each and every time we engage in theorizing? I sympathize with your plight of shaking yourself free of the sticky substance of culpability for the longest night of human history. And, at the same time, I refuse to betray the pledge I have sworn to the only theory of knowledge that I can at all envisage emerging from the darkness. If this stubborn oath condemns the two of us to antagonistic isolation, reinforcing the wall of solitude around me, I'll bid a morose 'goodbye' to you.

"I am relieved to see you vanish into the distance. The prospect of never again coming face to face with you lightens the baggage of burdens which I carry on my journey.

"And I *will* continue to speak. To myself, aloud. To you, silently (because you don't understand my words any better than you can penetrate silence). My eyes will remain eloquent. My silence will grow more implicative than your words. My words will illuminate corridors whose very existence you ignore."

"I have used a lot of words hoping to make available to you the centre of my world forty years ago. Today it is not my whole universe, neither is it my only universe. This, however, is the one with which you are the least familiar. I hope that what my words reveal to you is not just a mournful lament but an initiation into the realm of what *is*. I am labouring to reconcile what seems to be an unbridgeable schism: the exclusive pain of the past and the present power of awareness and social conscience. What I have unveiled to you is the rough blueprint of a new identity, no longer just a surviving victim but also a warrior and a teacher. I am battling to overcome past weaknesses so that a new strength can emerge. A strength able to contemplate past sorrows and failures as well as to honour distant tragedies. My intention is not to wallow but to remember. To remind myself of the version of life that seems to be an inescapable part of myself.

"These last words were not intended for you or anyone else. I articulated this itinerary for the road that lies ahead, a road that I now realize must be travelled alone. The solitude of reconstruction no longer has the flavour of loneliness, for the journey from here on will be lit by the clarity of a goal. I will continue to endure, however, the unsettling anguish of confusion whenever my glance is captive of the past."

Dialogue
with a
Survivor

WHEN NIGHT SENDS its messengers of death, ordinary mortals fall prey to an often fatal trance. The ominous tidings make no sense to the men or women whose daily diet consists of nurturing their young, replenishing their resources, tending to the routines of a profession, a job, a home. They who spend their precious moments of leisure meditating on the sometimes elevating, sometimes awesome commerce between the soul and its creator are not equipped to sink to the depths of darkness that some humans force on their brethren. They loiter helplessly on the edge of a nameless doom which they can smell and taste but which disorients them. They end up like lone toddlers on a frantic highway. By the time they emerge from the abysmal trance, with eyes and mind in control, they are condemned to a mournful contemplation of their own agony.

And the children? They know with a mystical prescience that life is becoming *other*. The litany of a hungry stomach, the absence of smiling blue skies reflected in a mother's eyes, the winter landscape of life on the periphery—all contribute to a morbid clarity that children were not meant to witness. Mother, child, and surviving ancestor weave new nets of nurturance through the holes of which howl nocturnal winds of panic and rage:

"Where is my man, the one whose vigour and tenderness sustained me through the torments of childbearing, whose wisdom, beauty, and human frailty are wedded to mine in the child who sadly whimpers in confusion for his dad?"

"What happened to the brightest star in the sky, the son whose flesh blossomed in my womb and whose love has guided me through all darknesses until this one completely absconded with the sun?"

In this panorama of horror, I remember the eight-year-old orphan I became without warning, without meaning. The cacophony of laments born in the air-raid shelters successfully muted all the voices of love familiar to my very young ears. My pallid sister, myopic of sight and heart, my cousins Tibi and Zsuzsi lost in the uncharitable maze of their hardly begun lives, my greedy grandmother (whose obese bulk demanded all her energies for survival), and my Aunt Sari were the only discernible outposts of friendly life in my version of the world.

"From this miserable remnant of a large loving family, you, Sari, emerge, surrounded by a unique glow that hasn't tarnished in all these years of dogged determination to forget the night. When all the erudite elders of the community stumbled from one fatal mistake to the next, when resourceful and wise matrons tore their hair in hysterical confusion, when athletic amazons collapsed, paralysed under the weight of the void, you, alone, stood as the indomitable power, the lioness, mighty in her love of her young, cunning in her invincible decision to shelter and to save the children. In the distance of years the details have faded; only your youthful face, hardened by the task yet tender to the touch and caressing to the eyes, looms larger than the opaque viscosity of our hidden existence. Sari, talk to me today from the depth of your mournful souvenirs. Tell me your heroic story so that I can pass it on to my children, whose offspring must hand down from generation to generation the tale of the simple woman who, with one body full of courage, triumphed over the flames of the death factories."

Her face is no longer vigorous. Her gait is tremulous under the bulk of her burden and the toll of nearly seventy years. Her rotund little body hides the giant she once endowed with the incredible mystery of a master magician.

Could it be that this undistinguished-looking old Jewish lady, whining and shivering in hypochondriac pain, once vanquished the ultimate torturer? I looked at her eyes, those dancing eyes that seduced the shades of the darkest night, and I wept and rejoiced. Because in her eyes I saw the triumph of life where death was supposed to flourish, *and* I saw the crowd of corpses of children who didn't have a fighting guardian angel such as my Aunt Sari. In her tired eyes I saw my body snatched from the snares of greedy murderers. In her tired eyes I saw the blanket of fatigue shrouding a tragedy she buried forty years ago.

"Speak to me, Sari, speak before you take your secret to the grave. Tell me your tale, *my* tale of survival, Sari, my mother's baby sister, Sari, who saved a sacred sliver of my mother's soul. When her life was near to its premature end—more absurd than any other death—you, alone, performed the miracle of giving me a second chance. Sari, my aunt, my miraculous mother, how did you do it?"

She remained silent. Yet I sensed her presence in all my bones and muscles. I was in the company of a unique presence. Beyond her petrified face a dramatic duel was being fought between the need to reveal, to empty, to let go, and the habit of covering up, lying lower than the eye can see.

In my selfish eagerness, I was tempted to push this frail angel. I bit back my breath with shame at the very instant I was about to become her insensitive torturer. The desire to know, to pierce the mystery of rebirth, to unveil the secret of her victory when most others were unconditionally defeated, was enticing. I almost succumbed to its seduction. How easy it must have been to become a torturer when one was promised something of value at the exit of the torture chamber!

I looked into my aunt's eyes again, to offer her a torrent of guilt and shame. And what I saw was a feeble flicker of tiny candle-lights. A faint softness melted the sepulchral contour of her face, while it remained still and colourless. I felt subterranean energy at work below the living mask. Her lips slowly parted and lapsed into a tired smile. Then, without modulation, her voice broke through:

"So you want to hear my story? Our story? Is it really *so* important to you that you are willing to wake up the dead just to know…? What can you do with such knowledge? You may not even believe what you hear. Or if you believe my words, you may become a monster full of hate. You may think that I am a vile merchant of life and death, or who knows what else....I have lived in silence, if not in peace, all these years, in a state of spurious but tolerable tranquillity. Years ago I lowered my 'story' so deep in my mind and covered it with so many layers of lies that even if it wanted to claim its place in today's sunshine, its voice couldn't reach my ears. Maybe not even my heart. And you want me to undo all this? Are you really this cruel or have you gone mad?"

She uttered these words of reproach and inquiry without the habitual melody accompanying these states of mind. Only her lips moved in the middle of her funereal face. She was making a mechanical inventory of what she had heard and felt upon my pressing requests for her to unveil her secret.

"Yes, Sari, in spite of all these years, no, *because* of all these years, and *because* of the few we have left to live, I crave to know how I survived. Need I feel guilty? Did I live to see the light at the expense of another's passing? Need I mourn only, or can I also celebrate? Can my children shout on the roof-tops the triumph of my mother's blood over a whole empire of darkness? Can I tell this story to strangers' children to inspire in them the real taste of life available to all when evil knocks on their door, in their soul? Or must I recount it at dusk in hidden corners to the select few whose appetite for survival doesn't shun the cannibal's teeth?

"Sari, my saviour, fear not my scorn. I owe you not only my life but also the life of my children and of my future grandchildren and of their countless offspring. In the name of this future nation of children, dig into your memories and I will sustain you in your struggle with the shadow people. You may even find living a bit lighter, more accessible to your frail flesh, if you allow the poison to escape from its captive vial. Sari, in the name of life, speak to me, tell me what you fear to know."

My voice, no longer the shrill shriek of a childish tantrum, was soft and clear, pleading and firm, the voice of a man in pain, of a man filled with love.

She remained motionless. Her lips were, however, quivering. Only the upheavals of her bosom betrayed the inner rehearsal that turmoiled in my aunt's body. "She is going to speak," I said to myself. What if her story is unexemplary, banal? Another wave of blinding shame flooded my mind. What is it that I *really* want from her? A front-page sensation? The plot of a Hollywood movie? A map to a buried treasure that would make me an instant millionaire? Indeed, to survive the empire of destruction with five helpless children, of which one was her own mother, could not be banal. It has to be the story of a triumphant hero, a story deserving only compassion and humility. I stood there, chastised by my own urge to protect this fragile creature. She is about to cut her bowels wide open to empty the steaming turmoil she stored there forty years ago so that she could be here today, with her children raised. She will tell her tale before the sun sets on her journey on earth.

I sensed that I had to make myself very small in order to penetrate the forbidding world to which entrance had been barred for forty years. Simultaneously I was aware of the need to be gigantic in order to bear the weight of a pain whose magnitude would overwhelm the sturdiest of mortals. And my frail little aunt had been living with this paradoxical conflict for nearly four decades. "What a price to pay for survival," I thought. As if guessing my thought, she spoke.

"Oh, surely not my own survival! I'd rather have died a thousand times. To safeguard my miserable life at this cost would make a callous murderer out of me. But the children, the *children* had to be saved, they deserved life, even if its roots grew in a soil saturated with foul madness. I didn't bear my precious son, my *only* son, to see him expire of hunger, or to witness his little fingers claw into the wall in his hopeless struggle to escape the murderous gas. Have you heard of the child tossed in the air by a so-called man and then splattered against the frozen earth while his assassin picked up the child's apple and mindlessly sank his teeth into the marks the child's teeth had made only a moment or so before? Well I have, and I knew then and there that those stories were all true and I was willing to do anything—you understand me?—anything to save my child from a similar fate. I owed my life to the son I brought into this world. He had already been robbed of the love and care of his father, he was not going to be swallowed by the world of orphans. I swore it to his father, to him. If I had to carve out the heart of my own mother to save that little life, that brand-new soul, I would do it.

"You may think I was possessed by an evil spirit, my own personal Devil, or that I was afflicted with a madness that demands to be fed human flesh. You must wonder why, if this is how mothers feel about their offspring, why didn't *your* mother, my poor sister, take the same road to protect you, why did she allow herself to be torn away from her home, from her children? You may have amassed a king's ransom in knowledge in the course of your long years of studies. But you have failed to leave your heart open to the parental wisdom that allows no compromise when your child's life is threatened. I pity your children if you don't learn from my story. Because, my dear nephew, the only reason that urges me to speak after so many years of tolerable silence is take you by the heart and teach you a lesson about parenting your little ones. Don't misunderstand me, I'm not pointing a critical finger at you for failing the four lives you helped to create. Your fatherly love is beyond reproach. I have decided to guide you with my story because I swore to your mother minutes before she disappeared into the endless night that I would treat you in every respect as if you had grown in my own womb. The son whose life taught me the real meaning of parenting is given the same bequest as you are. To have lived beyond the ultimate pain a human being can fathom would have been a further instance of torture if not for the chance to pass on the cursed legacy in the shape of this lesson on parental love torn out of my very flesh. No, I don't mean to say that these mournful shreds of wisdom make the howling worthwhile. What was, was, and no attempt at masking it or disguising it will alter its essence. The pain was what it was, and nothing can change its hurt. Not even time. Not even the survival of that life I cherish more than my own."

She stopped. Her face turned pale, her breathing shallow and rapid. Her tired eyes became animated with a peculiar kind of anguish that seemed to question her own sanity: am I *hearing* these words? Is this my own voice out there? Have I begun to indulge in the self-abandonment of senile hallucinations?

Uttering the message that haunted her for so many years sapped the energy from her tentative heart. Hearing the words, she wasn't sure whether the pain had thus secured a life over which she would have no control. And if that were the case where and whom was it going to strike next? "I should not have risked speech, it broke the seal of silence. It will thrust me into another battle for which I no longer have the vigour. Can it be that in the end I will have lost the war against the domination of evil over my descendants? Can it be that the struggle of forty years will lead to a cruel defeat? Can my fate be a cynical victory of evil over the purity of a mother's fight for the future of her son? I'm too tired for whatever an affirmative answer might unleash on my burnt-out existence." She didn't actually articulate these words. She didn't have to. Her shrivelled physiognomy spoke more eloquently of her last plight! I have no right to exact such a price from the only human being who remained faithful to the commitment of actively ushering me from shattered childhood through successive passages to tolerable adulthood. I must sustain her, ease her load at a time when just *being* is a burden! I was about to invite her to relieve herself of the chore of telling her tale when, upon a cleansing sigh, she engaged me with her words. Her voice sounded replenished and vigorous:

"Don't fret about me. There is still enough life in this old body to bear the weight of memories, however painful they may seem at the time. You were right, the story must be told. All the stories must be told. Silence breeds a fertile ground for forgetting. I have spent so much of my life's energy on pushing down the accounts of horror instead of freeing them from their unwelcome hearth! Now it's time to reveal the darkest side of human existence, it's time to expose the wound. Nothing will heal it, but seen it must be. You must learn to identify it, to distinguish it from all other wounds. Don't worry about me, my task is nearly completed; what needs to be done is the telling of the tale. You know that I'm stronger than the mightiest evil, so what have I got to fear? My age is not a burden to me, it is an immensely rich bag of wisdom not taught in any of your universities: in it you'll find all the recipes for survival. Oh, sure, some may leave your bowels twisted and discomfited. But it's better to feel the pain, it's a sign of life. And as long as I'm alive I know that I have a chance to alter my destiny. I'm a simple, uneducated old woman, but surviving the darkest of all nights has taught me lessons that make me invincible. I've learnt to rise above all forces, all powers, including death. I'll die when I am ready. And *I* determine when I'm ready, not some black magic in front of which rich and poor tremble helplessly. There is no mystery to it: people die when they lose the will to live.

"You must be blinded by so much arrogance in an old Jewish widow. You must wonder: if she's so powerful, if she knows so much, how is it that her life has been spent in the shadow world of pain? Why did she have to take refuge in endless silence to avoid being overwhelmed by that world? The answer is clear and elementary for me: after all, I invented it, I lived by it. For you it may be opaque and absurd. All I can tell you, my dear nephew, is that you learn to make sense of the absurd or you perish. You survived. Thus, you must know that I'm right.

"Whoever is responsible for the shaping of human nature made fatal errors for which I often wished the suffering of eternal hell upon him. But he did supply us with the proper disposition to learn to know our own pain, to familiarize ourselves with its caprices and weaknesses so that we might tame it through trickery, compromise, or flattery. He didn't provide us with the piercing sight required to perceive the pain in another. This innate moral myopia paints a self-centred picture of man. And I confess that at times it's a relief, a sort of built-in self-protection, to be blind to what ails the world around me. When my children suffer, it's a curse to be in the dark. And even then I can only be contained by one skin. To endow a mother with the ability to endure the plight of her offspring would have overloaded even the most extraordinary human. What helped me through my arduous past was my gift to feel only what's within me and to keep the rest of the world, even my loved ones, at a distance that allowed me the freedom to breathe. Deprived of the air I needed for my survival, I couldn't have been of any use to those whose existence was entrusted to me.

"No, I'm not egocentric, I'm not arrogant. I'm a survivor. A survivor must be a person who not only succeeds in breathing beyond the edge of night but also is able to make her heart harder than granite without chilling its pulse. The sometimes embarrassed, sometimes annoyed public, upon our return into what was left of the world beyond the barbed wires, received us with cold, polite applause. The masks were so awkward, so transparent, that even the blindest of us ghosts could feel our own intrusiveness. To have lived through the unspeakable singed our hearts, the frost of our clumsy neighbours' smiles chilled them. The wavering flicker of compassion bestowed on us in charitable corners failed to thaw the shield of ice. To me, to be a survivor means, above all, to have kept my heart intact for forty years in an indestructible safety box. Forged in the most unyielding wall of ice, it also allowed for the construction of a tiny door available only to the select few whose genuine love, friendship, and humility were not only welcome but essential for keeping the beat vigorous, yet vulnerable to authentic commitment.

"Don't misunderstand me, son of my sister, I silenced my lips for want of a language audible to the kind of ears that can hear *only* what the words don't say. Inside, however, the discourse never ceased to be fierce. It was the heat of this subvocal debate that scathed the endless succession of moments. My strength rested not in my inability to feel the burning licks of the flame, but on my construction of an edifice on top of that eternal pyre that sheltered the flame without allowing me to be incinerated by it. I have experienced encounters with every single burning light on earth and in hell and I am here, if not intact, at least life-worthy. Yes, I'm powerful, but no human is sufficiently potent to put out the fire nourished by six million lives; no human is strong enough to drench the flames reaching for the sky from the spot where *one* single child used to wave at the sun. To survive for me is to never forget that the war is over and to remember that the road ahead lends itself generously to countless ambushes. For the sake of my child I had to win every single one of them. For the sake of my sister's children, ultimately for all the children whose elders had been claimed by the pit, I had to live.

"My story is not the kind of bequest for which I would expect gratitude. You may curse me for this diabolical legacy. Once I tell it to you, it won't leave you a moment's freedom, even if you seek refuge in madness. And it will also free you to abandon yourself to explore a new territory bounded by someone else's story. You'll be master of a paradox: you'll fill your bag with a story that can't be yours and from which you won't be able to extricate yourself. One that will hurt you without the familiar sensation of aching memories. Because the memory I keep for myself. You'll be impoverished without lacking in luxury. No, indeed, the bequest of such a paradox doesn't earn me any thanks.

"My son, who keeps the sun shining even in the greyest of skies, is carved of a different substance: he is the sole keeper of our family's bewilderment, the stunned heir to an ashen empire. His lot is to invent a new version of life for what's left of us so that the awesome memory can find a balance in the form of staggering accomplishments and melodies that charm and soothe. I watched him blossom into a unique, exotic creature endowed with all the talent required to provide a suitable counterweight to the tons of ashes that remain from the once proudly populated house of our forefathers.

"Two heirs to two cursed thrones—but I leave you only one sceptre. If you hold it together, your fingers interwoven in brotherly love, it will prove to be a magical guide leading you toward a happier future for your houses. If you each want to have control over it at the exclusion of the other, it will turn on you and destroy what's left of our lineage. The choice will have to be made and lived by you. But remember, whatever you opt for will determine the future of your offspring. May my love guide you both toward the choice of fraternal harmony."

Again she stopped. She leaned back for a moment's respite. As she lay there in relaxed self-abandonment, her plump little body seemed lighter for the first time in years. She no longer appeared to be hovering above the ground in a constant state of readiness. Her wrinkled face lost its mouldy green undertone; instead, a youthful pink hue animated the two somewhat sagging cheeks. She seemed absent from her body.

"I wish she'd take me on her present journey," I said to myself as I watched this creature that meant everything to my life. "She must be visiting a beautiful place, very far from all that is known to me. She must be paying a visit to a child, perhaps to the child she was or the child she'd like to be. She seems thoroughly happy. I asked for a story and I am getting a whole education. How generous of her! How typical of her!"

I wanted to lean forward, to put a grateful hand on the shoulder of this frail little aunt who had saved my life. As I drew closer, I noticed that she was asleep. Her beautiful dream voyage painted a childlike smile on her seventy-year-old face. "I shan't disturb her, she'll need all the rest in the world," I thought as I tiptoed toward the door.

"Where do you think you're going? Are you no longer interested in my story? Did you lose your courage?"

Her voice surprised me. I turned around to find her sitting up, poised to engage me in the yarn of her tale.

"How did you awaken so abruptly? Did I make an intrusive noise? You seemed lost in the deepest sleep only a moment ago, and here you are fresh as the first smile of the morning in my baby's eyes. How do you navigate so quickly from one world to another? Aunt Sari, you'll never cease to amaze me." Her small, squinting eyes responded with a thankful glow. She obviously enjoyed the compliment.

"You always underestimate me, my boy. One of the many marvels you learn in the dubious rank of survivors is a new version of sleep: never completely sunken into the realm of dreams but always abandoned enough to gather all the strength the next moment may require. It's not a trick, it's a way of living the reality of the survivor. No one knows what the next moment will bring. The survivor is prepared for whatever it may be. You can think of us as eternal Boy Scouts. Forgive me the clumsy attempt at levity. It was disrespectful."

I was about to protest, to rescue her from her self inflicted embarrassment, when with an impatient flip of her hand she brushed the incident into oblivion.

"There is one more thing I want to tell you before I begin the story. You must have been torturing yourself for years with absurd questions such as, 'How is it that my own mother, this woman's very own eldest sister, didn't survive? How could she decide on leaving, how could she not notice that there were ways to stay? What does my aunt know that my mother failed to learn? How much of her death was her own fault?' I see you turn your gaze to the floor, so I am on the right track. You need not feel shame, for I'm not about to judge you. What I do intend to do is disabuse you, to help you put an end to the agonizing interrogatory you've set in motion for yourself. You know as well as I do that your mother is dead, she can't be disturbed by anything you may say to her, think of her. Whether you curse her or bless her, the dead remain untouched. Yes, I know my words cut into your flesh. There are truths that must be uttered in the most naked words to be *really* heard. I'm too old to waste my precious time on lulling you with a soothing discourse that doesn't reach your skin, let alone your soul. For you alone your mother is still your mother, for you alone she can still hear and feel. But only with your ears and your heart. When she speaks to you, it's with your voice, saying words that you want to hear. So when you put your mother through this internal third degree, you alone suffer. There are pains we can't avoid, they must be endured. But those that we impose upon ourselves should be put to rest as soon as possible. There are enough enemies out there, we don't need any within, do we?

"So let me tell you how it all happened. When you deal with survival the issue is simple: live beyond the moment or give into its violence. To live beyond, however, may entail living with pain caused by the very choice of solutions that secured you the escape route from the claws of death. If you are a survivor, you act in order to survive and you deal with the consequences later. This is not an invitation or a self-generated permission to commit acts of depravation. I shan't lecture you about amorality and immorality. I am a survivor, not a fabricant of moral survival kits. Suffice it to say, for the moment, that the dead take their toll from the survivors who part ways with them at the moment of truth.

"But I digress, you see, old fool that I am. I've kept silent for so long. I've been a participant in so many internal debates that all that incestuous wisdom is now gushing to the surface, each bit wanting to be the first one to the surface before it's too late, before I decide to close shop again. I don't have the discipline of formal education to bridle my thoughts, so I tend to ramble, to wander from one topic to the next, to leave one question unanswered while I attend to the next. You must be tolerant with the rambling edifice I am attempting to erect for your benefit as much as mine.

"Your poor mother is blameless, just as I am without merit. For her to have chosen my path she would have had to be me. You know as well as I that you can't understand the world at hand with someone else's knowledge. Man is rarely required to make decisions about his death, since life is given and, under ordinary circumstances, so is death. When the steel blade rested its point against my flesh, I had no use for expertise ingeniously forged by another brain, another body, another soul. It was my heart that was at risk; only I could find the wisdom required to save my hide. In a situation of an extreme nature, we ordinary mortals are all ignorant. I had not been groomed for making such decisions, for interpreting another person's words with the consideration that whatever I decided might cost me my life. How was one to remain rational, how was one not to lose the guiding light of common sense? Those who, like myself, emerged alive from the task of constantly interpreting the trivia of everyday existence with the consideration that 'this may be the last decision I ever make' can be said to have made the 'right decisions' only in hindsight, strictly because we lived beyond to tell what decisions we did make. What a cumbersome way to say a simple fact: I did what I did because I didn't know anything else that might lead to survival.

"I am here; I have a chance to make sense to you, whereas your mother is tragically absent. She can't explain to you that, among so many senseless alternatives, the decision she thought was the best possible one led to her death. Remember that none of us had any expertise in such nonhuman matters as 'will a simple *yes* result in being killed or will it save my life for now?' and '*yes* saved my life yesterday, is it going to do the same today?' In what diabolical dictionary are located such horrible meanings?

"None of us was any wiser than another, believe me. The only knowledge we had (and it was more a resignation than true wisdom) was that the very thought or deed that saved our lives could cost the lives of our sisters, the very thought that spared us from certain death or torture a moment ago could be our death sentence the next moment. With such an insane version of knowledge, we all did what seemed sensible at the moment, thinking of the moment. Your mother had the same commitment to her life, to her children, as I, and she lost both. For this she can only be blamed by the cruellest of men on earth. Those who, like yourself, praise my heroism for having survived are fools, immoral fools. Because each compliment paying homage to the poor devil who survived is an insult to the less fortunate who gambled for life and lost.

"There were no heroes in the depths of darkness, only martyrs, some with their hearts still beating, others totally engulfed by the pit. No, that's not quite how it happened: some lived beyond the murderer's schedule and others succumbed. No, even this is not quite right. Some survived and others were murdered. That's the closest that words can come to the reality we endured. It can never be more naked, for the victims can't speak, and those victims who are in our midst may not know how to speak. You'll have to settle for the only truth about your martyred mother, the only one to make any sense at all, and if you are a man of heart, and a man of respect, you won't even search beyond it: your mother lost her life because she didn't know how to save it. Period.

"All truths are simple; some so simple that we are ashamed to accept them as valid explanations. We need to hear lofty epic accounts in order to accept the limits of ordinary human beings squared off with the Devil. Except this time the Devil was a human being, no less ordinary than his victim. How does one rise above such a confusing reality?"

A morose, autumnal mist settled in my heart. The pain was so familiar that it was comforting: in its company I didn't feel the orphaned loneliness. My aunt's simple wisdom touched me at a depth whose existence was a discovery for me, a depth that I acknowledged with guarded enthusiasm. After all, if I accept her guidance, if I allowed myself to absorb the substance of her teaching, I might find myself exposed, without the layers of protective dressings sheltering the still open wound of that December morning.

"How *could* it heal, deprived of nourishing warmth and brilliance? For life to return to the mortified flesh, it must be allowed to imbibe the restorative flow of sincere tears, to thrive on the humility of a pure, open caress." My aunt was right, of course she was right, she was the living proof of her own wisdom. But I have trained myself to walk cautiously, step by step, along that segment of the road I have left to complete my travels. And she was inviting me to dance to the gentle cadence of a new melody!

"The pain inflicted on you from without must be endured, but the one you fabricate in response to it is an instrument of self-torture, that's the one that you use to destroy yourself, that's the one you must chase from your life." I can hear my aunt's gentle but firm voice reminding me that it's time to contemplate the road ahead. If I don't I'll continue to stumble, falling, hurting myself.

"You, too, are a survivor, don't forget that. You, too, are a struggler. And keep in mind that one doesn't survive in order to perpetrate the work of the torturer, that one doesn't struggle to finish the job of the executioner. To survive and to struggle must include elements of rebirth and moments of joy, boundless joy. And love, too: we must remember that we weren't spared just to hate, but also to show that even under the mountains of ashes there are living souls throbbing with the urge to love. You can't wallow in your hatred and in your bitterness so deeply that your eyes aren't able to spy someone to love and cherish. Someone who still breathes, someone who still grows. Our love has been so strongly anchored to the land that shelters our dead that we may fall into the trap of mistaking our sorrowful mourning for the only version of love left available to us strugglers. Come on, get up, leave the greyness of your dwelling and cautiously open your eyes, steal a glance at the sky and remember that it used to be blue. The red you see is only a memory of an ocean of floating blood hovering above an evil, guilty humanity; it's no longer visible out there. If you still see the sky as red, it's because your eyes are not facing the world out there, they are still riveted on an inner screen reflecting only the past. Come on, let the sun shine into your heart so that it can illuminate unlit nooks and crannies inside you that you have left somnolent, paralysed. To have survived also means to dare to *really* live."

No, she didn't utter these exact words. But I was able to read every one of them in her eyes, twinkling again with the fervour of youth. One last exhortation on the love of life and she can consider her oath to my departing mother fulfilled. If I let her down, I fail her. Am I so committed to the past, with all its torments, that I can't let go of it for the time it takes to embrace the present as a new kind of time? Am I really life-worthy if all I contemplate is grounded in the world of the damned? For what purpose did I survive if I am not willing to exploit the offerings of the moment? Don't I owe it to all the victims to live life to the fullest? My existence is not just mine, it's also theirs, perhaps mostly theirs. How can I live with one heart the unfulfilled dreams of millions? Yet, isn't it to this end that we survived? How can one man keep a promise his destiny extracted from him at a moment when he would have promised anything for the salvation of his naked existence? Of course, I remember the promise, it can't be forgotten, but it can't be kept, either. Are the dark flames that blind me to the light of life the punishment for my broken word? If so, shouldn't I spend the rest of my journey crawling on my knees begging for forgiveness? But I am a man, I won't crawl ever again, and when I fall on my knees it can only be out of reverence.

"You do what you can. Remember the lesson I have already tried to teach you. Then and now, we can do only what the knowledge available to us allows us to do. Your mother lost her life because she had to do something for which she hadn't acquired knowledge. You must not fall prey to the same diabolical request, especially not because, this time, the order would originate in you." Her wisdom rings in my ear as if I had been able to read her mind.

"I can tell from that dull, out-of-focus look on your face that you are in the middle of another one of your futile verbal duels with yourself, a duel in which you must lose. Stop the flow of words, nephew: live with your heart, lose your words, and come to your senses. See with your eyes, touch with your skin, hear with your ears. It's all so simple, yet you seem to be oblivious of this most elementary mode of existence. Learn some humility from your senses: they invite the world to pay a visit to you, but they don't get lost in a maze of interpretations. Before any other form of existence there is the one our senses offer to us. Become an expert in identifying, only identifying them for the time being.

"Forgive me, I'm making a dreadful mistake, I'm an old fool. The world of simplicity and honesty disclosed to us is the world of the innocent child. I clumsily forgot that if you stand before me today as a sensory cripple it is precisely because of the rape of your innocence. You didn't survive on the wings of a restorative speech. When one speaks breathlessly so as to block out the deafening silence left by the void of dead souls, the only sound one ends up hearing is the silence born of words robbed of meaning. No wonder my lessons are just another instance of confused speech. I'm crushed by my insensitive blunder. Blame it on my habitually well-disguised senility." And she leaned forward to underscore her desolation with a soothing caress.

"Your words, Sarika, have indeed unleashed a torrential turmoil inside me. No, I don't blame you for not remembering what only I and he should really know. My face is indistinguishable from that of ordinary men of my age. My voice is not any more lifeless than the sound of any declining flesh. It is the inner universe that sets me apart, into a solitary group of one: where others harbour a sanctuary of lavish treasures, I hide a lacklustre storage room of dark memories. No one has ever gained admittance to this lugubrious dwelling, so how could you have known about it?

"Understand me, please, I want to start to live in the shadow of the sun, and not just as the shadow of the night. I want to extend a powerful hand to that innocent child put to a restless sleep so long ago. Of course I want to be able to feel, I want to *learn* to feel just for the pleasure of knowing that feeling is an attestation of living. I want to feast all my senses with the discoveries that evoke spontaneous outbursts of joy from my baby. I want to own the wisdom of that innocent three-year-old. If only I could regain the blissful state of knowledge in which one is transported to heights of the purest ecstasy by beholding a peach! Don't you think I am burning with impatience to awaken the child in me so that he can guide me through the open gates of the simple pleasures of life? So much of me is enslaved by the past that I no longer really know if I survived. It is only when I hurt that I am sure of life flowing in my veins. How can I live with so much death in my body? Tell me, aunt, how is it possible to live beyond all those cadavers? You have a story to reveal to me, perhaps it will open my eyes to see the world of the living. Is your story endowed with the wisdom I need for my rebirth? Is it a story of survival or is it another tale of death?"

"You ask too many questions, nephew. The answer is not in the tale, but in the life of the teller, in the heart of the listener. The tale is similar to a prayer: it must be repeated through your lips as much as through your spirit. It offers endless avenues to explore, it even permits both the teller and her audience to invite God for a duel, but only within the boundaries of the tale. My story is about a tiny angel sent by God to save us all. As all of His work is beyond the meagre grasp of simple humans, this one escapes my understanding. So I don't even endeavour to make sense of it; I just live it with my bones, my heart, my womb. Yes, it is the story of a tiny angel—but it is also the story of another angel, a fallen one, who claims to have power equal to that of the King of Kings. Yet when God needs his services for one of His mysterious projects, the wicked creature can't abstract himself from His command. Wherever he may be hiding, the Lord puts him to the task and his only reward is God's limitless love: it permits him to go on living in the shadow world in spite of his treachery, in spite of his destructive endeavours. My story is about how the Lord ordered this fallen creature to help the tiniest angel to find her way to a fistful of His children so that she could rescue them from the very hand of the Devil. It's quite ingenious, isn't it?"

Now it was my turn to be confused and mystified by *her* flow of words. What was this senseless soliloquy about the Devil, the tiniest angel, and the Lord? Had she taken leave of her mind? Did the weight of the encounter break the thin thread of her aged faculties of thought and remembrance? I looked at her with concern, scrutinizing every wrinkle on her motionless face. She did appear very tired, as if just opening her mouth would prove fatal to her. Now I was immensely worried for her well-being. Could it be that this was the moment the Lord would choose to stop her heart to prevent her from revealing one of His miracles? Could it be that at the very moment she started her yarn about an angel she had just become one? No, this couldn't happen, I was slipping away from reality, I was the one given to madness. She just continued to sit, with her eyes lost in a distance not available to my eyes. I spoke to her, asked her if she needed anything, a drink, a pillow to rest her back against, her medication, anything. She didn't seem to hear me.

But she raised her right hand slowly to indicate that I should stop speaking. I was disturbing her. Obviously, she needed more than anything else to remain alone, to replenish her soul at a secret source. I obeyed. Patiently I contemplated the silence. After a time, she broke the spell.

"I was very alone when my husband was deported. According to the number of calendar years behind me I was an adult, but in reality I was a clumsy adolescent without him. I was tempestuous, rhapsodic in temperament, given to panic for a trifle, stubborn to the end if I had a goal to reach. The hardships of everyday life were mostly unknown to me. We weren't wealthy but he took care of everything so that I wouldn't have to 'grow prematurely grey hair' as he used to say with great tenderness. Now that he was gone, I was awestruck: how was I going to survive? I had never had to be in charge. He married me straight from my mother's lap. I was so young, so young, I hurt just thinking about how young I once was and how quickly youth vanished out of my life. 'But I'm scarcely more than a child myself, how am I going to take care of both my son and myself?'

"Because Tibi, my son, was just about two, I was counting on my mother to rescue me. The poor woman did what she could but she, too, was wrestling with the novelty of solitary life: father had been swallowed up by the great eater of men, the thousand-year Reich. He left one morning and we never heard from him again. He must have been caught in one of the numerous raids in which Jews and other undesirables were rounded up to be packed off to unknown destinations. My poor, old mother, whenever life became problematic to her, would surround herself with food and just eat ceaselessly as if she wanted to silence a horrible howl waiting to surface. 'No, I mustn't burden her with my childish incompetence.'

"I had some friends, but those days everyone had his own ordeal; it would have been indecent to burden anyone with my irresponsible inadequacy as a parent, as an adult. My brothers had already been rounded up and two of my sisters and their families had been murdered somewhere in the Ukraine. (I'll never forget the horror in my little nephew's eyes when the gendarmes showed up at our cousins' country house where the family had gathered to celebrate three birthdays: Agi's, yours, and Tomi's—that little golden-haired prince in whose smile you could recognize the best of God's creation. He knew with the uncanny clarity only children and madmen possess that these men had come for his life. He bit his tiny lips and he mustered up as much bravery as his four-year-old heart could yield. We never saw him again.) The morning they took my husband away I thought of Tomi, only of him. At his tender age, this martyred little prince knew the face of evil. I glanced at my baby and my heart turned to ice:

"'They'll kill you just as they killed him. Oh, my God, You'll let him be murdered at his age, what kind of a world did You create? What kind of a cannibal are You? I know I can rely on Your help, so just give me the strength to become master of my own destiny, don't let me succumb to weakness, to fear, to man, or to beast. If You won't protect him, let me do Your job, at least, I beg of You.'

"I was not in the habit of praying. I was much more attracted by singing and dancing. I was groomed for the thrills of youth, not for the horrors of war against women and children. I was blessed with a face men found charming and alluring and the carefree social life of young urbanite Jews rewarded me amply just for flaunting innocently the gift of God. My husband was as handsome as the brightest star in a midsummer night. We were the darlings of many circles. Now that he was gone I didn't frequent any of them, it wouldn't have been proper. For I may have been pretty but that didn't inspire licentious behaviour in me. I was your proverbial 'good girl'. I married the man I loved and in my heart I have never stopped loving him, and only him.

"I said a hasty farewell to the life of social teas, dancing parties, theatres, and innocent flirts. I dismissed the peasant girl looking after my baby boy and immediately resolved to assume the responsibility of full care for him. 'I must be mother and father to him,' I decreed silently. Your poor mother was my sole support. Without questions, without hesitation, she assumed the role of the big sister. In spite of being on her own, your father having already been taken to forced labour, she stoically performed all the duties of the household: bread-winner, mother, dutiful daughter, and now mentor to her younger sister. Your mother was the oldest of us all, and I was the second youngest. Almost a whole generation separated us in age, and our married lifestyles had been widely different. She was a stern, severe woman, a bastion of strength, a tower of love. I expected long lectures from her about how I was reaping what I had sown. Instead, the day my husband was deported to forced labour, when I ran over to your house to cry my heart out to her, she embraced me hastily, without a hint of scorn—she wasn't very comfortable with effusive demonstrations of affection. Then she held me firmly by the shoulders, at arm's length, and with the warmest voice I ever heard she said: 'Don't worry, I'll be here for you, I'll look after you.' She was a woman of few words. And she didn't need to say more. In a matter of days I became a competent mother and homemaker, thanks to my oldest sister, your mother.

"Forgive me if I'm boring you with what may seem to be trivial details. You see, my boy, for me every shred of memory is of the greatest importance. I promised you a story about the Devil and an angel saving human lives: in such an undertaking nothing is without weight. You can't build a skyscraper without paying attention to every brick, to every piece of material—even those no one will ever see. Besides, if you want to hear my story, I tell it to you the only way I feel it can be told. This is the first time I have let it out of my soul, it will *have* to be told the way it wants to get out, without artifice, without censorship. If you have the heart to hear such a story, you'll make the time and the effort for the caprices of the teller. If you don't, the story wouldn't have meant anything to you anyway."

I listened to her interjection with great embarrassment. How could she discern that I was impatient? Her eyes were closed, she seemed to be speaking to herself, apparently oblivious of my presence, yet she knew my unspoken reaction to her way of telling the story! But when it comes to my aunt, reason is often bankrupt to account for her perceptions or insights. I silently acquiesced and motioned to her that I agreed to whatever terms she set for telling her tale. It must be told, and I must hear it.

She closed her eyes again and I could practically see her leaving her body. She left behind the inert shell, what I had earlier mistaken for a sign of great malaise. "She has gone back in time and place. To tell her story, she must be there, she must relive the horrors as well as the petty details. She must recount them as they appear to her in the distance of time."

"We had quite a bit of savings, jewellery, and other valuables, so I didn't have to look for employment. I could devote all my time to cherishing my son. He was lacking nothing. As far as he was concerned, from the early stages of the nightmare all that was discernible was his father's absence. 'Apa! Apa!' he would call with hope in his voice in the first days, then with sad resignation mixed with resentment.

"Our life was quite safe, quite regular until March 19, when the Germans marched in and installed themselves as supremely reigning masters of our existence. From one day to the next the rumour machine changed into high gear, recounting horrors of which we had heard but which we always refused to believe. We couldn't afford to accept that those atrocities could become our reality one day. We would have lost all common sense and panic would have led us to our precipitated doom. So we chose to ignore the rumours. We were sufficiently fascinated by them, however, that we continued to traffic in them. They spoke of mass shootings into flaming pits, rape and pillage, torture and massacre of little children and their grandparents. 'No, they can't be true,' we parroted endlessly; but I knew we were lying to ourselves: if they weren't true, where were my sisters and their Polish husbands, where was my little ballerina niece, Vera, and my golden prince nephew, Tomi? 'We're cowardly liars!' I would flare up into states of frenzy and anger, only to collapse into despair and terror. Your mother and I supported each other every waking moment of the day and night. We decided that before the Nazis ordered us out of our homes as they usually did, according to the stories, we would move into one dwelling: mother's.

"Life in the crowded apartment was hard, but we had the warmth of the family. By that time our sister Boriska and her husband had also been rounded up and whisked away toward the bottom of the night. Their little girl, even younger than my son, became a common ward of the few of us left behind. Our mother was regressing into a pitiful state of helplessness; the only thing that made sense to her was to eat and worry:

"'You'll see, they'll grab the two of you just as they did with the other five. And I'm going to be left behind with all these orphaned children. I'm too old, too tired to take care of them. When the air raids shower the city with a rain of death, my old legs freeze to the ground and my heart turns into a flaming piece of stone. What can I do to save them? How can I even save myself? They'll kill us all one way or another. It's harder and harder to find enough food for all of us. When the two of you are gone, I'll starve. Who will want to feed a useless old woman, how can I fight with my weak hands for another loaf of bread? What a frightening end to a life of toil! I deserve some reward for having sacrificed my time for the sake of seven lives! Now, where are my children to make my declining days more restful than the sixty years of constant struggle? The good Lord has no heart, I'm afraid, He's a cruel master. He has no regard even for the old who have served Him with every waking minute of their existence or the little ones who haven't even had time to sin against His laws. Curse on a God of such vicious temperament.'

"I listened to her endless ruminations with an immense sadness in my heart. Indeed, she did deserve to be cajoled, revered, and pampered after tearing her flesh seven ways for four interminable decades.

"Often while she was murmuring her indignant laments, I would hear the sorrowful moan of one of the children or the awful outburst of terror of another, as the little ones were wrestling with evil forces in their disturbed sleep. What a cruel, pitiless version of existence when a mother can't even reassure a child: 'Don't worry, darling, it was only a dream.' Your dreams were not any more terrifying than the brazen reality of the frozen world spreading its icy tentacles closer and closer to our tiny shelter. One night, I heard my son scream out in horror and premature indignation and gallantry: 'No, not my mommy, don't you dare to touch my mommy, get away from her!' My heart stopped for a moment. And that sacred moment may have been long enough for God to sneak into my soul. I exploded in a fit of cleansing rage:

"'He's right, that tiny babe is right! Damn their perverted hearts, I'm not going to let them take me. I'm young, I'm strong, and above all I'm a mother: I have no right to let them defeat me. I'll find a way to outsmart them, to defeat them all, the whole cursed Kingdom of Death! They won't destroy my child or my sister's brood. I swear on his head, he will live and I will accompany him on a long life's journey. If I don't, may my soul never rest, may it haunt a whole world's conscience for eternity. My children must and will survive, so help me God!'

"I felt relieved. Not only thanks to the outburst that purified my inner world of the shame of cowering but because I had faith in my stubbornness. I collapsed into a deep sleep, one of those peaceful self-abandonments afforded only to the pure of heart.

"The next morning I visited my old friends the Lehel sisters: one was blind, the other her contact to the world.

"'Rozika, for once, be thankful to the Lord that He spares you the horrifying spectacle available to Jewish eyes. We walk the streets branded like cattle prepared for the slaughter. We want to hide our shame by practically disappearing into the wall but the tormentors, with their diabolical astuteness, force us into the middle of the street where only dogs and horses used to roam. I would gladly trade places with you these days so that I wouldn't have to witness the humiliation of my mother, my son. I'm not even speaking any more of myself— I'm strong, I can put myself above and beyond it. When all this madness is no more real than yesterday's nightmare, I'll demand satisfaction of man and God equally. But my child, my tiny innocent child is learning life through daily lessons of shame and degradation. Be glad, my friend, be glad that you don't have to see that.'

"'Stop your stupid ravings! The shame is not the Star of David you have to wear, it's a mark of distinction I gladly sport any day of my life. Before all hell descended upon us, didn't we all wear the Star of David and other tokens of our proud Judaic heritage around our necks? The shame rests in the despicable fact that ordering us to desert our faith in public fills us with a sense of inferiority, as if a whole people had been raped. For thousands of years our laws have governed our conduct, our values, our actions. Our wise men incited us to the love of the Lord through their exemplary way of devouring His teachings. We have become so pacific, so erudite, so spiritual that we have forgotten to prepare ourselves to be strong against the continuous waves of attack on our people. Our wisdom has never included the mastery of the sword to stave off the slaughterer. Our men's backs (prematurely bent under the weight of so much knowledge) and myopic eyes (overburdened by the texts) have inspired the vicious to straddle us with the pain and hardship of their existence. For centuries, too many centuries, we have been the willing screens on which the Gentile has projected the images of all that he hates about himself. It's so much easier, and so much wiser, I must confess, to hurt another than to hurt oneself, especially when the other doesn't defend himself. All the cruelty the Gentile fears and defends about himself becomes the image of the Jew. All the greed, the hatred, the nefarious schemes he secretly harbours in his mind, he projects onto the screen made of innocent Jews whose only real guilt is an excessive commitment to the King of Kings and a weakly grounded footing in the world He bestowed on men.

"'I don't want to quarrel with our *tzaddikim*, this is not the time, our enemies do a superb job at disuniting Jew from Jew, alienating him from his ancestors. I don't want to add accusations from this precarious vantage point: hovering over the pit day after day sheds a peculiarly clear and unique light on past wisdom. But believe this much, my friend: if we had been taught by our forefathers the art of being and appearing strong, our cousins in Poland would still populate the streets of Warsaw, the *shtiblech*s of countless *shtetl*s, our men wouldn't be dying by the thousands every day in labour camps, our people wouldn't be rounded up in the streets and sent off to more or less certain torment and death. And you and your child could wear the Star of David when you so desired.

"'On the other hand, the Jewish people are never completely lost. The price we have to pay over and over again is stifling, for we have to assess it in human souls. Those who survive the successive pyres conscientiously rebuild the world in the image of the one burnt to the ground by the evil hands and below. This time, though, when the flames are doused by all the Jewish blood the world thinks it can spare, we'll need to start not only rebuilding, but sketching new blueprints for the Jew of the future: he must not lose his place in the reading of the holy texts but he must also burn with the desire to learn the use of the rifle so that he and his offspring can continue reading the Torah forever. The Jew of the future must have Talmud in one hand, machine gun in the other.

" 'You're blasphemous when you wish my affliction upon yourself to avoid the sight of the Star of David in the street. The more we see this glorious emblem, the more we can rejoice at the number of Jews still triumphant over the Kingdom of Death. I would love to partake in the glorious celebration where Jews and even Gentiles voluntarily display the star to freely announce to the world: "Yes, we are Jewish and we are proud of it," or "We may be Gentiles but we love our Jewish neighbours, we're children of one God."

" 'You're strong and healthy, you have no right to give up the struggle and wallow in self-inflicted shame. You have a family whose survival is in your hands alone. No matter how much food you provide for them, no matter how safe a shelter you build around them, if you don't pour into their hearts an unconsumable dosage of dignity and pride about who they are, they may as well be dead. Remember: he who walks like a victim, is a victim. The Nazis excel at instilling the god of shame in our hearts, in our souls. Would you collaborate by abandoning yourself and the little ones to that very feeling of worthlessness with which the sons-of-bitches want to gorge us? Who is the worse of the two: the Nazi who *really* believes in the inferiority of the Jew or the Jew who assumes the posture of the inferior creature? When you think of how low humanity sank in producing the Nazi, what does that say about those who allow themselves to sink even below him? Do you judge yourself to be full of shame because you are a Jew? I certainly don't. If you don't experience elation at the thought of being one of God's chosen, don't you find in your heart at least a clear sense of equality? If you do harbour such a wisdom, you'll rise above this brotherhood of mediocrity—for he who truly feels equal to the next person is a superior man. The ordinary member blindly believes in his superiority over others, and he'll commit infinitely stupid, senseless acts in his dogged determination to prove his superiority. But isn't he who embraces *all* of humankind as his equal superior to such bigots? Your ancestors' faith or nationality has nothing to do with the matter, it flows from your own soul, from your own generosity.'

"I must admit she planted in me the seed of a new version of shame, very different in texture from the one inflicted upon me by the enemy outside. Under its yoke I felt smaller and more transparent: this sightless girl read me as if I were an open book. No, I didn't rush to cover myself up. I harboured nothing that she shouldn't see in me. My conscience was pure, except for what she labelled my 'willful collaboration with the enemy in my own victimization'. She was right, I was guilty as charged. But I was willing to redress. How wise she was, this blind friend of mine, to think of the heart of my child, a heart that should never grow dark in the shadow of the Star of David. On the contrary, it should glow with pride, it should mean to him and to all of us that it distinguishes us from the guilty mobs. Those who wear the mark of the house of Israel can walk with their heads high, for their innocence is proclaimed by the very act of having been branded. But can we say that of those not displaying the star? Can we be sure that we are not face to face with an assassin of children, or a torturer of women? Their unmarked chests may hide what lurks in their veins: the guilty blood of murderers, indifferent spectators, or greedy profiteers.

"Who knows?

"'Thank you, my friend, you have provided me with the spiritual wisdom I need to begin my struggle with the nation of cowards. Now, I'm internally armed with the moral weapons that will protect me when I look in the mirror or into the eyes of a Gentile.'"

"'I can hear your heart beat again, Sarika; I think you have let my words reach you. I am grateful to you. We all have to do our share for survival. We don't have the right to just lie down and wait for them to rob us of our existence. I do my share by inspiring courage in those who are paralysed by the shadow of the pit. I urge those whose life is dominated by darkness to cut a window in their soul to let the Lord's light shine in, to awaken their dormant humanity. You, what do you do for survival?'

"Not without pride, nor without conviction in my voice, I replied: 'I'm saving the children and my declining mother.' Then with much less assurance I added, almost in a whisper: 'But don't ask me how.'

"'Have you thought of lending your soul to the Devil for safekeeping so that another demon can't hurt it?' Her words had no meaning to me. I thought: 'Rozika has always been a bit weird with her mystical world of supernatural creatures. I guess in that world even the blind can see.'

"'No, my dear, this is not some mystical mumbo-jumbo, I'm not speaking of voodoo. I'm being serious, serious enough to suggest that this may be the only (and certainly your surest) way to accomplish your sacred task. Let me be clearer: it is not only a matter of your soul, but the shell that harbours it. You are a pretty woman, one who has mastered the fine arts of charm and poise. You have all the expertise of a *grande dame* without the depravation of her heart. So, my dear Sarika, I propose to you the road, maybe the only road, to your freedom: find yourself a Nazi lover, preferably a highly placed one. Yes, I'm suggesting that you become a whore. Not a common one, but a holy one: the access to your groin, for the life of the children.'

"'But you're insane, how can you propose such a base, such a depraved scheme? I would never be able to look at my face in the mirror for fear of finding the reflection of a monster laughing at me! I would never be able to look my son in the eye fearing his hatred for having defiled the vow I made to his father. I would never dare to come face to face with a Jew who has lost a loved one or a friend or who accepts with his head held high the fate that was prescribed for him by forces beyond human control. No, I couldn't live with myself, I'm sure. One has to wager for the survival of a better day, a purer heart. If I am to partake of its light, I must keep my conscience clear to deserve the extraordinary gift of life beyond the pit. Otherwise what would I say to those who shared my destiny? "I am still breathing thanks to the generous protection of a torturer for perverted services rendered"? I'd rather die today, I'd rather never see such a day!'

"Rozika's face turned crimson with the energy of rage. She jumped to her feet and without the slightest hesitation so typical of the sightless, she lunged at me as if she wanted to pin me to the wall.

"'I don't believe what I hear! Who is the blind one of the two of us, really? The one who can see with her mind and her heart past the object world surrounding her or the one whose conscience and commitment to survival are so feeble, so rigid, that they bar the view beyond the tip of her nose? Your eyes are riveted on a wall within your soul which doesn't allow you to see that there is a world outside of your precious virtue. If your eyes don't spy the dreadful fate of your son, can't your ears discern the moan of souls hovering in the air, souls that chant the tragic lament of those murdered in indifferently cold Polish pits? Can't you hear your own son's whimpers in the night? If your ears are deaf to his terror what *can* you hear above the petty whines of a snivelling heart? I'm ashamed of you! Today, he who doesn't do everything and *anything*, you hear me, *anything*, to save his life, but especially the lives of the little ones, has innocent blood on his hands, and that blood will stain your face forever, even beyond the grave. If you fail to save the children through no matter what means, in what way are you morally superior to the murderer?'

"I abandoned myself to the breathless flow of her fury. How could I do anything else? I knew she was right. The chill of her accusing finger robbed me of even inarticulate sounds. There was no use arguing with her, she wouldn't tolerate that anyway, nor did I have the inclination to do so. How could I disagree with my duty of saving those brand-new human beings at whatever cost? I had no right to cling to my purity while the children starved to death. Indeed, what would my successfully defended virtue amount to in a new world beyond the mountain of tears if it was stained with children's blood? How could I ever dream of some sort of eternal peace if we succumbed to the murderer's strangle-hold with the dismal knowledge that there was one avenue of life that I had failed to explore, however muddy the road might have been. Mud stains can be washed out with a sincere flow of tears, whereas blood shed in vain blemishes forever. I had no argument to offer to my friend, she bore in her words the hallmark of the ultimate truth: the uniqueness of human life and the unconditional commitment we owe to it. My excuses were pompous and self-righteous.

"'You're right, of course, Rozika,' I finally gathered sufficient presence of mind to respond. 'The children must live or there won't be a tomorrow even if the parents survive. However diabolical your suggestion is, I have to surrender my repulsion to the seduction of the Devil's bargain. My stomach turns at the very thought of allowing a murderer of children to spill his lust on my belly. But if he can protect the children, I'll make myself as strong as I can. I'll suspend my existence as a woman, a wife, a member of an ancient community, I'll permit only the one-track mind of a desperate mother to govern my actions. If we live to give account to posterity, I'll plead for its charitable pardon. If we perish, may the Lord's heart be informed by the true motivations of my groin.'

"'Now you're making sense, my friend; now I can hear in your hesitant voice, from beyond the veil of anguish, words of strength, words that lead to the future. I only wish I could practise what I preach, but, alas, the Lord didn't bless me with an alluring physique. My struggle is limited to the ferocious wielding of incendiary words, words born in a powerful heart harboured by a scarcely adequate body. Well, that doesn't mean that I just sit here waiting for them to whisk me away to the Danube. If I can convince others to fight against this plague born of human mothers, if just one of our children is saved because his mother heard what I had to say, I'll go to my death undefeated. Nothing will compensate me for the years of which their bullet will deprive me. But at least I'll have the sense that, in my very small way, I have forced one gun to a moment's silence, just long enough to spare one life. And saving one child is like saving the world.

"'So you see, Sarika, we all must do just that: the world is in such extraordinary danger, especially the miserable little world of the Jews, that it needs to be rescued over and over. You'll do your share, I'm sure. And don't worry about the moral consequences. Only those who survived in the safety of their indifference and their guilt will judge you. The victim will know the rule of the abyss, the real tribute we pay to the sanctity of life. Besides, there is so much to do today, with such limited resources, with so little energy, against such formidable odds, that we can't wallow in the luxury of musings about the future beyond the next moment and the one after that. We can no longer look at time as a vast, limitless expanse, an untamed wilderness. If we want to live it, we must break down its awesome bulk to a manageable string of moments, each bounded by the awareness that we have survived the previous one, and that in order to reach the next one, only the one at hand has any meaning at all. But these are only words, wise words to be sure, words that must be included in our daily diet along with the dry bread, the bit of sausage, and the drop of molasses. Their nutritional value is right, for they feed the soul and the mind, they fuel our entire being for the battles ahead. But for now, enough words; we must spring into action before it's too late. Do you have any contact with Gentiles who could introduce you to an influential Arrow Cross officer? One who is likely to have retained a shred of the civilized man, one whose heart is still available for passion aroused by life rather than death?'

"I was already resigned to the ignominious plan; in fact, I remember the sensation of warmth at the thought of a possible chance of survival for our decimated little family. Rozika's practical question reminded me of the price of survival. It filled me again with fear mixed with unquestionable disgust. However, nothing could have dissuaded me from going through with this last effort to live beyond the night.

"'No, I have no contacts. The people I frequented prior to my husband's deportation were all Jews, and the few Gentiles with whom we had any rapport at all were simple workers and domestics, not likely to have any intimate relations with any men of power.' I knew that everything depended on the proper choice. It would have been the cruellest joke of destiny to allow me to soil myself with a lowly executioner with no power to extract us from the communal flames. When Rozika heard my discouraged answer, she held out the gentle hand of a true friend, one who feels the struggle without words.

"'Don't worry, my dove,' she said. (She hadn't called me 'my dove' since the Germans had marched in. Her heart must have been too trampled by the ominous sounds of the goose-stepping murderers to give expression to ordinary feelings of love and friendship. For the first time since that wretched day, my friend seemed to remember again the taste of the warmth that had animated our friendship ever since we were children.) 'I think I know someone who may fit the bill. Remember the son of our super, the one we used to call "Potato Head"? He was in the provinces for a while. I heard from neighbours that not only is he back in Budapest, but he has succeeded in distinguishing himself and he has been promoted to the rank of Chief Inspector. We both know that for him to go from simple detective to Chief Inspector he must have tormented a lot of souls in the provinces. But you can't let that stand in your way. What counts is that he has the clout to satisfy his whims even if that means the violation of some anti-Jewish laws. And what's equally important is that we both know that he used to be rather sweet on you. ("Come with me Sarika, I'll make you into a happy woman, a true patriot's woman. What can that little Jewish tailor have that I couldn't give you tenfold better or bigger, if you know what I mean, hee, hee, hee....") You remember how we used to make fun of him behind his back?) Well, luckily he doesn't know about our little charades when I would pretend to be Potato Head and woo you with mushy pathos mixed with a caricature of his ridiculous patriotism. We were silly and free in those days! Anyway, he doesn't live in the building but apparently he comes to visit his parents every few days, to bring them succulent pieces of food as much out of filial duty as to show off to us miserable Jews his newly acquired status. My sister Anna ran into him only a few days ago in the courtyard, and he didn't fail to inquire about you. I think he'll do just fine. What do you think?'

"I was singularly silent. My God, how easily she arranges this hideous deal, as if it were a matter of trading bread for sugar. I was horrified at the concreteness of the plan. I was also unjustly bitter toward my friend, the only person in my world who hadn't lost her head in the chaos. Yet I looked at this pallid young woman, resembling an awkward pubescent girl more than a woman in her mid-twenties. Her whole being seemed intent on executing the plan that she seemed to have already formulated in her head without any sort of difficulty or impediment. 'She is selling *my* flesh, she's arranging the surrender of *my* body to the lust of this torturer as if we were in the market dealing with poultry. How easy it is to make decisions over another person's body, even if one is only motivated by love and concern! Or is she? Could she find some sort of vicarious perverted satisfaction in committing my groin to the kind of man who excels in brutality as a profession? Can she really be thinking only of our survival?' I couldn't chase away the dark cloud of suspicion about my friend's intentions. I did feel the heavy weight of shame at the pit of my stomach, and I also felt a bitter taste in my mouth. I could neither exorcize the devilish thoughts about some hidden pleasure that would propel Rozika's imagination nor confront her with my dark suspicions. I just remained silent.

"'You're not answering me, my dove; your silence disturbs me. I've known you practically all my life, there is precious little I couldn't sense in whatever way you communicate with me. I wouldn't be surprised if you harboured feelings of hurt and disgust toward me. No, my friend, I don't enjoy the role of the matchmaker, especially not when the partners are my best friend and a freak of nature. I hate the thought of this monster embracing you. I don't even allow myself to dwell on how the image of your husband is burning a hole in the dark screen of my sightless world of fantasy. All that I care about is the rescue of the children. And if it means that I have to convince you, to cajole or manipulate you, to sermonize or threaten you with eternal damnation, I'll do it. As much as I love you, and I've always loved you as if you were my flesh and blood, I don't *really* care about your finicky repulsion at the thought of surrendering your body to Potato Head. If it helps you at all, I would do it without a moment's hesitation if I were in your shoes. And I know that what I've just said is an absurdity. You may think of me as a monster. I can live with that a lot more easily than with the guilt of the death of those four children. And if it means Potato Head, damn it, Potato Head will be their saviour. So what do you say, Sarika, shall I speak to the super to drop a hint about your being available these days and interested in her son? What do you say?'

"I just nodded. There was nothing I could add. My heart was dead, my tongue turned to stone. Sure, arrange everything, I'll deliver the goods. Life can be cruel, very cruel, I thought. Of course, it's my duty to do everything to rescue the children from certain death. I'm a mother before all, am I not? But, from a yet unknown corner, I heard a tiny but decisive voice: 'No, that's not true. Before all, you're a human being, a person. You have your own life independent from the child you bore in your womb. You are a separate entity. You hurt, you feel shame, you feel disgust, and nothing will change that. You have the right to be repelled by this bargain in which everybody stands to gain except you. Don't be so hard on yourself, give permission to the person you are to experience despair and horror at the thought of being sacrificed for the survival of your child. Of course you'll do it, how can you not do it? But don't deprive yourself of the right to be yourself in addition to and independent from the role of the mother. Keep the fire of your hatred burning for the ravisher of your purity: you'll need its warmth to sustain you in the chill of his embrace. You'll need it to remind you of this moment should you be tempted to forgive the evil in men when the world only wants to know of rebirth. For you to emerge from the night, it is essential to keep that flame vigorous.'

"The voice was unfamiliar, as was its message. But, strangely, I welcomed it. I seemed to breathe with greater ease after it vanished. I felt encouraged by its wisdom. It helped me discover the strength I needed to resign myself to my own slaughter and to resolve in good conscience that I indeed wanted to go through with this absurd plan of my own free will. I had to know, *really* know, that I was still a human being, making decisions about my own body, about my own life. I couldn't go through with it as a puppet whose strings were being manipulated by forces beyond my power, even if one of them was my very best friend acting in my best interest. I needed to know that the person I was had the right to experience revulsion at this vile prospect. It was one thing to endure it out of the choiceless resignation of an overwhelmed mother; it was an entirely different experience to decide to submit to the beast because I wanted to do so in order to reap the harvest of five lives.

"'Yes, Rozika, go ahead, I'll do it, just set up a date with Potato Head, I'll be all right. And don't worry, I'm not angry with you; on the contrary, without you I could have never done this, we'll probably owe our lives to you.'

"We hugged very tightly, as if guided by a prescience that this might be the last time. Indeed, I never saw my friend again. She and her sister fell prey to one of the numerous raids terrorizing the Jewish population of the capital. I never found out where they finished their ordeal on earth.

"She did have a chance, however, to speak with the super. A few days after we had developed the plan, Potato Head showed up at our door. His real name was János...."

My aunt's voice trailed off into a void populated only by her memories. Searching her face for traces of the flame of hatred that fuelled the painful decision forty years ago, I found only clouds of dark smoke in her tired eyes. I could detect in the depth of the two vertical wrinkles dominating the centre of her face signs of an ancient pain.

"There is more to her secret than what I have so far heard, as if this awesome bargain doesn't suffice," I thought. "What loneliness is she still harbouring in that weather-beaten body of hers? Those two wrinkles stand silently on either side of her pale lips like two mournful sentries, two flameless candles to commemorate a life." Trying to discover words for the untold lament mirrored in those two speechless witnesses to her ordeal left a heavy sadness in the pit of my stomach.

"I don't really know the meaning of suffering, my pain is not in the same league as hers," I thought. "A futile, self-punishing exercise," I added, "after all, pains can't be measured or compared." Yet, mysteriously, I must have had some indefinable need to humble myself in front of my aunt's story.

"I'll spare you the tasteless details. They are most unedifying. I am also embarrassed to reveal the material aspects of my shame. Besides, no son born of a human womb can penetrate the degrading world of a woman who submits herself to a lust she endures with unconditional disgust. To suffer his slobbering embraces was beyond my ordinary limits of tolerance. To know that before and after our dark encounters the same hands that touched my timid flesh gleefully tortured innocent people thrust me into the depths of a depression that stilll visits me every time I allow myself to remember his hands. That's all I can recall of the beast, his hands, those meaty butcher hands running up and down my skin with urgent passion. At times his caress felt as if any second he were going to rip my flesh. This was his version of love.

"Yes, he claimed he had never loved anyone as he loved me. 'Do you want me to prove it to you? Just ask me to do anything that would convince you. If you want, I would deport my own mother to the East if that would make you trust me, if that would make you love me once more.' ('If this is love, I don't even dare to imagine what he does to the poor devils he interrogates,' I would think.)

"So I told him: 'If you love me, don't let them deport us. Not just me, but my whole family. That's all the proof I need. You save all our lives and I'll be your woman as long as I live.'

"'And if I don't, you'll still be my woman as long as you live because the minute you want to leave me, I'll kill you,' he'd reply with a big belly laugh. I had no doubt, either, that he would keep his promise. I was reconciled to this fate, for I knew that it was just a matter of time before we'd be freed of these blood-suckers. So I pretended with the artistry and skill of a seasoned actress to be devoted to him body and soul. But he was really interested only in my body. I must say, that made it easier for me. At least there was a corner in my existence where I could be inviolate.

"Then came the darkest day of my life. As I lay next to his meaty body in his chaotic, dilapidated room, thinking of my poor husband from whom I had not received news for months, he interrupted my reverie:

"'I'm not sure I can save the bunch of you. All Jews will be liquidated in the near future. Some will be deported, some will be lined up by the Danube, some will be gathered in a ghetto and blown up. I'm not sure I can do anything for all of you. If you were alone, sure. But like this, it's very risky even for me. Unless....' He stopped for a moment and during the space of that moment I was already dying. 'Unless,' he continued, 'you rid yourself of all parasitic excess weight you won't be able to hide. You must let go of your mother as well. She is too much of a fat pig to hide. Besides, who can feed such a tower of meat?' And he fell back in the bed continuing to smoke as if he had just announced to me that we were invited to dinner by one of his underlings.

"'No, my family and I are inseparable. You'll have to kill me or deport me, I guess, because they are my flesh and blood the same as if I had carried them in my belly. As to my mother, I don't negotiate about my mother's life. The Lord gave her a long and painful life, I refuse to share your dirty game of playing God.' My words were sharp as the cracking of a horsewhip. He had never heard me speak like that. I was always the way he liked me: timid, submissive, mostly silent. As much as this new voice was unknown to me, it had some effect on him, accustomed as he was to such emotionless outbursts in the practice of his cursed line of work. I needed time, I needed a miracle to keep him under my spell. This was our only chance to survive.

"And the Lord sent me a miracle.

"You chose an unfortunate time to make your brutal announcement. I, too, had something to tell you. Something I thought would make you the happiest man on earth. But I guess it's not the right time. Since I'm going to accompany my family to their death, it makes no difference to you that I'm carrying your child.' Yes, it was a miracle, I tell you. In my life I had never been one to be ingenious with words, nor was I particularly talented as a liar.

"My words were rewarded with the desired effect:

"'My child, you're carrying my child? Oh my God, I can't believe it, I'm going to be a father, and this wretched Jewess is hiding the most fantastic thing in my life. You deserve to be lashed fifty times or more. But I won't hurt the woman carrying my son.' He was ecstatic. He picked me up and carried me around the room like a victory trophy. 'Now I've got you captive,' I thought to myself. 'Go ahead and celebrate, because I'm going to get from you what I want.'

"'Either you save the whole family, or I take your child to the grave before you ever lay eyes on him.'

"'You calculating little whore, you mercenary Jewish bitch, nothing is sacred for you people, everything is a matter of business, even human life!'

"I thought I had misjudged him. I lost my composure; in fact, I was ready to throw myself at his feet when I realized that he was making sport of me.

"'Now, now, don't get too morbid, I'm just kidding you. You shouldn't take everything so damn seriously, you'll end up upsetting my baby.'

"'Well, are you going to save us all, including your child and my children?'

"'You win, woman. I'll see what I can do. Just make sure nothing happens to my baby or you'll all die a death you can't even imagine.'

"He dressed without a word. For once, he really seemed to be thinking. I knew I had won.

"Only, I wasn't pregnant. I had made sure it wouldn't happen. There was only so much curse I was willing to inflict upon myself. So now I had to get pregnant.

"Need I say that an avalanche of moral conflicts plagued my waking hours? My nights were haunted by the spectre of my anguish. It is one thing to submit to a loveless embrace for the sake of life. It is an entirely different matter to conceive a human being with a perverted man. What kind of a life would I bring into the light of God? Would it inherit its father's cruelty? Would it be stricken with the curse of its ancestors and turn on its maternal lineage? Can a mother love and sustain such a progeny born out of hatred and a diabolical contract? How can I hold that child to my bosom without having its father stare at me long after he has disappeared from my daily horizon? How can I explain to my child, to my family, the drama surrounding the conception of this baby? Have I, too, become a heartless creature bartering with human lives as if they were lifeless commodities? How will I account to that child when it is old enough to pose questions? How will I reveal to my child then, in the long-distant future when all the shadows of the night have dissipated, the tale of my bargain with the angel of death? How will I live with this flesh of my flesh reminding me every minute of my existence that I bestowed upon it the gift of life on top of a mountain of ashes as part of its birthright? How can this human child live with the knowledge of having been conceived in the union of a lustful man and a revulsed woman? Do I have the right to create such a life? Will that child not be condemned by me to an existence of hatred and rage? Can such a child not grow into a self-detesting monster taking revenge for its unfair history on every human being born out of a happy embrace? Can I give birth to a human being who will have neither the wisdom nor the inclination to love?

"And the questions just continued to gush from my confused conscience. They surfaced at such a rapid pace that even if answers existed to them, they could not have come to light. Don't the living have priority over all potential considerations? Doesn't the scarcely begun existence of my son demand the time and space to blossom into a man? For the life I received from my mother's womb don't I owe it to her to sustain her, even if I have to rip my own flesh in two, until the moment the Lord sees more suffering in her earthly existence than He sees joy?

"I spent the night in the throes of these duelling forces, both wanting to extract from me a price I couldn't see myself paying. As the first rays of the new dawn began to take hold over the night, I was gradually gaining clarity over this opaque stronghold: we must live at all costs. The child must save us from certain peril. It would never have to learn the sad truth about the absurd decisions that culminated in its conception. And even if the lie was unveiled, and if it cursed me for coercing upon it a perverted biography, I had to save the living. I prayed the Lord to bestow upon me the strength and the wisdom to lavish on this miserable child all the love and tenderness a human mother could gather. Perhaps that would free a path to its heart teaching it the power of parental love in whose name I summoned it to my womb. Perhaps....

"There were also other nagging uncertainties about how to explain to your mother the awesome decision I had made without losing her love and support. What if God performed another miracle and He sent my husband back to us at the end of the war? Would he ever forgive me for soiling his home with the living proof of the beast trespassing in the womb that I had sworn to him and only to him? Would he ever be able to understand or are such choices the dubious monopoly of desperate mothers?

"It was so easy to allow myself to wallow in uncertainty. Words would flow inward with the ease of a vigorous brook in the spring. I eventually came to accept my plan as an honourable one, a decision which was likely to preserve the few precious members of our family not yet requested to feed the pyre. I made peace with the future child by taking the solemn oath to raise *her* with the respect owed to a saviour. I began to think of her as a female child, a future mother whose instincts would predispose her to accept her mother's desperate gesture. All the rest lapsed into a shapeless background from which only one figure emerged: this child will come to save us all, blessed be the child whose life warrants those of her lineage. Such a child is the true gift of God regardless of her human heritage.

"Being so totally committed to my responsibility to the survival of my family, I triumphed over all negative considerations, all that could have erected obstacles before my design to conceive. My only concern was: what if my body refuses to collaborate and I can't conceive? What if he is sterile? But my stubborn dedication carried me over the treacherous territory of self-torment and self-defeat. I banished all queries from my mind that pointed my attention in any other direction than the one leading to our salvation.

"Your mother worried me the most. I so much needed her approval. I had the respect for her that one owes to an elder whose wisdom is not displayed in words but through the example of her conduct. I feared her condemnation, her rejection, more than the scorn of my own mother. But, as is customary with such rare human beings, she remained consistent with her habitual sober understanding of life's requirements, however extreme, however outlandish they might be. I realized that it was my own doubt I had projected onto her. When she heard my story, she lowered her gaze as if she needed to see inside herself to unravel her own feelings, her own thoughts, in response to what I had just unveiled to her. Waiting for her assessment seemed interminable. She was charitable: she embraced me without a word. I felt the warmth of her tears on my cheek. They were shed in a moment of sad love and compassion:

"'I understand you, I admire your courage, may God bless your womb and the child He'll send to save us all.'

"I was able to breathe again. Having shared the awesome secret with my sister liberated me from my occasional remorse and guilt. The angel of life was definitely on my side. At times I felt ashamed to admit to my special fate. 'What have I done to be so singled out from among my parents' seven children? Do I have the right to accept such an extraordinary distinction? But do I have the right to refuse it and thereby collaborate in the murder of us all?'

"'Questions, more questions,' you must be saying to yourself impatiently. Remember, nephew, that the time we endured created its own speech limited to the inquisitive mode. Answers, on the other hand, had to be lived.

"Then I encountered an unexpected obstacle: János, governed by his ignorance, refused to allow me into his bed.

"'We can't do that until after the baby is born. It may hurt the child. What kind of animal do you think I am, anyway? I know what's right.'

"The expression of a sense of propriety stunned me in this man who, without scruples, tortured and murdered as a day's routine. While I secretly thanked him for allowing me to sneak a glance at the only vulnerable spot in his heart, I nearly panicked at this new impediment. Words were useless, I knew with certainty. If I behaved in a manner contrary to my usual shy, retiring demeanour, he might react in an unpredictable manner. 'I must get him dead drunk when my womb is most predisposed to engage his seed,' I decided. I was no longer surprised at my uncanny resourcefulness. I was learning fast the wisdom of the moment. 'Live, we must live, anything to live beyond this hell on earth.' This was my only motto, the only energy that fuelled my otherwise not particularly alert mind.

"My plan bore fruit. On the day when my fertility was at its peak, I paid him a visit in the early afternoon, as was our custom. From his provisions, which seemed regal compared to our pitiful daily fare, I prepared a quick meal. He loved to see me play homemaker for him.

It allowed him the illusion that ours was the normal relationship of an ordinary couple. I refilled his glass with rum as often as he emptied it. In a matter of an hour the tiny flicker of concern he harboured for the safety of his future offspring was extinguished, leaving in its place the flames of his unbridled lust. He embraced me with a brutal passion from which all signs of tenderness were absent. I didn't complain, I even encouraged him, for I feared failure. Need I say more?

"I conceived that afternoon. It was May Day, lily-of-the-valley day in times of peace. For me and for that bud of life it was the first step on a brand-new road.

"The course of the next few months was fraught with a succession of tragedies and traumas. The lot of the Jew worsened with each day. We were fair target for any demented mind. To venture into the streets was a likely risk to one's life. The nights were endured with anguish and hope: bombs were raining from the sky as if to wash away this rotten corner of the earth and make way for a new version of life. My baby was growing, unaware of the madness dominating the city of her imminent birth. I saw János less and less frequently. As the Soviet troops were approaching, his cursed occupation took on an increasingly frenzied pace. It was clear to him and to his superiors that it was only a matter of time, a short time at that, before the débâcle.

"Even a simple mind such as his or mine would conclude that the only way to escape the wrath of the occupying forces pointed toward the west. That would have meant that they couldn't finish their fanatic endeavour to kill every single Jew in the country. From mid-October on, when his demented Party managed to prevail over the decaying vestiges of the admiral's regime, he gave himself to the task with a zeal comparable to a kind of absurd religious fervour. I couldn't say I missed his embrace or even his presence. But each time he disappeared from my sight I feared for his life. Oh, no, I didn't allow him to sneak into my heart: with him dead or permanently absent we had no security. Who would believe a Jewish woman's claim that the child she was carrying in her belly had been sired by a Chief Inspector of the Arrow Cross Police? I needed his presence, I needed his protection. He told me that it was just a question of days or weeks before the ghetto opened its gates. Those who escaped deportation or the quick bullet in the neck along the Danube would be gathered within the walls of the ghetto.

"'Sarika, stay away from the streets. As long as you are inside, no one will bother you. But out there I have no power, nobody has. The mob is king. If an enthusiastic youth doesn't get you, you'll end up in the net of a raid and you'll be taken to a camp. I can't save you from there. Be careful with my child, this child that will avenge his father's blood should he fall victim to treason or to those damned Allied bombs. That baby is my entire future. Can you understand what I mean?

"What a myopic monster he was! I am living the terror of a slow death-march under the yoke of his friends and he asks *me* if I can understand his paternal concerns for the future? During a moment when evil triumphed in my heart, I wished death upon my unborn child to see him suffer the way my people had been suffering the loss of their blood. But I'm no slaughterer, I could never be one. I paid with sleepless nights for that one moment. 'Suppose God heard my insane plea and suppose He listens to its cursed message!' While I was tormenting myself from within, wretched neighbours fearing for their lives openly attacked me day after day for the child I was bearing. The closer they felt to their untimely demise the more energy they spent on venting their hatred for 'the slut who sold her womb to the enemy.' 'She is special, she can't have the same fate as the rest of us,' they would say. Or 'she won't listen to God's plan for the Jews.' Or, 'she will sell us all if it suits her, the lousy little tramp, may God curse her with a monster....'

"I felt assaulted from all directions: the bombs kept pouring from the sky, as did the insults from the building and the self-torment from within. I thought that any moment I would lose whatever was left of my sanity. Madness surrounded me on all sides, its callings were powerful and tempting. And then, when I thought that I was no longer able to cope with what had been dished out to me, another blow came to toss me beyond what I had believed to be my threshold of tolerance. 'How many times do I have to adjust my capacity for pain in order to stay alive?' I asked myself on the edge of despair.

"Your mother was taken away on an otherwise ordinary December morning. As they were calling the roll in the courtyard, I mumbled to myself: 'Now I am truly alone, in charge of the bare bones of the family. If I succumb, we all perish. I can't afford the luxury of dwelling on my pain and anguish for my sister. If the children and mother are to be saved, I must remain in control. I have to become hard and selfish. Nobody counts from here on but the children and mother. May God be with all our loved ones wherever they may be enduring their ordeal. Worrying about them will not help them, and it will only undermine whatever meagre resources I have left. May God forgive me for what may be mistaken for lack of compassion or care. But we must prevail. We have come so far, freedom is so close to us, we can't abandon ourselves now. I must be strong and concentrate my efforts.' I knew that I'd never see your mother again. Another wasted life, more innocent blood, more orphans.

"My poor gentle sister never came back.

"The next day I found out from János that she was one of a transport of middle-aged women taken to Bergen Belsen for hard labour.

"'Why were the younger, healthier ones saved, why did they take the weak?' I asked János, hoping to gain some insight into the workings of their lugubrious minds. (I never knew if his protection might someday prove to be useful. It might save my life to know how to make sense of selections.)

"'Wait a minute, you're asking me to reveal state secrets to you,' he replied with mock seriousness. He enjoyed playing the role of the powerful official in front of me. The mightier he made himself appear, the weaker I emerged by contrast.

"'You wouldn't be passing information from our bed to the enemy by any chance? You wouldn't be making some extra money from spying, would you?' His morbid humour was not entirely free from a layer of doubt. 'Could it be that this Jewess will lead me to my destruction?' I imagined him mulling the morose thought over in his increasingly frightened mind. He, too, knew that nothing would really save his Party from the might of the Allies.

"'The job must be completed. We are all soldiers, we must do what we have been ordered to do. History will express its gratitude to us for having done the work no one wanted to do. But no one stopped us from executing it, either! Your precious Allies, they could bomb the camps, they could bomb the railroad tracks, they could bomb the roads leading to the camps. But they don't. Why? Because they know as well as we do that the Jew must be exterminated from our midst so that Western civilization can continue its progress toward a pure future. The Jew would just pervert it in whatever way he could. But none of the Allied countries has the courage to act on its heart's desire to be rid of the Jewish vermin. We started the job, we will complete it; then we will be ready to face the price of defeat. But mark my words: you won't be here and I won't be here, but posterity will benefit from the improved quality of life we are making possible for it in these few thankless years. We assumed our place in history, even if it is not a very pretty one. It does open vistas no other nation could secure for its brave sons and daughters.'

"'What about me, my children, what about *your* child who will be born in less than a month from a Jewish womb?' I inquired not without anxiety.

"'I am not sure that any of you will survive what is in store for all of you, and I can't say any more. But even if you do, you will be part of a small group whose fate I don't envy. When millions have perished, what do you think the victors will ask themselves about the handful of survivors if not "just how did these select few escape the might of the Third Reich? What favour did they grant to the conquerors so as to walk out of the lion's mouth with their heads on their shoulders?" You'll have to account daily for your miserable lives. You'll have to tell them how you slept with a Chief Inspector the day after your sister had been taken to her death by his colleagues. You'll have to confess that you owe your life to having sold your womb to the enemy as if it were a piece of real estate. You'll have to reveal that your newborn child is born from the flesh of a Jew-killer. I tell you, the job we haven't completed, the spectators and the conquerors will. And if they don't, your own conscience will tear you to pieces when you see the extent of our accomplishments. You yourself will decide that, face to face with the millions of dead Jews, you have no right to live, that their fate demands solidarity from you. Your own madness will drive you to your grave. One way or another, Europe will be Jew-free. As for my half-Jewish child, he will be guaranteed survival if you live long enough to release him from the captivity of your Jewish flesh. Just as he will have saved your life under our rule, he will save mine in the new order. He will be the living proof of my courageous attempt to save an entire Jewish family. Your tribunals will absolve me of any culpability. They may even bestow upon me a medal for valour and gallant behaviour.

"I couldn't stand any more of this horrible discourse. Had I been able to grab his gun, I would have put an end to his miserable existence with my own hand. I knew that he was right in every cynical detail of the picture he painted of our future. He would win, and one way or another we would end up losing. I did not crave victory over him. I just wanted my children to live in the light of freedom. But he was absolutely right—there would be no place for the survivor among the victors. We were outcasts, people would treat us as cannibals, we'd be judged along with the murderers. We'd be accused of selling our brothers and sisters to the enemy. The neighbours would be right. If any of them lived to tell the tale, I would be sentenced for the betrayal of my people. No one would care about my predicament to save the young ones. The judges wouldn't have lived through the hell on earth that forced a mother to bargain with the only commodity the torturers forgot to steal from her, the ability to bear offspring. They would decree that under such conditions the honourable way to act would have been to perish with dignity. But these virtuous folks didn't know what they would do if they had to endure our lot. How many of them would succumb to the primeval call of self-preservation? How many of them would kill their own parents to save their children or themselves? He was right, the victors wouldn't know the nature of our existence at the extreme edge of darkness. They would banish us from the midst of decent communities. We'd be branded as the 'Jews with blood on their hands, blood on their tongues, blood on their hearts!' And he would have the last diabolical laugh with his hero's welcome. No, damn you, no, you must learn the full truth even if you kill me right here and now, since there seems to be no exit for us anyway.

"'Given that you didn't take the trouble to assuage my doubts and my anxieties with lies, I will reciprocate in kind.'

"And I unveiled the whole plot, with every detail of the subterfuge, including how I coaxed him to the abyss of total inebriation to attract him into my womb. He listened most attentively, without a muscle moving in his face. I had never seen him so involved with my words. He never had patience for 'feminine chatter' as he referred to women speaking their hearts or their minds. This time he drank up every sound I uttered. When I finished the story of his entrapment, I expected him to get up, go to his night table, draw his gun from its holster, and kill me with one well-placed bullet. 'Or maybe he will lose control,' I thought, 'and he'll beat me to senselessness!' Instead, he just sat there, speechless. He seemed to scrutinize the shine on his boots.

"Finally he looked up, raised his gaze to meet mine straight in the centre, equal to equal. For the first time since our disgusting liaison began, I saw him look at me almost as a friend.

"'You may find this hard to believe, but I knew it all along. I let you carry the yarn without ripping it out of your mouth because I thought of the future. For a short while, I even entertained the dream that if you gave birth to my child, you would consent to marrying me after the defeat. Oh, don't think I was as naïve or as stupid as you thought I was. I knew that your sudden interest in me was not due to my masculine charm but to the position I occupied in the new order. My friends and I have all been approached by numerous Jewesses with similar designs. Most of them just laughed at the miserable whores offering their bodies for a chance of surviving in a world that was bent on their destruction. It's quite absurd, you must admit. I succumbed to your opener because I had always loved you with a devotion one may even call abnormal. I had no illusions about your feelings: you hated every moment you spent in my presence. In spite of your habitual theatrical performance, I felt to the marrow of my bones how violently you recoiled at my slightest touch. So when you informed me of your pregnancy, I first jubilated with all my heart. I thought: if she allowed herself to conceive my child, she must have some tender feeling for me. No woman, not even the most desperate, the most cunning Jewess would consent to bearing the monstrous offspring of a fascist murderer. After the first waves of elation calmed down, I began to think and I realized that I had underestimated you. I was going to put you to the test. That's why I refused to make love to you—not because of ignorance about the health hazards to the child. I told you, I'm not as idiotic as you all imagined me to be. When I saw you actually *wanting* to fall into my arms, I knew I was right. I knew that you were desperate to make good your bluff. Your efforts were touching but transparent. I was perfectly aware of your plot to get me so drunk that I would lose self-control. I went along with your scheme. My heart was so broken when I pierced the balloon of your trickery that I wanted to get drunk. As I was eating the only meal that you *offered* to prepare for me, I, too, became cynical and calculating. If I have a child from a Jewess, it may save my life after our final demise. You'll be an outcast, you'll be the mother of my child, you'll need me more than ever. Now, at least, you are counting on the victory of the Allies to rescue you from your sad predicament. Then, there will be no one to save you from the scorn of the victors. Yes, the further I pondered the more sense it made to me to let you "use" *me*. So you see, my dear Sarika, we are two of a mind, two of a similar fate. The more we think to win, the more we end up losers. There is no way out for either of us. I feel pity for both of us.'

"He looked animated by what I interpreted to be compassion, the sympathy of a man who himself knows the depth of hopelessness. Yet, except for the coldest hatred short of freezing my own heart, I felt nothing for him. No matter which way I turned, he triumphed over me. I could have killed him without the slightest hesitation, the slightest remorse or guilt. He was not a human being, he was the angel of death in human disguise. Then my instincts saved me from wasting any more energy on this unimportant little man. 'No matter, my goal is the same as ever. We must survive. I don't care if he does, too, all that makes any difference for me is that we must prevail.' And to that end, I still needed him. I didn't forget his tale about the impending ghettoization of all surviving Jews.

"'Look, János, no more lies, no more games. Whatever happened is in the jealous claws of the past, it will never release any of it for revision. The reality is that very shortly I will be giving birth to your child, to our child. This unborn baby does establish between us a relationship neither one of us can deny. For our selfish reasons, we both wanted this child. The fact remains that I am quite relieved that we can tell our progeny without lying that we both wanted its birth. That's already a gain over what we both thought he had as the sad foundation of his life. As for the rest, the facts remain unchanged: I must survive with the children and my mother. I will do everything in my power to escape the attention of any harmful group or individual. Which leaves me with an absurd alternative: the hope to make it to the ghetto. I will no doubt give birth in the ghetto. If that child is to survive, you must help us. We will need accommodation and food. In exchange, I will not testify against you after the liberation and I will not raise our child to hate you, to despise you, to fear you. We shall never live under the same roof. You are right, I find you physically and morally repulsive, and I feel guilty to have inspired love in you. From here on, we shall not continue our physical contacts. In fact, we never need see one another, except when you must come to make sure that your child's interest is best served. Ours is an arrangement of convenience in which the stake is no longer the sum total of six lives but eight. As long as your life and that of your unborn child mean anything to you, I no longer need to barter with my groin, am I right?'

"I think I hurt him deeply. No more theatrical performance, no more fantasy of a possibly happy ending to his imaginary romance. Wartime business deal, that's all that was left of the world woven of secret rendezvous, make-believe passionate embraces, the romantic thrill of loving a hidden enemy. He looked like a shadow of himself. His immense mass seemed to have collapsed into an amorphous shape in which the supportive backbone was shattered. His ruddy complexion took on a funereal whitish mask. Without lifting his head, he acquiesced with a silent nod. I was about to take leave without any further words to the father of my child, when his voice stopped me:

"'I promise that you will see the liberation and that my child will have a better life. You needn't fear the ghetto, I'll protect you from the outside, not just because of the child but because I will always love you. Your spite, your hatred—even your lies can't change that. I don't love the woman who stands in front of me full of disgust for me. I love the young bride I saw years ago, so innocent, so beautiful, so devoted to her brand-new Jewish husband. In my dreams, it is that woman who keeps me happy and confident in the future. Go now.'

"With this chapter of my life closed behind me, I concentrated my thoughts on the next days to come. I had his assurance of protection, but, my God, there would be many thousands of people in the ghetto, how would he find me? How would he let me know where to find shelter...? My faithful companion, the one who puts answerless questions in my mind at times of crisis, was by my side again. I thought, 'Now that we are so close to victory I can't allow myself to lose my sense of orientation, my confidence in our survival.'

"And the order to move into the ghetto came two days later. We abandoned our flat and with heavy hearts we joined the endless procession of homeless Jewish women and children, with an occasional old man in our midst. As the line of broken lives snaked through the streets to the rhythm of frequent gun bursts and continuous insults in Hungarian and German, I took stock: we had four little children, a senile old lady, and a young woman ready to release the life she had been growing in her belly for nine months. We had no food, little money, and a few pieces of jewellery; the balance of the past. That was what must support the edifice of the future.

"Our entire history didn't amount to anything that would inspire optimism. To accentuate our dismal present, arriving at Klauzal Square, the soft underbelly of Jewish life in Budapest, we had to defile in front of large urns set up to swallow all our valuable possessions. Our only chance for survival rested with this amoral murderer, the father of the child in my body.

"We spent the first night in a room with nearly a hundred people, without any food at all. The next day an Arrow Cross messenger came to fetch us and led us, amid whispers of envy and hatred, to the apartment my husband and I had occupied in nearby Akácfa Street. I began to feel some warmth for János. I wanted to banish any upheaval of gratitude in my soul; after all, he was just keeping his end of the bargain, protecting *his* child. But still, because he was protecting his child, I again concluded that even the most depraved of assassins has points in common with the purest of heart and deed.

"I shall not go into the details of life in the ghetto; I'm sure you will remember them vividly as long as you live. We never saw János again, nor did we receive any food packages from him as he had promised. Our starvation diet terrified me for you little ones, especially you, the most haggard of them all. And I trembled for the unborn babe's life. I had nothing with which to nourish her in those final days of her uterine security.

"And finally the day came. The rhythmic contractions announcing the onset of my labour filled me with optimism. This sign of life was an announcement, a message from the other side of life, from beyond the ghetto walls, that freedom was nearby. In that unlit, damp, air-raid shelter, between two buildings, in an emergency escape hatch, I gave birth to a healthy little girl on the eve of our liberation. She was not even a day old when the first blood-and-sweat-covered Soviet soldier appeared in the frame of the shelter's entrance. That exhaused warrior, saturated with the mud and filth of thousands of combats along the long road from his home to ours, was my personal Messiah.

"Judit was in fact the tiniest, the youngest, angel in God's stable, on loan to our little family to bring us the gift of life. She remained with us until we resettled in our old family flat from which we had been deported. She waited until your dad came back to make sure that you two had a parent, a real parent to huddle against in that January that marked the beginning of a new order of life. She patiently graced our humble existence for another two months, until my youngest sister and her husband returned in their camp uniforms to collect their daughter on their way to Palestine. And then, one night, she left our lives, certain that we could continue with the restoration efforts without her guidance. God recalled His tiniest angel, the one whom He had loaned to us in our hour of greatest need.

"But the cynical bitter truth is that the poor infant had starved to death on the meagre diet of my watery milk. There have been times when I felt the dark pangs of a guilty conscience: we are all thriving today at the expense of her little life.

"I know that I didn't keep my word to cherish her, to sustain her, to raise her into a strong woman. And I also know that I did what I could, what any mother could for her brand-new treasure.

"Believe it or not, I don't even remember her face, nor her voice, and sometimes I am not even sure that she really existed. The only proof I have is that we are all alive. Isn't that enough?"

Sari slowly lapsed into her deep armchair. She was visibly exhausted from the long road she had just travelled backward in time, a road whose milestones looked more like tombstones on closer scrutiny. She was gently sobbing. Her eyes were closed and from behind the heavy lids two trickles of tears moistened the deep wrinkles on either side of her mouth.

Moistened with the ointment of her memories, the wrinkles lost some of their dark depth. I thought I noticed the faintest sketch of a smile softening the hitherto rigid lines.

Recently I went back to Budapest for my annual pilgrimage to the memory of my youth. I searched for a record of my tiny cousin's birth or death. Time, *that extraordinary version* of time, swallowed all traces of her brief earthly visit to us. Now and then, when I revel in the purity of my baby daughter's face, I seem to detect a memory. Or could it be a message or a blessing from Judit, the tiniest angel of life?

Dialogue with a Boy

*T*HE ROAD has been long, the journey fruitful and oppressive. In my quest for light and peace I have encountered all the fragmented actors of the drama that shook the earth under my feet forty years ago. The voices are still familiar, even if their words bare regions of a lost universe I had hoped never to discover. Visiting the spectres who used to have palpable dimensions for me, I elicited tales of horror from them. Their tales. They each spoke from a hidden locus revealing that, in essence, nothing has changed in all these years.

So what is left unfinished? Why not stop this lengthy visit with the phantoms of the past?

Looking into the blurred distance I am aware of the reply: I have meticulously avoided engaging one voice, the only one that still intimidates me. I have made a few oblique attempts at testing whether he heard my words. A bitter question here, a shameful throw-away confession there. Only silence resonated as an echo to my voice. Preoccupied with following the prescribed road, I remained conveniently aloof for as long as the others held my attention.

But now I seem to be at the end of the road. I have closed all the gates I needed to open. Except his. I am tired, I want to rest. But how can I rest without making peace with him? Yes, we must speak. Even if this dialogue lapses into a forced soliloquy, I must make sure that he hears the essence of the pallid wisdom which allowed for no other option but survival. He must at least have a chance to listen to the story that we wrote together, he and I, with or without intention.

But how do I find him? What do I call him? Speaking into a dark void is my sole memory of past endeavours to tease him out of hiding. How can I summon up enough sincerity, inspire him to encounter me for just one final meeting? How do I tell him that in spite of all my compassion for him I am also overflowing with swollen rivers of resentment, rage, and sorrow?

After so many words, so many ill-fated lives, so many tears that failed to cleanse the ashes from my eyes, I am left wondering. Still unsettled, I thirst for some truth that would make sense, some truth that would show the restless wound how to heal. None of us has a source of light to dissipate the penumbra left as a legacy of the night.

I stop the flow of my words. With tentative eyes, I visit the opposite end of my study, resting my gaze on a vacant corner. Its blinding whiteness is mesmerizing. In self-defence, I close my eyes. I turn the beacon of my awareness inward, as if to search for a refuge from the tremors of our meeting.

He is standing in the corner. He looks cold. My God, I forgot how deep his cavernous pallor was, how vulnerable his brittle body. His clothes, soiled and ripped beyond mending, inadequately cover his anemic stature.

"You look hungry and cold. I'd like to take care of you," I hear my disembodied voice utter. He doesn't seem to have heard me. Can I blame him? He probably felt my anguish and took it for cynical hospitality. I am discouraged by my initial failure to breathe trust into his meagre soul. He seems so unprotected, so weather-beaten, yet I am the one behaving like a beggar's apprentice. I search for his eyes. I can't speak to him without embracing the depth of his eyes. A dry well of darkness fills their bottom.

"I forgot how small you are. And how brittle. You are scarcely taller than my six-year-old son, and certainly you can't weigh more than he does." For some reason I resort to an instinctive whisper.

"Is it the banal work of time? Looking back everything looms smaller than it really was."

He just stands there, with his back barely touching the wall, as if he fears contact with any part of my world. I am unable to engage him.

"Look pal, I tried my best. You must admit you left me precious little to start with. And today I am here, having concluded our affair quite honourably. I have achieved much more than either one of us would have predicted back then. I have extricated myself from the captivity of the silence of fear and shame. I've transplanted our family into this fertile New World and taught millions of words I thought you'd have liked to hear. I've raised the red flag of doubt in several generations of students. I have published inspired prose and poetry paying tribute to our family's tragedy. I have done the best I could to guarantee the vigilance of my children over the shapeless graves. And, in spite of all the evil, I survived. And I remained sincere."

"You talk too much," he says flatly. "And all your sentences start with 'I'. Yes, you remained sincere. But all you care about is you." There is no accusation in his voice; he proclaims his statement without making it a verdict. And yet, his words hurt.

"Now listen, young man," I say, "you come here as if you just dropped in from the air-raid shelter for five minutes to let me know how much you despise me and to disappear forever leaving me with another cursed batch of guilt and shame. You behave like a brat. You've forgotten the desperate shape our existence took on at the moment you so conveniently disappeared from the scene. The wisdom you left behind may have saved you from falling into the trap of madness. But new evil calls for new knowledge. The bomb craters were mended, the ghetto walls were pulled down, and the yellow star no longer burned our chest every time we stepped into the street. Little by little, the stores began to sport meagre but sufficient food supplies. Father came home, blind and burnt out, but he came home. Mother didn't. And grandmother, well, you know grandmother....Agi and I were left to our own creativity for sprouting new roots on our own. I know, you wanted limitless vengeance, you wanted meticulous retaliation, you wanted me to dig a hole big enough to fill it with the rotten blood of all the assassins, torturers, and smug spectators. You wanted me to become strong, triumphant, and invincible. You wanted me not only to heal the wounds of the broken but also to fortify the fragile so that they could never again shatter. But even more, you wanted me to bring the dead back to life. You hoped with the stubborn doggedness of eight-year-olds that I could perform some kind of miracle and bring mother home alive. You inspired desperate tales about reasons for her inability to return. You wanted me to set the horizon ablaze and live to tell the tale in magnificent words. Well, my poor, misguided boy, you expected too much from me. Not only did you hand me a broken staff to lean on, you also expected me to run and never stop for a moment's fresh air. No, I couldn't put into human words the spectacle of the flames beyond the horizon, I just couldn't...."

"I see." My words fail to elicit in his battered body the urge to embrace me, or even to shake my hand. "I expected you to stand up and climb out of the pit. Instead, all this time, your wobbly legs have been teetering on the edge, imploring the whole world to see your pain. Imploring, how ridiculous! You failed to learn the real words of strength that leave no room for pity, for self-doubt, for hesitation. You have lived for forty years without goal, without aim, without knowing how to begin to live.

"I left you enough pain to break your agonizing heart when you stumbled over the threshold of the first dawn. But I also left you the strength of an eight-year-old who couldn't be killed. That should have been sufficient to create a new heart, bent on starting all over again. I wanted you to build us not a shelter but a showcase so that everyone could see that I had survived. I may be the one who looks like the martyred orphan but you are the one who has never stopped fighting the war. You are the one who has never stopped fleeing long enough to notice that we won a long time ago. You spent forty years running from shelter to shelter. Every time you met a human being, you used his shadow to hide you from the sun. Whatever happened to building the most powerful nation of history, the State of Israel?

"Well, Ben-Gurion was older than I, he did it for me. And he did a rather decent job. Israel may not be the most powerful nation in history, but it certainly is the only one that will never be conquered."

"I see," he says again, not honouring me with his gaze. "And what about a League of Nations to safeguard the sleep of every child on earth, what did you do about that?"

"The United Nations was founded almost immediately after the hostilities ended. It may not be able to paralyse the hands of all assassins, but it is as vigilant over the destiny of children as any assembly of humans can be."

"I see," is his laconic acknowledgement. My hope for a fraternal embrace is dwindling catastrophically. "And what about your oath to settle our account with God? Did you at least keep that one?" His face is animated with growing anger. Tiny red spots in his sunken, chalky cheeks shine like traffic lights.

"He has never given sign of life. Not once did I have any indication that the sky was not vacant. Be reasonable, how can I force God to account if I have no proof of a divine presence? I have implored Him in the hope that the purest prayer of a young boy would inspire in Him the desire to exercise His limited generosity. Surrounded by a monstrous infinity whose depth has filled me with boundless horror, I have knelt on the naked ground to attract His attention. But He was not moved either by the endless fright or by the fictional posture."

"I see," he rewards me with his blind cynicism. "You used to swear night after night before we hugged farewell that you would be a doer, man's watchdog; that you would preside over the trial of God and His prophets. You uttered solemn oaths attesting to your commitment to action instead of prayer. Instead, you have spent forty years in contemplation and avoidance. You are a petty traitor of children, a dream-giver and a wordsmith, a fabricator of dead tales. I despise you because you are pitifully small, because for forty years you have been throwing tantrums over the world's unwillingness to see and honour your pain. Wake up, little man, the world has seen enough of your pain. Will you ever wipe the sterile tears from your pain-ridden eyes to replace it with the sunlit gaze of an empire builder? When will you turn off the light in the family tomb so that you can brighten the days of the living! You pat yourself on your stooped shoulders for having had the courage to partake in the creation of four lives. Aren't you moved by the thought of your children having to endure my history? Where is the fortress you were supposed to erect to shelter the children from evil projects? Where is the language you were going to invent to compel man to follow you, the unknown prophet, into the land of eternal peace on earth? Whatever happened to the Republic of Childhood you swore you would found? Answer me! You are singularly silent right now. Have you run out of shabby excuses and apologies?"

Before I can gather my wits to compose a suitable answer, he abandons his corner and, weightlessly, he closes in on me. We are almost nose to nose.

"You were supposed to rebel for me and all the other children of the ghetto. Instead you waged your war strictly for yourself, to appease your rage. You were going to grow into the shoes of an adult who would shield the children like the bark of a tree. And look what you have done....I am still not life-worthy. Look above your head. The sky is sinister and undefended. I had been hoping to find you behind me with a ferocious sword protecting me. And now? I keep looking behind me and there is no one there. I am covered in rags and unhealing wounds; I am hungry and exhausted. I want to escape to a vacation in the land of dreams, dreams that speak of life as it used to be. But I can't because your endless, sterile, plaintive words drown all sounds of hope. With your pain howling throughout the years I can't even expect to die as a child. I drag my restless existence in the shell of an eight-year-old man.

"I hate you, I hate you more than anyone else....For you, alone, were meant to free me. It is for your sake that I made all the efforts to not succumb to the call of death. I am full of a useless, crippled hatred stuck in my heart like constant indigestion. If only I could experience anger and rage! Alas, I am too spent for that. There is no anger in my heart, and revenge doesn't interest me. Are you surprised? Are you shocked to hear that all your fantasies about me were wrong, just as you were wrong about everything else? You never took the trouble to look into yourself deeply enough to really find out about me. You fixed your eyes on the mirror and imagined that you saw me. You never saw me as I am today. Had you found me this way long ago, you wouldn't feel the oppressive urge to make peace with me. You exploiter of homeless phantoms of the past, how can you say that you are at the end of the road? You don't even know where the road starts or in what direction it unfolds. Let me hear you explain your treason!"

"I...I..."

He moves in so close that I feel robbed of my own breath. "Tell me about how you implored God instead of putting Him in the box of the accused," he continues. "Tell me why you didn't demand that He not only confess but also atone. How is that you failed to indict Him? I wanted to hear you talk to him like a man weighed down by the burden of his truth:

"'Almighty King, ruler of us all, you have been hiding from me for almost four decades, you the Creator of all beauty, you chose to remain unmoved by the suffering of millions of your children. Doesn't pity ever stir your heart? Have you gone mad to allow the destruction of your creation? Or are you as cruel and evil as man, the crown of your creation? Is this what shamed you into hiding your face from our accusing glance? Or are we victims of a monumental error which you cynically perpetuate by remaining silent? And since you don't answer any of my questions, I indict you for your gratuitous wickedness in being the ultimate perpetrator of evil.'

"I wanted to hear you spit in His face truths that I learned under the darkness of that violent doorway followed by my unscheduled visit among the dead. I wanted you to paint His portrait with my wisdom:

"'You, sir, are a puppet manipulated on endless strings of barbed wires performing acts of tightrope walking in ghettos and camps. No, contrary to what other tales of darkness recount, You were not hanging on the gallows in Birkenau, You were guiding the executioner's hands in planting the Tree of Death! While the victims addressed to You their silent prayers before surrendering their last breath, You tacitly blessed the toils of the slaughterer. Could it be that poison gas is Your real breath? Could it be that You carefully avoid meeting with me so that You don't have to answer my unequivocal demand: where were You in December 1944? What panorama captivated Your gaze with such seduction that You couldn't see my bleeding flesh? What divine delights held Your ears captive when my mother implored You in her typhus-ridden delirium to rescue her from the insatiable fever? Where the hell were You being entertained to have been insensitive to the roar of that tiny angel's hunger pangs?'

"I see horror in your eyes, I see you frozen with terror while listening to the words I have been whispering into your ears for forty years. And for all those years your heart has been dead to my words. How wasteful, how useless you are to me, and to the rest of our family of victims. You have not only betrayed me but you have also defeated me. You have robbed me of my hope and my words. You buried the voice of rightful indignation in numerous layers of self-serving laments. I don't doubt the sincerity of your pain. I only regret its futility. I see the anxious flickers of blasphemy-by-association dance in your eyes. Don't worry. I may be audacious and I may have chosen a perilous journey before I return to the disturbed world of silence, but I really have nothing to lose. No, I fear not His wrath; I already know the ultimate. His curse and abandonment liberate me. And yet, to be banished at the age of eight...to be condemned to familiarity with such a language...I had hoped for so long that you would relieve me...."

"Damn it, I tried, at least with God I spent myself on countless exhortations, virulent threats, humble laments; but nothing seemed to attract His pity, His love, or even His ire. Our story left Him bathing in distant passivity...."

"Well then, speak to *me*, defend yourself, show me that in spite of your unforgivable fear you don't have my blood on your hands. Show me the wound in your soul, show me the rage He chose to ignore...."

"All my words to Him were parched by His arid silence," I tell the boy. "Finally I confronted Him for one last time.

"'You never respond to my pleas, my challenges, my bitter confusion.' I said. "I must speak for both of us, right? You leave it to me to carry you, a wounded brother needing my unconditional love for survival. You want *me* to produce the conclusive diagnosis: *Deceased. Cause of death: rejection by his own victims*. You leave me this unfair task, without even a sign to guide me through my second tunnel. Indeed, Your cruelty is what endows You with Your infinite nature.'

"And to my bewilderment I hallucinated His voice! Or could it be that He actually reached down to me?

"'The boy is alive, and so are you. The pile was rich with a hundred lives; one more would have simply proven the consistency of human projects. But no, he provided the counterpoint that sheltered the seed of hope in the centre of the mountain of doom. His flesh may have been bruised by the rigid tumult of frozen cadavers, his tiny heart may have been tainted by the taste of defilement, but his soul is intact. He was spared. Thus, so were you. Did you fail to recognize the charitable hand of your Creator catching him at the crest of the edge? Or does it serve your brooding anger to keep your eyes closed to the good in order to confirm your commitment to the unconditional evil of all that lives, including your Creator?'

"No, He didn't actually break the seal of silence with these words of reproach. They emerged from a carefully camouflaged nook of my conscience where bits of remorse are stored. Be reasonable, my young friend, it would be absurd to expect His attention to the meagre spectacle of our being. And yet, I know what you are thinking: He could have intervened. His eyes are capable of absorbing even the tiniest portrait of suffering. But this is only a floating possibility...."

With an impatient gesture, he wipes out the end of my sentence.

"As usual, you speak too much, saying nothing worthwhile. You are still chasing the mirage of a divine solution to your solitude. I, on the other hand, don't love Him for His possible help in my escaping the eternal void, but rather I often overflow with hatred for His unbreakable silence. Only accusatory and reproachful words feel at home in my lungs. Violent fantasies of killing Him afford me greater relief than do entertaining fables about His protective omnipresence."

His bitter words bubble with the teeming wisdom of a prematurely aged survivor's dark potion. Indeed, I wasn't there when the pit was crawling with lives ending violently and in vain.

"What if He did lean down from a sequestered sky to prevent your imminent destruction? What if He did intervene at the first opportune moment to preserve father's life, if not his sight? Maybe it *was* He who sent that tiny angel to Sari's womb to protect the wretched vestiges of our once thriving family?" I ask rhetorically.

"No matter. I don't owe Him one grain of gratitude for saving my miserable existence. If it was He who saved me from premature and inappropriate death, He just did what He was supposed to do. And if it *was* He who fished me out of the waves of fire, why didn't He act sooner? He couldn't fail to see the pervert violate children's innocence with the gleeful ease with which one shoots for stuffed animals at an amusement park. Why did He allow the degenerate to demote me into a lifeless target? Why did He wait until I had entered into the servitude of the ruler of darkness? Did the two of them have some sort of wager in which the children of Israel were the stake? Or did He need bloodstains in my groin to convince Him of the soiling of nature's most beautiful project?

"Never mind me, I am just one of the countless. Where was He when our angelic little cousin with the forest of golden curls crowning his tender years lost his right to live? Where was *He* when mother was imploring Him from the pit in Bergen Belsen? I tell you, my pathetic keeper of the only future I will ever know, should He ever make an appearance before me, this is what I would spit at Him:

"'You sustained the villain by forsaking the innocent. You lulled the children of Israel into the alluring fable of them being Your chosen people. But to what purpose had You chosen us? To satisfy some obscene need to condone and to produce evil? You are a cruel father who should die before any more of Your children perish to feed Your perversion. I want You to die!'

"That's what I would tell Him, but I don't believe that He would dare to appear on this cursed earth."

With fervour animating my breath, I rush to blurt out words of bizarre inspiration: "And He would respond to you:

"'You're too young to know that My work was completed on the eve of the sixth day. From then on, man has involved himself in nothing but defiling the beauty I bestowed on him. Now, after many generations of wicked cruelty, I am left with the sad knowledge that whatever I created for the enjoyment and the thriving of all living creatures, man has belittled, soiled, perverted. This panorama of ashes, this forest of frozen cadavers, this sea of blood is no longer My creation, it belongs to man. He has engineered it, he must live with it. When I choose to rescue some of the innocent, I feel hesitant and the prisoner of a bind. The children deserve a chance, otherwise why let them come to life? But aren't all assassins the product of a distant innocence? So when I don't save all the children, I may be allowing fewer assassins into this guilty community. Why give the dubious gift of life to children at all? Because I haven't completely turned sour on My human project. I have given life to man. Man's duty is, therefore, to live to the best of his ability in the most humane manner. That is the most appropriate way to prove his devotion to his Creator.

"'But I fear that I made a mistake in making man. He is not content with what he has been given. He wants to occupy My throne, to usurp My sceptre, to trade places with Me. No, indeed, I didn't go to Auschwitz, because, for the first time in our joint history, I feared for My own life. Man has reached such perfection in producing evil that I feared I could succumb to his might. I snatched as many pure souls from the pit as I could without falling into the flames Myself. You owe me gratitude for the breath in your heart, but, more important, you owe Me gratitude for risking My divine existence to save your mortal life.'"

The boy is immensely agitated. He paces back and forth in my study. Now that he has turned his cavernous eyes away from my face, I notice that his pitifully bony shoulders are shaken by a rhythmic upheaval. He is crying without tears. Then he stops, fixing his gaze on my eyes. There is such a fire burning in those dark pits of his eye sockets that I feel startled. I sit erect in my chair to receive his words. There is pain, deep pain, in his hurried speech.

"No, I won't fall prey to your clever professorial apology for the biggest hoax of human history. I can't believe my ears. You are actually pleading His case to me—to *me*! You turn His unpardonable sin into a fate deserving compassion and even pity. How dare you sermonize to me about His benevolence? He created us with a disposition for good and evil, He has the power to safeguard His creation. He is either a master of perversion or a Wizard of Oz, a sham masquerading in the cloak of justice and love. I don't even want to continue our dialogue about this spurious master. The spectator of six million deaths from the safety of the firmament beyond the screen of ashes is the guardian angel of the man who feeds the furnace with human fuel. Let Him peddle His power amid the assassins! And you, you romantic weakling, you seeker of superhuman solutions, I want to hate you with passion. And yet, I can't evict you from the privacy of our attachment. You are my only link to hope, to tomorrow. But listen to me carefully: if you have one ounce of me left in you, write down faithfully the tale of our last encounter ever. For, to be sure, we will never meet again. Tell the world that on one last desperate attempt I came to you, I appealed to you to save us both from falling prey to perverted masters of all sorts. Tell the world that I am still alive and that you, too, are struggling in spite of your smug torrents of words."

As if a mysterious messenger were about to deliver a response on my behalf to my disappearing young friend, a ray of the clearest and warmest sunshine inundates the spot where he stands. It proceeds, then, to enwrap me. Beyond the brightness can be seen an unmistakable blanket of mist. Turning my glance toward the clouds that seem to usher the source of this brilliance directly and exclusively at my study, I think I hear him whisper: "Thank you."

It may have been a hallucination. And yet....

To the
Angels of Life

WITHOUT YOU, children of tomorrow, the journey would not have been possible, nor would it have been worth the avalanche of horrors I needed to relive to set free the demons of the past. Without you, my precious children, I would not dare to sing ancient laments in a minor mode for fear of falling prey to their mesmerizing lull. For nearly twenty years your bountiful smiles and vigorous wailings have kept cherished company with the candles burning in the sanctuary of my memory. Your energy and lust do not resuscitate the snuffed-out lives of the murdered members of our family. But that's not what you are here on this earth for. You owe nothing to the past: your commitment is to building the future. And if your laughter doesn't fall prey to another assassin, if your efforts bring a garden full of the sweetest fruit of new lives, then you will have defeated the infamous who dedicated his wicked genius to ridding the earth forever of Jewish children. He who kills Jewish children is the enemy of all children. He who murders children is the enemy of all life. I pray that you will triumph over this angel of doom.

One of you, the one whose dark diamond eyes sing soothing melodies in my tentative heart, wrote, at the age of eight, an open letter to my martyred mother: "Dear Grandma who died in a concentration camp, who I never met and I love, Boy am I sad and very mad, but that's the way life goes, love, your Granddaughter." Your compassion and the purity of the anger of an untamed child are more eloquent than the preceding volume. And I know that you spoke with the authority of your three siblings, robbed of the love of a grandmother, of a lineage. I also know that all of you will be strong in your indignation and in your sorrow whenever you lean over the gaping holes in our family albums, the empty chairs at family gatherings, or at the very thought of another avaricious night trying to rob your children of their birthright.

You with the name of the mother of all gods, you have already taken up arms against the madness of a nuclear doom. May the tale of your grandmother's death guide you on the righteous path leading us back to life.

My little boy, my only son, your six-year-old naked curiosity has already been pricked by the black mystery of evil, you have already lost the shining innocence of your brand-new life: you discovered evil when you learned the words: "The Nazis killed my dad's mother." May you never lose the brilliance of your vigilant intelligence. May you devote as much of it to safeguarding life and peace as you reserve for improving the quality of the flame warming your private hearth.

And you, tiniest of them all, who have just discovered the mixed blessing of speech, you who the mystical yarn of dreams claims were sent to me by God as a token of His sincere desire to make amends, may your sensual bond to this earth lead you to a version of existence in which the word "evil" is only a distant memory and a vigilant warning.

Yes, together the four of you may just set the horizon ablaze....